NEW ENGLAND INSTITUTE
OF TECHNOLOGY
LEARNING RESOURCES CENTER

Civil Rights and the Social Programs of the 1960s

CIVIL RIGHTS
and the Social Programs
of the 1960s

The Social Justice Functions
of Social Policy

MARCIA BOK

Westport, Connecticut
London

Library of Congress Cataloging-in-Publication Data

Bok, Marcia.
    Civil rights and the social programs of the 1960s : the social
justice functions of social policy / Marcia Bok.
        p. cm.
    Includes bibliographical references and index.
    ISBN 0-275-93654-6 (alk. paper)
    1. Social service—United States—History—20th century.
    2. Social service—Moral and ethical aspects. 3. Civil rights
movements—United States—History—20th century. 4. Social justice.
    5. United States—Social conditions—1960–1980. I. Title.
    HV91.B59 1992
    361.6′1′09730904—dc20   91-46996

British Library Cataloguing in Publication Data is available.

Library of Congress Catalog Card Number: 91-46996
ISBN: 0-275-93654-6

First published in 1992

Praeger Publishers, 88 Post Road West, Westport, CT 06881
An imprint of Greenwood Publishing Group, Inc.

Printed in the United States of America

∞™

The paper used in this book complies with the
Permanent Paper Standard issued by the National
Information Standards Organization (Z39.48–1984).

10 9 8 7 6 5 4 3 2 1

Copyright Acknowledgment

The author and publisher gratefully acknowledge permission granted by The University
of Chicago Press to reprint extracts which appear in chapter 4, from "The Current
Status of Community Action Agencies in Connecticut," by Marcia Bok, originally
published in the summer of 1988, *Social Services Review* 62(3): 396–410.

To My Family, With Love

Contents

Preface

While each decade in a century has its own specific characteristics, it is the contrasts between decades that often dramatize their distinctiveness. Such is the case in comparing the 1960s and the 1980s. The profound differences between these two decades reveal the many complex social, economic, and political forces active within the United States. Although it might appear that the 1960s were more an anomaly and the 1980s more of a norm (because of the prevailing conservatism in the country), from both a historical and a political perspective either decade could, and did, occur. One decade is not necessarily more representative of this society than the other. Herein lie reasons for optimism in the possibilities for social change.

This book is about social policy: How it develops, its historical antecedents, its political context, and its implications for society and the poor. It is also about the civil rights movement and social justice and how these events and ideas contributed to the unique character of social policy and social programs in the 1960s.

It is not a book about the history of the civil rights movement or the antiwar movement or the women's movement. These important stories have been told many times—much better than I can tell them. It is also not about rock and roll, drugs, and sex nor an attempt to objectively evaluate the outcomes and impact of the civil rights movement, the Great Society, the War on Poverty, or the counterculture of the 1960s.

In addition, this book does not address all of the social programs that were initiated in the 1960s but discusses a few programs as examples of the types of social policies that represent the era. In fact, it is difficult, and almost arbitrary, to decide what constitutes a social program because all human services could be included. Alfred Kahn (1973), in an attempt to tackle the difficult task of defining "social services," excludes health, income supports, housing, and education as "larger, separately institutionalized systems" (p. 5) and includes such programs as "family and child welfare, services to the aging, and the various counseling and assistance programs in schools, hospitals, and similar facilities" (p. 5). These he refers to as general social services or personal social services.

In this volume, I apply a much more inclusive definition of social programs that includes health and mental health, antipoverty programs, and preschool education. For example, the book contains material about Medicare and Medicaid, which are primarily health programs, and Head Start, which is mainly a preschool education program. And, although the emphasis is definitely on public policy, rather than on social service programs in general, I do not include the policies and programs of the federal Departments of Housing and Urban Development and Labor here. Thus, the classification system used in this book is certainly not definitive.

The programs included were selected both for their diversity and as representative of the Great Society and the War on Poverty; they were major federal initiatives in the scope of their service provisions and the total number of people served; and they have had enduring value and powerful individual and societal ramifications and consequences. I could have included other programs whose principles are similarly illustrative of the era of civil rights.

Clearly, the subject matter is so vast and so much has already been written and said about the 1960s that the boundaries of the present volume need to be specified. Naturally, I believe this book has a unique contribution to make. I agree with most poverty theorists that much social policy is based on the political economy of a nation: That is, public policies are motivated by both political (electoral and governmental) and economic (labor market and monetary) considerations. But the political economy is not static; it changes in different decades and under different kinds of leadership. It is important to ask about the forces of change and why the political economy changes the way it does and when it does. Social control theories of social policy—particularly policy targeted specifically for the poor—also have validity. These theories refer to public policies and programs that attempt to "cool out" and co-opt minority leadership to neutralize demands for social justice.

Both political economy and social control theories have been written about extensively (Piven and Cloward, 1971). However, one other dimension does not get as much recognition: the social justice functions of social policy. Indeed, social justice (defined as equality) is often disputed by both progressives and conservatives—by the latter because they believe that social justice means fairness (the right to keep what you earn) rather than equality (the redistributive principle) and by the former because they believe that social policies generally reflect social reform and not true social change and rarely go far enough to correct inequities. This book emphasizes the redistributive social justice functions of social policy.

I have been concerned about this subject matter for more than twenty-five years as student, social work practitioner, researcher, and teacher of social policy. I have chosen to write about the programs of the 1960s because it was a special time with respect to individual rights and societal obligations and because there are lessons to be learned from that experience. The programs of the 1970s and 1980s (and now the 1990s) with New Federalism, cutbacks in social spending, so-called welfare reform, and a general mean-spiritedness toward the poor, are very different from the expansiveness and redistributive aspects of the social programs of the 1960s. The reduction in the percentage of the population living below the poverty level from 22.4 percent in 1959 to 12.8 percent in 1969 attests to the fact that something different was happening in the decade of the 1960s and that it left a noteworthy legacy. The objective of this book is to address these issues, trying to account for some of the differences that occurred and are still taking place, with specific reference to the relationship between civil rights and the social programs of the nation.

The terms "progressive" and "conservative" are used throughout this book to denote a specific political agenda, specific kinds of social legislation, and specific roles and responsibilities of government. I believe that the use of labels is not insignificant. Those who do the most name-calling often argue disingenuously that labels are largely meaningless and "only" symbolic. But, as we saw in the 1988 presidential election, these labels can be enormously powerful and are used, by design, to conjure up images that have strong connotations.

A conservative agenda always begins with a statement to the effect that the basic problem in America is the breakdown of traditional structures, like family and work, and that conditions are made worse by government intervention and social programs. The recommended solutions are always less government and fewer social programs, along with restoration of traditional work and family values through mandatory workfare for poor people and a return to two-parent families within a patriarchal structure as an antidote to the feminization of poverty. In this context, principles of self-help are taken to mean the need for personal change because of personal deficiencies, rather than self-help as methods of social cooperation, mutual aid, and grass-roots initiatives to deal with social and economic problems.

These days, the liberal agenda continues to be more neoconservative than progressive. Currently, many liberals agree that society has become too permissive; that redistributive principles and the welfare state are outmoded and counterproductive; that class, race, and special interest politics are divisive; and that partnerships between government and the business community are inevitable and necessary for social programs and growth of the economy.

Within a progressive agenda, social justice and greater equality are seen as responsibilities of government, and redistribution of resources and power are considered the means to achieve these goals. Social legislation represents the policies of government that operationalize these concepts. Some characteristics of a progressive scenario are a combination of universal entitlements for all citizens and programs only for the poor, based on need (i.e. means-tested); an emphasis on the rights of individuals; class, race and gender consciousness; and generally negative attitudes toward private delivery of social services and New Federalism, which delegates responsibility for services to state and local officials without local authority, and away from the federal government.

As I consider the audience for this book I think broadly about the many students, professional social workers, activists, and academics I have worked with and known in the classroom, in my office, in my home, and in the community. Many work with the poorest people in society, the most sorrowful, and the most oppressed. I am particularly interested in social programs in the public sector where work is almost always discouraging and frustrating. I have always been respectful of public service and inspired by the determination, hard work, sincerity, and knowledge of the people who work for public agencies. If the world were black and white and there were "good guys" versus "bad guys," I would place most of these often maligned individuals into the "good guy" group. I have learned from them. I hope this book helps make their jobs easier and more fulfilling. I believe that most of these individuals view social justice as I have defined it, and the ideas expressed in this volume will resonate with their ideals. I particularly want to acknowledge my friends and colleagues at the University of Connecticut School of Social Work, many of whom I love dearly, and the help of Dean Nancy Humphreys, who critically read and commented on the manuscript of this book.

Civil Rights and the Social Programs of the 1960s

Introduction

Among the many glaring contrasts between the decade of the 1960s and 1980s are differences in moral direction and definitions of social justice and the manifestations of these differences in social policy. This book takes the position that, although the limits of the civil rights movement and the limits of social legislation are often emphasized, the decade of the 1960s was, in fact, progressive—it was a time when lasting social change occurred and when the expectations, aspirations, and quality of life for poor people, minorities, and women improved.

Some of the tangible legacies from the 1960s are the extensive amount of new social legislation that was enacted, the increase in social spending that occurred, the large number of people who were served, the decrease in poverty, the longevity its legislation has enjoyed, and the conscience and consciousness of the American people that were aroused. Except for legislation during the decade of the 1930s, the social legislation of the 1960s is the most important of the twentieth century in the number of people reached and the changes that occurred in peoples' lives as a result of legislative and judicial actions.

This book deals with selected social legislation programs from the 1960s, chosen for their diversity and reflection of Great Society programs, specifically in relation to the civil rights movement. In addition to programs included in this volume, other 1960s legislation included, for example: the Juvenile Delinquency Prevention and Control Act of 1968; the Health Manpower Training Act of 1968; the Manpower Development and Training Act of 1962 (the precursor to The Comprehensive Employment and Training Act—CETA); the Housing and Urban Development Act of 1968, which dealt with aspects of urban renewal and the Model Cities Program;

and the Older Americans Act of 1965, which extended elderly services from income and health into social services, recreation, nutrition, and transportation. Education programs, in addition to Head Start, are identified in Chapter 5. The impact of the social legislation and the civil rights movement are viewed as positive and far-reaching in their consequences for the quality of life in the United States.

Although social legislation in this country is always in the tradition of social reform, rather than fundamental social change, the 1960s is considered a progressive period—and this is central to the theme of this book—because of the role of government and societal obligations. Class consciousness was aroused, and the redistribution of power and of resources was a salient issue. In addition, the empowerment of both minorities and the poor was a prominent goal, and respect for cultural diversity began to resurface. The term "progressive" is used here to denote a time of change when the civil rights movement and the social legislation of the period were inextricably tied together by the constitutional and democratic goals of social justice and equality, when social legislation recognized the basic rights and entitlements of citizens, and when government was revered as a force for improving and protecting the quality of life for individuals and groups. Thus, the fate of civil rights and social programs is considered to be linked by Constitutional guarantees and democratic ideals: It is contended that, in a conservative era, the erosion of civil rights and social programs runs in parallel with the deterioration of Constitutional guarantees and democratic ideals. Thus, we find setbacks in such areas as affirmative action and abortion rights for women occurring concurrently with cutbacks in social programs and federal social spending.

The civil rights movement is often denounced for being insufficiently economic in its orientation and outcomes. It is alleged that the movement failed to achieve its goal of economic empowerment for minorities; in fact, it is suggested that the demise of the movement occurred precisely because it turned its attention to this issue (Hamilton and Hamilton, 1986; Heclo, 1986). Similarly, insufficient recognition is given to the accomplishments of the social legislation of the decade. Much more emphasis is placed on the limitations of social programs, with criticism emanating from both the political right and left (Murray, 1984; Glazer, 1988; Block et al., 1987). An emphasis on social justice and equality as the basis for social programs also receives relatively little attention in the literature. When the purpose of social legislation is discussed, political economy and social control theories are usually invoked. However, in addition to these theories, social legislation is also motivated by more lofty principles. Societal changes occur when particular behaviors are rewarded or punished or when shifts in values and beliefs occur. During the 1960s it was the transformation in values and beliefs that was particularly important.

A political agenda that includes the importance of the moral principles of social justice and equality fosters social legislation that improves the social and economic status of the poor (Gil, 1976). A political agenda that invokes the morality of the free market and traditional gender-based work and family structures cannot be in the interest of the poor, many of whom are women, caring for children, in nontraditional family and work environments (Abramovitz, 1988). Thus, a moral agenda operates within a political and economic framework, although this fact is often overlooked.

Michael Harrington (1984) makes the point that "in the sixties, Kennedy and Johnson had persuaded the people that social justice was smart economics. Johnson, in particular, emphasized how rebuilding the cities and educating the poor would create jobs, profits, and increased productivity" (p. 35). Today there is a prevailing sentiment in the United States that a progressive agenda is either irrelevant or irresponsible because, it is alleged, social legislation contributes to immorality, drains the economy, and adds to the federal budget deficit. Since evidence exists that these charges are not true, there is a need to counteract these beliefs (Block et al., 1987).

Unfortunately, the Democratic party, which had been identified with the victimized in society since the 1930s, is currently unable to mobilize old coalitions or to forge new alliances, and Democrats are particularly mired by racial conflicts within and between social and economic groups. In addition to having no ideological conviction about social justice, the Democrats are unable to provide the kind of leadership needed to mount an aggressive assault against conservatism. It appears that a progressive third party, articulating a reawakening of the principles of justice and equality, after the void created in these principles during the 1980s, is needed if social justice principles are to reemerge in electoral politics.

The emphasis in this book on democratic principles of social justice and equality as the basis for social legislation within a progressive agenda does not negate the importance of dominant political economy and social control theories. Rather, it is considered timely to call attention to other factors— moral factors—in the analysis of social welfare programs. A focus on democratic principles in social legislation at this juncture in the country's history seems particularly relevant since neglect of these issues has shown itself to be an economic and social disservice to all people in our society.

Thus, this book has a number of objectives: It describes the background, analyzes the process of decision making, and traces the passage of selected landmark legislation of the 1960s from both a historical and a political perspective. It details the changes that have occurred in this legislation in the last two decades, and it deals with the current and possible future status of social policies and programs. The work includes analysis of historical, political, and legal aspects of the civil rights movement and concurrent events, and the concepts of equality and social justice are considered as the basis of the social legislation that is discussed.

Chapter 1 discusses and attempts to explicate the major concepts used throughout the book: civil rights, social justice, and social policy. The basis for civil rights is considered to be the Constitution of the United States, which purports to guarantee the rights of citizens against infringement by government. Thus, there is a discussion of the post–Civil War Constitutional amendments that freed the country from slavery, guaranteed all people the right to vote, and offered protection for citizens through due process of law. The civil rights issues of nondiscrimination in public places, voting rights, school desegregation, affirmative action, and equal protection under the law are reviewed.

John Rawls's theory of justice helps clarify social justice in a progressive agenda. His ideas are contrasted with the writings of Nathan Glazer, which represent a more conservative viewpoint. The concept of social obligations from an individual and a societal perspective is also considered, as is the role of leadership in influencing public beliefs and attitudes about justice and equality.

The section in Chapter 1 on social policy suggests the limitations of political economy and social control theories and discusses specific provisions of policies that enhance or impede a progressive agenda. These include, for example, means-tested programs versus entitlements; privatization versus public service; centralized versus decentralized administration; and income maintenance versus in-kind service delivery.

Chapter 2 highlights the major contrasts between the 1960s and 1980s. This includes discussions of changes in the economy from the "Golden Age of Capitalism" to the "deindustrialization of America"; racial attitudes and affirmative action; the feminization of poverty; the need for a class consciousness for social change to occur; the role of government and changes from confidence to hostility in public attitudes toward government; and changes in the moral imperatives of the society from public responsibility for the poor to a resurgence of social Darwinism and the belief that the poor are immoral and the affluent are virtuous.

The discussion of the Civil Rights Act of 1964 in Chapter 3 emphasizes the political, Constitutional, and historical antecedents of this legislation and subsequent events. It addresses the changing status of the Civil Rights Act, mostly the deterioration of gains, especially in relation to current attitudes and policies emanating from the executive branch of the federal government and the new conservative composition of the U. S. Supreme Court. Challenges to affirmative action in the workplace and set-asides in construction, continued segregation of public school, distortion of the intent of the U.S. Commission on Civil Rights, the use of the judiciary to circumvent the legislative branch of the federal government, and challenges to the fundamental right to abortion are some of the current threats to civil rights and civil liberties addressed in this chapter.

The struggles and violence that accompanied the civil rights movement also raise questions about the nature of social change in the United States.

Because of economic and social gains made by minorities and women and changes in electoral politics (particularly on the local level) where new kinds of empowerment were occurring, the late 1960s and early 1970s marked the beginning of the end of the progressive politics of the earlier part of the era. In the 1980s and continuing into the 1990s, conservatism has strengthened, and racial tensions and conflicts in the nation have intensified.

The Economic Opportunity Act (EOA) of 1964 discussed in Chapter 4, is the legislation most closely identified with the antipoverty programs of the Great Society and the War on Poverty. The federal government was the major funder for the EOA, and funds were provided directly to newly created private, nonprofit Community Action Agencies (CAAs), thereby circumventing established state and municipal government. CAAs were expected to spend their money on social action and social services, initiated locally with "maximum feasible participation" of the affected populations in the planning and implementation of programs. The history of the EOA is replete with attempts to dismantle the program, and if this was not possible, to strip it of its autonomy and empowerment features. The survival of over 900 CAAs today is testimony to the tenacity of the antipoverty warriors and the reciprocity that has been achieved between CAAs, local and state government, the business community, and the poor in many geographic areas. An appraisal of the accomplishments of this cornerstone antipoverty legislation is almost as controversial as the program itself.

Project Head Start is examined in Chapter 5 as an exemplar of programs in the War on Poverty, which emphasizes education and opportunity at the earliest levels of intervention. The supporting legislation and the underlying principles of environmentalism are discussed, including the controversial concept of "cultural deprivation." The controversies around parent involvement between parent education (to become more middle class) and parent activism and local control are an intrinsic part of Head Start history, as is disagreement over the methodology, content, and meaning of numerous evaluations of the program. Head Start continues to be a vital program today, with more demand than available resources. It emulates other antipoverty programs in its retreat from political and social activism, at the present time, but it has the potential to ignite actions based on the principle of indigenous control at the local level.

In the 1960s, it appeared that comprehensive, national health insurance for all Americans was about to happen. What actually transpired, however, fell far short of expectations. Chapter 6 deals with the background and passage of Medicare and Medicaid in 1965 and the subsequent history of that landmark legislation. Broader issues of health care and privatization in the society are also examined. Higher deductibles, additional co-payments, reduced coverage, Health Maintenance Organizations (HMOs) and other prepayment plans, Diagnostic Related Groups, and Catastrophic Health Insurance all form part of a jumbled mixture of public health policies that have been considered or which now exist, together with a large private, for-profit component that is uniquely American. Despite health care expenditures that far surpass the rate of national inflation in the United States, and the rate of such spending in Canada, an often quoted poll of Canadian and U. S. health consumers indicates that the latter are more dissatisfied with their health care than are the former. The spiraling cost of health care, the millions of Americans without any health insurance, and the continual restrictions on benefits for those who are insured are some of the sources of discontent. The issues of entitlement and universal health policies, and the challenges to these principles in social insurance and public assistance, are also discussed.

In Chapter 7, the Community Mental Health Centers Act of 1963 and deinstitutionalization are discussed. This chapter begins with an exploration of the relationship between social class and mental illness. The notions that the poor are disproportionately represented among public mental hospital patients and that mental hospitalization is not simply a psychiatric issue cast a different light on a very old societal problem. The intrusion of sociology and politics into the otherwise pristine field of medicine opened up new areas of inquiry into mental health practices that had not been scrutinized by the public for many decades. The mentally ill, who were meant to be invisible, generally lacked advocates after the interest in mental illness and hospitalization among social reformers and muckrakers waned at the turn of the century. Family members who were being held responsible for their relatives' mental problems, according to the psychoanalytic theories of the day, were unlikely to come forward and aggressively bring attention to themselves or their problems. Thus, if the plight of the mentally ill was going to be exposed and if conditions of mental health treatment were going to change, it was outside advocates who needed to rise to the challenge, and they did, often as young attorneys in legal aid practice.

Although the introduction of psychotropic drugs is usually credited with beginning the movement toward deinstitutionalization, many other factors were operating, including civil rights issues that accompanied debates about the alternatives to institutionalization of the mentally ill.

Certain lessons from the community mental health movement apply today to the long-term, custodial care of the elderly in nursing homes and to the homeless. Quality of life issues for institutionalized elderly raise the consciousness of society about treatment versus custodial care. The current condition and treatment of the elderly and homeless mentally ill attest to the unfulfilled promises of the deinstitutionalization movement and the civil rights issues that are involved.

The programs and policies included in this volume were chosen for their diversity and, paradoxically, for their commonalities as representative of

Great Society legislation. The number of programs dealt with represents just a small portion of total new programs initiated during the 1960s. The common elements across programs discussed in this volume are the principles of (1) the rights and empowerment of citizens and the obligations of government toward its citizens; (2) the issues of social justice and equality in opportunity and access to the goods and services of society; (3) the limits of social legislation even in a progressive political environment in the United States; and (4) the decay of social legislation in the last two decades.

Taken together, the Civil Rights Act, the Economic Opportunity Act, Head Start, Medicare and Medicaid, and the Community Mental Health Act deal with issues of opportunity and access to education, employment, health, and mental health and the right not to be harassed in everyday life. While this is hardly the full array of contingencies in the life experience of individuals, these programs all touch on social justice issues and core conditions that determine standards and quality of life.

Given the nature of political compromise and the limits of social policy in a reformist framework, the programs of the 1960s obviously left the rights and entitlements of many citizens unfulfilled. For example, not all mental patients' rights are protected; enforcement of civil rights legislation continues to be weak and controversial; eligibility, coverage, and privatization in health care limits access to services and the kinds of services that are insured; means-tested health care was enacted rather than universal health care for all; and antipoverty programs emphasized opportunity and local control, but were not totally successful in achieving group empowerment and redistributive goals. Yet even with these limitations, major changes occurred.

Indeed, the civil rights movement altered the nature of the relationship of black people to the rest of society in important and permanent ways. This includes legal, organizational, and structural reform, cultural norms, and attitudinal, interpersonal, and personal change. As Margaret Burnham (1989) states:

Had nothing else come out of the body of legislation enacted under the rubric of John Kennedy's War on Poverty and Lyndon Johnson's Great Society, it would still not be possible to call any era that heralded the end of legalized apartheid in the United States a failure. How telling that few of the most vocal critics of the 1960s choose to laud it (p. 122).

There is also strong evidence that social programs make a difference. The status of the poor improved during the 1960s and early 1970s, at least in part due to income transfer and antipoverty programs, whereas conditions of the poor deteriorated in the 1980s due to cutbacks in services (Burtless, 1986; Ellwood and Summers, 1986). Frances Fox Piven and Richard Cloward (1983) note, referring to the American welfare state:

In the face of popular pressures during the sixties, expenditures were greatly enlarged, and the procedures governing the social programs were liberalized. Furthermore, welfare-state protections have transformed the distribution of power in private spheres, especially in the market, and they substantially increased the capacity of vulnerable groups to influence the state (p. 64).

Expectations around participatory democracy, a loosening of puritanism, and self-actualization of individuals and groups are other changes that are also noted (Miller, 1986).

It has been suggested that some of the backlash that occurred after the 1960s might have been mitigated if different tactics or strategies had been used (Miller, 1986). For example, perhaps too much emphasis was placed on the rights of the people—implying that reciprocity and citizen responsibility were ignored, or that the nation became too litigious, or that targeting the poor for special attention was bound to create divisiveness and acrimony between groups, or that, precisely because the growth of welfare empowered the poor, resistance and backlash occurred. And there is criticism that progressives were out of touch with the majority of people in the nation who came to resent alleged give-aways to special interest groups, particularly racial minorities (Edsall and Edsall, 1991).

In this volume, the Constitutional rights of individuals in a democratic society are considered core values to be upheld, and government is viewed as the mechanism for protecting and enhancing these rights through judicial and legislative actions. Government leadership can be unifying or divisive; in the case of the last two decades, it has proven more divisive. Similarly, the role of the Democratic party could be a lot more constructive than it has been. Issues of race, which previously had seemed to be contained in the South, became national issues in the 1960s, and the Democratic party has been unable to unify itself since that time. Democrats have also buckled under allegations of permissiveness around work, family, and other traditional values (Ehrenreich, 1989). Thomas Edsall and Mary Edsall (1991) state that the Democratic party did not foresee that being champions of the excluded and disenfranchised would lead to conservative accusations of being soft on crime, criminals, and other so-called deviant behavior. Unfortunately, Democrats have been unable to build new coalitions or to staunchly defend party actions, so they have become apologists instead.

It is intended that this book fill a need to restate the accomplishments (as well as the shortcomings) of the civil rights movement, to illustrate the progressivism of the 1960s that was evident in the social legislation of the decade because these achievements are often underestimated, and to attend to the moral imperatives of that era. Attention to the moral precepts of the 1960s is meant to remind us that disregard of such principles undermines a democratic society and deprives Americans of their

Constitutional rights, such as occurred in the 1980s and continues today. The American people benefit when principles of social justice and equality continue to be present on the public agenda and subsequently become incorporated into everyday life.

1

The Major Concepts: Civil Rights, Social Justice, and Social Policy

The disparity between expectations and reality is the source of much bitterness and frustration in the United States. This disparity is also the basis for social action and social change to bring about convergence between what actually exists and society's basic ideals. Thus, the civil rights of all individuals are guaranteed by the U.S. Constitution and other laws of the land. Included here is social justice—the right to equality of access, opportunity, and outcomes for all individuals. But social justice and civil, or private, rights are yet-to-be-achieved goals and cannot be taken for granted in the United States. Social policies and social programs, the societal commitment to pursue a particular course of action, are the mechanisms through which Constitutional principles of equality and social justice are implemented and enforced and through which democratic processes are expressed.

This chapter first discusses the Constitutional basis for the civil rights of all citizens and the salient civil rights issues of today. Second, it explores differences in definitions of social justice and the role of leadership in influencing public attitudes and beliefs. Finally, it considers various provisions of social policy that enhance or impede a progressive agenda.

CIVIL RIGHTS

The purpose of the civil rights movement was to assure that the fundamental rights of citizens, guaranteed by the Constitution of the United States, to be free, to vote, and to receive equal protection under the law, were protected and upheld (King, 1964). This struggle continues.

Post–Civil War Constitutional Amendments

Although Article VI of the U.S. Constitution sets forth the concept of federal supremacy, the first ten amendments to the U. S. Constitution, added in 1791, reflect the reluctance of the "founding fathers" to submit to a strong central government. Far from embracing a spirit of unity within one nation, the Bill of Rights expresses a fear of nationalism and indicates a commitment to state sovereignty, property rights, and individualism. These sentiments and fears were so strongly felt that the idea of federal supremacy was not fully accepted in all the states, even after the Civil War. Thus, states in the South continued to practice racial discrimination in open defiance of Constitutional law. As Archibald Cox (1987) notes: "The Bill of Rights . . . protects the individual against oppression by the federal government. It would be three-quarters of a century before the Constitution of the United States was amended to safeguard individual rights against violations by a State" (p. 38). Even then, the newly enacted, post–Civil War Constitutional amendments were largely disregarded.

Historically, arguments for states' rights have often masked racial prejudice. In the aftermath of the Civil War, for instance, the newly freed slaves were hardly free at all. In defiance of federal law, ostensibly protecting individual and states' rights against the tyranny of strong central government, Jim Crowism and racial injustices flourished throughout the South (Franklin, 1976). In undermining affirmative action today and arguing against the proposed Civil Rights Act of 1990, for example, conservatives insisted that the Civil Rights Act of 1964 was designed to protect individuals and not groups of people. However, conflict between the powerful and the powerless, and whose special interests should prevail, as well as individual rights, has always characterized this society.

The Thirteenth, Fourteenth, and Fifteenth Amendments to the U. S. Constitution, enacted shortly after the end of the Civil War, are generally regarded as the benchmarks that imprinted the equal status of all Americans. While the Thirteenth Amendment abolished slavery, it was the Fourteenth Amendment, containing the due process and equal protection clauses, that is cited most frequently as the basis for much of progressive legislation. The Fifteenth, or voting rights, Amendment, forms the basis for the Voting Rights Act of 1965. However, each amendment contains the statement that the "Congress shall have the power to enforce the provisions of this article by appropriate legislation." Herein lies the foundation for the never ending judicial and congressional struggle to alternately undermine and protect these Constitutional principles.

The Civil Rights Issues

Derrick Bell (1987) believes that problems for blacks in this country were institutionalized by the U. S. Constitution in its protection of property rights over human rights. The Constitution created individual rights to protect property rights, and, because black slaves were considered property, their civil rights were not even relevant. Thus, there has been an ongoing and never ending struggle to interpret and "fit" the Constitution to uphold the civil and human rights of blacks.

The specific issues dealt with in the civil rights movement are the major societal problems of discrimination in public places, voting rights, school desegregation, employment rights and affirmative action, and equal protection under the law. These issues are briefly explicated here and expounded upon further elsewhere in this book.

Rights in Public Places

The Montgomery, Alabama, bus boycott and nonviolent civil disobedience and sit-ins at lunch counters throughout the South were efforts to overcome racial discrimination in public places, such as stores, restaurants, hotels, gasoline stations, rest rooms, amusement parks, and movie theaters. Of all the battles of the civil rights movement, this is the area of most unequivocal success. More than any other accomplishment, the breakdown of apartheid in public places impacted on the everyday lives of all blacks living in the South (Brooks, 1974).

Voting Rights

Overcoming barriers to voting was even more of a struggle than ending discrimination in public places because of the obvious redistribution of power that might result from such change. State laws prohibiting blacks from voting (despite the Fifteenth Amendment), poll taxes and literacy tests (implemented with great local and personal discretion), and gerrymandering and reapportionment manipulations—all had to be struck down. Interracial Freedom Rides in 1961 and voter registration drives in Mississippi in 1964 and throughout the South were some of the most violent episodes of the civil rights movement (Hampton and Fayer, 1990). Perhaps most famous of all was the march from Selma, Alabama, to Birmingham in 1965 in support of voting rights (Fager, 1974). Although the Civil Rights Act of 1964 deals with voting rights and the Voting Rights Act of 1965 upholds the principle of "one person, one vote," it was not until 1966 that the Court struck down state poll taxes. This action was based on the Fourteenth Amendment–based principle that a state cannot dilute a citizen's right to vote on account of economic status or ability to pay a fee (Bell, 1987).

School Desegregation

Although school desegregation became law in 1954 with the U. S. Supreme Court action in *Brown v. Board of Education*, even thirty-seven years later, battles around school desegregation continue. As neighborhoods continue to be segregated and middle-class people continue to live in suburbs, where low-income housing is opposed, inner-city public schools, with populations that may be anywhere from 80 to near 100 percent composed of children of color, suffer from racial and class discrimination and neglect.

Today, there is disagreement within the black community about busing children to achieve racial balance and skepticism about the outcomes of school integration. In fact, as Bell (1987) notes, the emphasis should be on "equality of quality education" with local control and parental involvement in decision making as educational goals.

Employment Rights and Affirmative Action

It has been argued that the civil rights movement made its fewest gains in the arena of economic rights. Although the Civil Rights Act of 1964 deals in a limited way with employment rights, this is the area that has probably been most disputed in the courts. As recently as 1988, under Ronald Reagan's administration, there were at least six challenges to antidiscrimination laws, which the courts upheld.

Possibly most controversial of all are affirmative action principles in employment and education. While there seems to be little question that affirmative action laws have benefited educated and skilled blacks, these individuals still earn less than similarly educated whites; whites continue to be favored over equally qualified blacks in employment (according to a recent study by the Urban Institute); and black job mobility and job security remain more precarious than those for whites. Additionally, the gap between the economic and social status of middle-class and poor blacks has been widening. Affirmative action is implicated in the intransigency of black poverty in urban ghettos, but this shifts the blame to the victim.

Public opinion polls indicate that Americans appear to support affirmative action in the abstract, but are generally unsupportive of its implementation. Charges of quotas and reverse discrimination, beginning with the Bakke case in 1978 (Cox, 1987) and continuing into President George Bush's veto of the Civil Rights Act of 1990, renders affirmative action, the way the leadership of this country has recently defined it in economic, rather than civil rights, terms as one of the most divisive racial issues today.[1]

Equal Protection

Currently, the equal protection clause of the Fourteenth Amendment requires strict evidence of "intent to discriminate" before it provides protection for minorities. Since the passage of antidiscrimination legislation, acts of bigotry, prejudice, and discrimination are apt to be more subtle and covert than in earlier days, thus making it more difficult to demonstrate intent:

Today, while all manner of civil rights laws and precedents are in place, the protection they provide is diluted by lax enforcement, by the establishment of difficult-to-meet standards of proof, and, worst of all, by the increasing irrelevance of antidiscrimination laws to race-related disadvantages, now as likely to be a result as much of social class as of color (Bell, 1987, p. 5).

In commenting on the intransigency of institutional racism, Bell touches on another struggle for equality and human rights for all: classism. However, antidiscrimination judicial and legislative actions cannot be overlooked. These actions continue to provide a needed supportive foundation for new challenges that can be expected against women and minority groups in civil rights. The issues of social class add to the complexities of race and gender discrimination in the United States.

SOCIAL JUSTICE

David Gil, in 1976, outlined the role of social justice and equality in a way that continues to be relevant to a progressive analysis of social policy. To Gil, the criteria for a just policy are the degree to which the goals of equality of access, opportunity, and outcome are achieved (Gil, 1976). His ideas run somewhat parallel to those of John Rawls in *A Theory of Justice* (1971). According to Rawls, justice is the moral basis for a democratic society and thus is the first and most important virtue of social institutions: "In a just society the liberties of equal citizenship are taken as settled; the rights secured by justice are not subject to political bargaining or to the calculus of social interests" (p. 4). Social justice, viewed as equality, would thus require equality in the assignment of basic rights and duties and presupposes a conception of social justice that provides a standard for assessing the distributive aspects of the basic structure of society. Rawls includes the concepts of social cooperation and fairness in his formulation of distributive justice and emphasizes that "inequalities of wealth and authority are just only if they result in compensating benefits for everyone, and in particular for the least advantaged members of the society" (p. 15). A class analysis of socioeconomic differences is implicit in Rawls's formulation.

It is totally inconsistent with Rawls's conception of justice to argue that, because it is inherent in individuals and in society, inequality is therefore immutable to change or that equality really can never be achieved. Rawls would contend that just institutions correct such inequities through a fair distribution of resources and power; a just society sets a fair distribution of these resources as a goal to benefit the least-advantaged members of society:

The most obvious injustice of the system of natural liberty is that it permits distributive shares to be improperly influenced by these factors [e. g., chance contingencies as accident and good fortune] so arbitrary from a moral point of view. . . . The liberal interpretation . . . seeks to mitigate the influence of social contingencies and natural fortune on distributive shares. . . . Free market arrangements must be set within a framework of political and legal institutions which regulates the overall trends of economic events and preserves the social conditions necessary for fair equality of opportunity (Rawls, 1971, p. 73).[2]

All of this is in sharp contrast to libertarian views purporting that tampering with personal inequality violates individual rights and privileges and is antithetical to principles of liberty and freedom. Alan Brown (1986) notes that libertarianism, including the concept of minimal state and natural rights doctrine, "isolates the value of individual liberty from those of welfare and equality" (p. 87). In contemporary parlance, the primacy of social and economic equality over economic liberty fits into the progressive tradition, whereas economic liberty (particularly free market mechanisms) is more apt to be identified with the conservative domain. In the latter framework, concepts of fairness and entitlement come to mean "any distribution of holdings that results from legitimate transactions concerning legitimately acquired holdings is itself legitimate—and thus may not be interfered with on grounds of justice. In fact, to interfere (say by taxing the rich to help the needy) is unjust" (p. 95). In the extreme, it can be suggested that the entire welfare system is unjust because it takes away private earnings from their rightful owners.

Writers such as Nathan Glazer (1988) are able to support conservative public policies by asserting that it is not the role of government to implement social justice. While Glazer concedes that "social justice means equality" (p. 156), he argues that the United States lacks equality because "most people don't want much more equality than we have. . . . and even among the poor, only 55 percent (at most) strongly support redistribution" (p. 159). He further contends that most Americans would like to restrict the role of government to limiting distress and not have it redistribute income. Within this framework, if government tries to implement social justice, it makes people "greedy and resentful" (p. 167).

In addition to differences in definitions of justice, there is also disagreement about what is meant by the concept of social obligations. While all citizens and corporations have rights and obligations, from a conservative point of view, it is mainly the poor who have obligations to society in a welfare state. Mandatory workfare programs discharge part of these social debts. Other such obligations include behaviors that uphold the work ethic (Katz, 1989), the family ethic (as described by Mimi Abramovitz, 1988a), and other institutionalized expectations of middle-class society, such as cleanliness, politeness, gratitude, and other cosmetic accoutrements.

An opposing position views corporations and the affluent as having special obligations to society. This includes the duty to replenish used and abused natural resources; the protection of workers from insecure, dangerous, and capricious work environments; and the responsibility to uphold the laws of the land in business practices, including banking, stock market activities, and real estate ventures (Gil, 1976; Piven and Cloward, 1987). This point of view asserts that government has an obligation to protect the basic rights of individuals, including access to such rights as housing, health care, education, and adequate income.

Given such opposing views of justice and the obligations of government and the wealthy in society, it is not surprising that major differences in beliefs about social legislation exist in this nation, leading to cycles of expansion and retrenchment in social programs.

Despite what Glazer (1988) cites as evidence that Americans do not support goals of equality within their society, survey data indicate that Americans are not as niggardly as conservatives suggest; in fact, conservative leadership asserts and reinforces public negativism about social programs and the poor. It cannot be denied that increased racial tension exists in the United States at the present time. Certainly there is backlash from the 1960s. But, at least as important is the fact that the political leadership has failed to unify ethnic and racial groups within and between socioeconomic classes. Conservative leadership under Reagan and now within the Bush administration has exacerbated, rather than mitigated, racial tensions and conflict.

A study conducted at Smith College in 1989 revealed that people emulated racist and antiracist sentiments. While antiracist remarks tended to be echoed by other antiracist statements, the opposite was also true. Dr. Fletcher Blanchard, a psychologist who conducted the research, is quoted in the *New York Times* as saying that a few outspoken people who are vigorously antiracist can establish the kind of social climate that discourages racist acts. Dr. Stuart Cook of the University of Colorado is also quoted, "I have no doubt that the absence of strong disapproval by our national leaders of racial and ethnic hatred has found its way into our schools and businesses" (Goleman, 1991). Many studies indicate that simply placing black and whites in proximity to each other may not reduce stereotypes and bias but that working together for a common goal does, in fact, break down negative stereotypes. Americans are not inherently mean-spirited or egalitarian, and racial bias can be reduced in a non-discriminatory environment.

In fact, changes in social policy are known to change social attitudes and behaviors, as well. For example, when asked in surveys how they feel about the homeless and social spending, Americans will usually say that homelessness presents a serious problem that is getting worse and that the government is not doing enough and should do more to help homeless people. Some people even go so far as to say they would be willing to pay higher taxes to pay for this. On the other hand, a large minority of people say also that homelessness is caused by lack of personal effort and that people on welfare getting too much money is a bigger problem than people on welfare not having enough money to live on (Heclo, 1986; ABC News and Associated Press, 1988, 1989). These sentiments change as the sentiments of the nation's leadership change. The current economic recession creates greater support for some social programs, but more antagonism toward others. Where programs are supported, alleged government waste is often deplored.

Although backlash from the civil rights movement is often emphasized as a negative outcome, the drama of the civil rights movement heightened awareness of what could be achieved by mass movements and the responsibilities and obligations of government toward its citizens. During the 1960s, people were optimistic that government could solve social problems. As the federal Department of Justice intervened, however tentatively, to protect the rights of individuals and to uphold the laws of the land, the concepts of social justice and equality became politically palpable. These principles lie sufficiently dormant, or are actively suppressed, during conservative periods in the United States so that it takes events of sufficient magnitude—like the civil rights movement—to reawaken and revitalize these foundations of American democracy. In fact, progressive social movements in the United States restore equilibrium when the tendency toward conservatism becomes overly dominant.

When the consciousness of Americans is aroused, as a result of charismatic leadership, popular discontent, or mass movements, there are opportunities for constructive action, and this occurred in the 1960s. But countermovements are also awakened. The leadership and power centers in society shape the sentiments of Americans into social policy, and social legislation becomes the tangible evidence of these beliefs. Social protests like the civil rights movement can, and do, radicalize the populace, on the right and on the left. Thus, the civil rights movement led to progressive actions, as well as to strengthening neoconservative and right-wing politics. The resurgence of conservatism in the 1970s probably can be accounted for, in large measure, by the fear of empowerment of previously oppressed groups that occurred as a result of the social activism of the 1960s and by the perceived threat to the status quo and personal well-being of the wealthy. In the conservative decade of the 1980s, there was either lack of attention to the problems of the poor or further blame and victimization of the population in order to undo empowerment gains and expectations. So far, in the 1990s, a lagging economy adds to the beliefs that the nation cannot afford social programs and that the poor are a moral and economic drain on society.

SOCIAL POLICY

Kahn (1973) takes on the difficult task of trying to define and categorize components of social policy. He states that policy is:

The explicit or implicit core of principles, or the continuing line of decisions and constraints, behind specific programs, legislation, administrative practices, or priorities. . . . General social services are programs that protect and restore family life, help individuals cope with external or internalized problems, enhance development, and facilitate access through information, guidance, advocacy, and concrete help of several kinds (pp. 8, 19).

Kahn considers such diverse programs as day care, homemaker services, personal and family counseling, child welfare services (including foster care and adoption), probation and parole work, family planning, food stamps, and information and referral services as "social services," excluding (somewhat arbitrarily, it seems) income maintenance, health, housing, education, and employment programs.[3] While Kahn's analysis reveals the many facets of social policy, and his approach is universal rather than solely targeted to the poor, he does not attempt to provide a theoretical perspective on the functions and purpose of these policies. An attempt at theoretical explanation follows below.

Political Economy and Social Control

When the purpose of social legislation is questioned, political economy and social control theories are usually invoked. Within a political economy perspective, social legislation serves the ends of political and economic power rather than has the needs of citizens as its primary goal. Social programs and civil rights legislation are viewed as politically expedient and based on economically and politically opportunistic motivation. From this perspective, legislation not only supports the traditional power structure within society but also, in the process, actually strengthens existing institutions. In this framework, John F. Kennedy, in his quest for the presidency in 1960, and Lyndon B. Johnson, in 1964, supported progressive legislation because they viewed this as politically necessary for their election. After signing the Civil Rights Act of 1964, Johnson allegedly declared, "I think we just delivered the South to the Republican Party for a long time to come" (Moyers, 1988). Support for Judge Clarence Thomas for the U.S. Supreme Court by Southern Democratic Senators in 1991 reveals the growth of black electoral power in the South. And the recent approval by President Bush of the compromise 1991 Civil Rights bill is believed to reflect his best political instincts. From a political economy point of view, such laws or actions do not redistribute wealth or power or expedite social change but, rather, consolidate the status quo within preexisting structures and institutions and among specific individuals. It can be argued, for example, within a political economy framework, that President Reagan constructed the federal budget deficit to justify curtailment of spending for social programs. The reification of the status quo in family and work values can also be explained by principles of political economy. That is, these values support the maintenance of a pool of workers, men and women, who are available when needed to fill menial, low-paying, dead-end jobs (Block et al., 1987).

Social control theory mirrors political economy theory in its maintenance of the status quo, but adds to the principles of opportunism and exploitation of the poor the dimensions of regulation and cooptation in the name of personal improvement and social stability. For example, through beliefs, rules, regulations, procedures, and levels of income that demean and punish the poor, the welfare system prevents the empowerment and mobility of women and minorities and reinforces their dependence on the patriarchal system in society (Miller, 1990). Incarceration of the mentally ill "for their own sake" is an example of social control. Although Harrington (1984) makes the point that the social legislation of the 1960s actually encouraged and increased social turbulence and militancy, rather than curbing these tendencies, as suggested by Frances Fox Piven and Richard Cloward (1971), this only attests to the complexity of social behavior and social movements and does not necessarily disconfirm political economy or social control ideas.

Progressivism and Social Reform

But it is more than political economy or social control theories that account for the social legislation of the 1960s. Such factors as the growing attention to issues of socioeconomic class and poverty, increased sensitivity to considerations of race and cultural diversity, the moral imperatives of the civil rights movement, potential and actual social and economic unrest, and the power of trade unions and the Democratic party all converged to support enactment of progressive social, as well as civil rights, legislation.

Despite the progressivism of the era, in reality of course, the legislation considered in this volume had serious shortcomings. That is, the goal of social change was only partially achieved. Contradictory principles contained within specific social policies illustrate the constant political struggles between progressive and more regressive elements in society. As discussed earlier, redistribution of economic resources and political power were limited, although the latter has grown somewhat more than the former in recent years. The limitations of specific social policies can be illustrated by a discussion of the contradictory principles of universal entitlements versus means-tested programs, public service versus privatization, cash versus in-kind services, and centralized versus decentralized service delivery.

Universal Entitlements

Progressive politics are generally associated with more universal entitlements in social legislation rather than with means-tested programs based solely on need. Public assistance, however well intended and needed, stigmatizes the poor and is the target of public recrimination. Even though minority group members are not the major recipients of public assistance, popular beliefs to the contrary persist. Thus, racism and racial divisiveness combine with existing negative attitudes toward welfare and welfare recipients to create an inadequate and unstable welfare system.

Universal programs, such as education and Social Security, because they serve all social and economic groups, generally have more popular appeal and political support. They are likely to be of better quality because the poor are often poorly served, the stigma associated with welfare is reduced, the criticism of bowing to special interests is mitigated, and legislation is not viewed as undermining the morality of society but, instead, is seen as an integral part of society (Wilson, 1987). Income transfer programs such as Social Security, also narrow the gap in income between the rich and the poor through taxes and benefits, respectively.

Public education, an entitlement that should benefit from universalism, does not receive the kind of public support that would be expected for several reasons: Children are a special target group with insufficient recognition in the society; separatism in education, between urban and suburban cultures, renders education almost means-tested, based on capacity to pay (Kozol, 1991); and there is a conservative movement afoot to undermine all universal programs. Among other factors, means-tested programs, because the poor are generally powerless, are easier than universal programs to regulate and retrench. On the other hand, just as full employment policies will not reach all segments of society, means-tested programs are needed, even when universal entitlements exist, to meet the special needs of poor, oppressed, and disenfranchised people.

Legislation has recently been enacted that begins to undermine basic rights and entitlements to adequate income from unemployment insurance and Social Security retirement benefits by imposing taxes on both programs. There is substantial public support for taxing Social Security retirement benefits, particularly for the more affluent elderly, as a cost-saving mechanism. In fact, an economic backlash against the elderly currently exists.

President Bush proposed that premiums for Medicare Part B be tripled for the more affluent elderly, and, in 1991, the maximum wage base for computing the health insurance portion of Federal Insurance Contribution Act (FICA) increased to $125,000 while the wage base for Old Age Survivors Disability Insurance (OASDI) remained at $53,400. This resulted in substantially greater Social Security taxes for the higher wage earner. Proposals such as these represent attempts to divide the elderly population and to erode popular support for Medicare, and all of this really represents prejudice and discrimination against older citizens and universal programs in general. Because they have benefited from income transfer programs and many are no longer poor, and because they have formidable political clout, the elderly are no longer considered helpless and as deserving as they had been when they were submissive and compliant and poor.

It is true that social spending in the past twenty-five years has gone disproportionately to programs for the elderly, most prominently Social Security and Medicare. In 1990, for example, the government spent $353 billion on Medicare and Social Security, but only $100 billion on programs such as food stamps, school lunches, tax credits, Medicaid, and welfare that help the poor. For the elderly, the spending has made a great difference. The poverty rate for older Americans dropped from 35.2 percent in 1959 to 11.4 percent in 1989. As it fell, it crossed the poverty rate for children, which has risen from 15.5 percent in 1970 to 19.6 percent in 1989 (DeParle, 1991). What is not mentioned, however, is that the cost of Medicare is a problem of the health care system in the United States and not the fault of the elderly. There is a need to applaud, rather than deplore, the improvement of conditions for older citizens.

It is the erosion of universal entitlements that is at stake here. If Social Security benefits become means-tested, it will ultimately be the poor and minority elderly, rather than the rich, who are most adversely affected because they will be stigmatized and will receive the fewest and lowest benefits, while the affluent will have choice and other alternatives. When the Catastrophic Health Program (within Medicare) was repealed in 1990 because of strong opposition by the elderly, it was the affluent elderly who were blamed. But members of Congress petulantly threatened to throw their allegiance to children and away from *all* of the elderly. Suddenly, the deserving elderly became the ungrateful and undeserving rich elderly.

Society should be progressing toward greater income security and health benefits for all, rather than sliding into more demeaning means-tested programs. In the realm of health benefits, Medicaid, a means-tested program with state and federal financing, is experiencing major cutbacks and public antagonism. Again, the poor elderly who depend on Medicaid for long-term nursing home and home care are victimized, as are the poor of all ages.

In response to President Bush's budget request for fiscal year 1992, a *New York Times* editorial proclaimed the following:

Everyone over 65 is entitled to Medicare health insurance. Entitlements serve noble causes, but there's a problem: They're eating up the budget. All other non-military federal operations account for only 7 percent of the budget [the cost of the war in the Persian Gulf is estimated at between $164 and $268 billion]. . . . For the sake of controlling federal deficits, entitlements will have to be reined in. And for the sake of fairness, what is spent for entitlements will have to be targeted on the needy. . . . They [the Democrats] are already ridiculing Mr. Bush's persistent desire to cut the tax on capital gains because it would hand over billions to wealthy families. The Administration is unlikely to win this battle of populist appearances; its overall budget weighs heavily toward the affluent. . . . And according to estimates by the Center on Budget and Policy Priorities, the budget would reduce non-entitlement programs for low-income families by more than $750 million. . . . What warrants immediate welcome is the principle of directing entitlements to the people most entitled: the poor (Who's Entitled?, 1991).

President Bush has already proposed the diversion of funds from one set of children's health programs to target infant mortality in ten cities, rather than increasing funding for all children's programs. Reagan also proposed the "safety net" concept while cutting aid to the poor.

Privatization

Although during the 1960s the role of government was viewed relatively positively, the public sector in the United States generally does not enjoy the respect and reverence experienced in other Western nations. For example, the enactment of Medicare, which was generally considered progressive legislation, provided a major role for the for-profit sector in health care. In fact, the original legislation specifically limits any encroachment of public regulation on the free enterprise system in medicine. Under the Reagan administration, the private use of public funds for profit—that is, privatization—spread much beyond health care with a substantially increased role for the private sector in delivery of all kinds of human services.[4] Although the nonprofit sector in health care and social services has a long and honorable history, and even here there has been concern about an invidious two-track system of public and private services, growth of the for-profit sector is a relatively recent development. Negative attitudes toward government and deregulation of private industry by the Reagan and Bush administrations renders privatization even more worrisome. Privatization in this context is not consistent with a progressive agenda because profit in health care and social services is generally incompatible with social justice goals.

There is a strong likelihood that standards of availability, access, and quality of care may be differentially applied to low-income and middle-income clients where service for profit is the norm. Paul Starr (1989) states this objection:

To alter the public/private balance is to change the distribution of material and symbolic resources influencing the shape of political life. Privatization ought to be frankly recognized as part of an effort of conservatives to reinforce their own power position. Since I do not share the values for which that power is deployed, I distrust privatization. . . . As we move public provision into the private sector, we move from the realm of the open and the visible into a domain that is more closed to scrutiny and access. And in the process . . . we are likely to narrow our involvements, interests, and visions of a good society and a good life (p. 44).

There is current belief in the inevitability and appropriateness of public/private partnerships. However, the question of balance between the two sectors is raised, as well as the possibility of other kinds of partnerships. For example, partnerships between labor, church groups, nonprofit community-based organizations, new coalitions of citizens, and municipal government should be considered. Which sectors shall prevail, in what areas, and at what social cost? Arnold Gurin (1989) suggests that the criteria of access, quality, and cost be applied in evaluating the mixed economy of public and private funding and operations (Kamerman, 1983); efficiency, flexibility, and innovation are other criteria that might be included in this assessment. Sheila Kamerman and Alfred Kahn (1989) in discussing child care, comment on the availability of these services in a demand-based marketplace: "The decline in direct funding (supply subsidies) has led to fewer low-income children being served within the organized service system—and in some instances to the unavailability of formal services for them—while service options and subsidies have increased for the middle-income groups" (p. 249).

With regard to services provided by the for-profit and nonprofit sectors, without an ideological direction and taking only a pragmatic approach, many professionals contend that there is little discernible difference between the quality of services in, for example, home health care, day care, nursing home care, or acute hospital care administered by for-profit or nonprofit organizations. These conclusions may result from eyeballing the situation rather than from rigorous, empirical research. Again quoting Kamerman and Kahn regarding child care: "Our own very limited assessment of the for-profit and nonprofit services reveals no consistent patterns. . . . There has been no comprehensive and rigorous research comparing the quality of programs under for-profit and nonprofit auspices, so the issue remains unsettled and important" (p. 251). Clearly, pragmatic considerations are significant, but ideological issues are also relevant to the private/public partnership debate.

In-Kind Services

One of the major limitations of the social legislation of the 1960s was the lack of new, expanded income maintenance programs. Beginning with the 1962 amendments to the Social Security Act, which increased the service provisions of public assistance, most Great Society legislation provided in-kind services instead of increased financial aid (Burtless, 1986). This was part of the access and opportunity strategy of the War on Poverty.

While it is true that the rolls for Aid to Families with Dependent Children (AFDC) increased during the 1960s and early 1970s, this was a spin-off from the civil rights movement rather than the direct result of new legislative action. Michael Sosin (1986) makes the point that a strong legal rights perspective in welfare developed during the 1960s, and this resulted in greater protection of the rights of individuals eligible for public assistance. But Betty Mandell (1990) notes that:

The NAACP, the Urban League and other middle-class black groups chose not to ally with a welfare rights group advocating a guaranteed annual income, preferring instead to emphasize jobs. . . . The most useful and long lasting relationship, continuing to the present, was the coalition between the National Welfare Rights Organization (NWRO) and Legal Services. . . . They struck down the man-in-the-house and suitable parent laws and residency requirements, all of which had been used to harass welfare mothers for years. They also established the right to a fair hearing before welfare departments could terminate benefits. However, this winning streak ended in April, 1970 when the Supreme Court rejected a suit which sought to establish a constitutional right to welfare (p. 113).

Piven and Cloward (1971) also discuss the development and impact of the NWRO on increased public assistance enrollment. However, all of this built on what already existed, rather than initiating new income programs. There was little or no government support for additional income maintenance. In fact, one distinguishing characteristic of programs in the 1960s was an emphasis on "no hand-outs." Thus, what has come to be seen as an important criticism from some poverty policy analysts, in contrast to 1930s New Deal programs, was a 1960s strategy and ideology.

All of the social programs chosen for inclusion in this book provide in-kind services, rather than income, and these programs are typical rather than unique. In fact, policy analysts, advocacy groups, and citizens have different basic approaches to alleviate poverty through income or service programs. Adequate income programs tend to be favored by more left-leaning individuals and groups and low-income citizens, especially for women with young children, whereas income programs (such as welfare) are rejected by individuals and groups with a more conservative, middle-class orientation.[5] Ironically, it wasn't until the Richard Nixon administration that the Family Assistance Plan was introduced, which included new legislation to provide a guaranteed annual income, but with powerful work incentives and regressive discretionary mandates.

Decentralized Services (New Federalism)

A fourth area of controversy that impacted on the goals of 1960s legislation was the role of the federal government in social policy. Beginning in the 1930s, New Deal legislation involved the federal government in social programs to an unprecedented degree. The growth of federal government participation generally continued unabated and expanded in the areas of funding and the provision of services for several decades. In the 1960s, lack of minority representation in social programs and the desire for local control created pressure for the transfer of program administration and operations to state, local, and nonprofit community-based organizations, but with continued federal funding. Herein lies the irony that was created. Centralized services, generally identified with liberal government, had been preferred because of uniformity and objectivity in service delivery, and the potential for redistribution of resources on the national level. In contrast, decentralized services had tended to be discretionary, uneven, and generally poorly funded. In addition, the history of states' rights (and racial inequality) and local control conjure up images of conservatism. (How many of us associate "support your local police" with police brutality?) New Federalism, as defined by President Nixon and later by Reagan and Bush, has, in fact, been identified not only with decentralized, local services but also with cutbacks in funds and less government responsibility for domestic affairs (Griffith, 1989). Indeed, New Federalism has state and local governments fighting over limited federal resources and has almost bankrupted the coffers of many states and municipalities. Decentralization, under the Reagan and Bush administrations, has meant local responsibility without local control and empowerment.

The decade of the 1960s was a transitional period in this regard. Major resistance to indigenous local control was expressed by established, mainstream local governments who feared redistribution of goods and resources and loss of power. This local government resistance undermined the achievement of citizen participation and empowerment, particularly for minorities. However, beginning in the 1960s and continuing today, local control, grass-roots organizing, and community initiatives are progressive goals. In the uphill struggle to protect the right to abortion, state legislatures and state courts are now looked to for support, and there is a resurgence of grass-roots, coalition building that is changing the nature of electoral politics on the local level. A viable progressive agenda, using special interest politics to build coalitions of women, people of color and multiple ethnicity, the disabled, gays and lesbians, labor unions, and the working poor, is enjoying local electoral victories.

It may be helpful to differentiate the political process and electoral successes from social policy, funding, and service delivery. While in programs and service delivery the goals are local movements, local provisions, and local operations, it is in policy formulation and funding that often "a decentralized, community-based strategy cannot make up for the absence of national, universal benefits in crucial areas" (Gurin, 1989, p. 203). There is no substitute for universal national health and employment *policies* and funding, for example, with health and employment *programs* carried out on the local level, with local control, input, and authority.

Unfortunately, cities currently do not have the money to govern adequately, and states are also experiencing extreme economic downturns. The politics of the Reagan administration, with deregulation of business, budget cuts that favored the rich, and a massive military buildup, all of which resulted in a huge federal budget deficit, is generally acknowledged as a major culprit in the current recession and fiscal crisis being experienced by many states and cities. Only the federal government has the capacity to equalize regional, state, and local differences through redistribution mechanisms. There is a need for federal funding patterns and a national policy in such areas as abortion, civil rights, fiscal policy, and market and labor conditions. But this should not substitute for local empowerment in citizen movements, programs service delivery, and electoral politics.

Despite the progressivism of the 1960s and the moral imperatives of the decade, all of the social legislation enacted combined provisions that enhanced and impeded a progressive agenda. Thus, Medicare was a universal entitlement that provided health care for all elderly, irrespective of need, while Medicaid was a means-tested program only for the poor. Antipoverty programs were designed to provide services and community action for the poor, but often poverty is most effectively alleviated through income transfer programs. The public sector is often the most important source of affirmative action and pro-union policies, and while the history of the nonprofit sector in social services is honorable, the advent of the profit motive in human services does not usually serve the best interests of distributive justice. Moreover, while local control and citizen participation are quintessential progressive goals, there may be no substitute for national policies in areas such as health and employment.

A PROGRESSIVE AGENDA

A progressive agenda is not unattainable nor is it subversive. The history of the Progressive Era in the United States, in the first two decades of the twentieth century, for example, is a fascinating account of the many contradictory forces that influence social change. The same arguments are raised about that era that are brought up about the 1960s in relation to assessing the accomplishments and legacy of those noteworthy years. Some parallels between the Progressive Era and the civil rights movement are instructive.

In a general sense, both were attempts to democratize society by broadening the powers of government to help overcome the social injustices that were occurring as a result of the rapidly growing economy. In 1900, five percent of the population owned nearly half of the property, while more than one-third of the nation's 76 million people subsisted below the poverty level. Not the least among the achievements of the era were women's suffrage and the legacy of the women's movement (e.g., Chamberlain, 1965; MacKay, 1966; Mann, 1964; Gould, 1974; Cooper, 1990; Dawley, 1991). Today, full-employment policies would be advocated, the minimum wage would have to increase substantially, a minimum income would be guaranteed, there would be universal health insurance, and welfare reform would provide economic security and job mobility and raise working peoples' incomes above the poverty level. Rather than controlling inflation by increasing unemployment, other planned economic strategies would be implemented. As Ray Marshall, Secretary of Labor under President Carter, is quoted as saying:

We know that a full-employment program would be good business. With a jobs program, $15 billion could save the federal government $30 billion. We've demonstrated that in the past. The main reason we don't do it now is the neoconservative mythology that it didn't work. We ought not to let them get by with that. The contrary evidence is overpowering (Burnham, 1989, p. 123).

And in contrast to traditional liberalism, a new progressive agenda would have a class consciousness (Ehrenreich, 1989). In fact, the purpose of social policy would be to correct social and economic inequities and ultimately to create a classless society.

The successes of the 1960s reflect a confluence of factors: a compelling moral message about desegregation and the rights of individuals and groups; the practical challenges of confrontational tactics and urban unrest; and, with reservations, a government willing to provide some programs and some money to begin to achieve social justice for all (Miller, 1986). Piven and Cloward (1983) believe that the welfare state has been empowering to all citizens:

The rise of the welfare state has contributed to the extension and deepening of the idea that democratic rights include economic rights. . . . The idea that economic rights are political rights is strengthened because there are organizational forms and political relationships through which these ideas can be turned into action. . . . The development of the welfare state has contributed to the expansion of democratic aspirations, and to the articulation and organization of democratic influence (pp. 58, 69).

Issues of civil rights, social justice, and social policy can be translated into questions of race, social class, and democracy. In U. S. society, these issues are ubiquitous. The unique aspect of the 1960s was that these difficult problems were addressed. Even the war in Vietnam and the antiwar movement dealt with some of the same concerns. However, since the 1960s, the U. S. government has been unwilling to even acknowledge these problems. This requires that people on the grass-roots level force these issues onto the national agenda.

NOTES

1. Melvin Urofsky (1991), citing the 1978 Bakke case and more recent Supreme Court actions on affirmative action, points up the Supreme Court's inconsistency on this issue. The American people share this ambivalence.

2. Citing Rawls in this brief way is not meant to do justice to his formulation nor to critically evaluate it. His ideas about distributive justice and social justice help in our conceptualizing the goals of social work and social policy.

3. Kahn (1973) defines social welfare as "all those policies and programs by which government guarantees a defined minimum of social services, money, and consumption rights, through the employment of access or distribution criteria other than those of the marketplace and through demand management of the economy" (p. 24).

4. Privatization does not refer only to the use of public funds for profit. It generally also includes the nonprofit and not-for-profit sectors, as well as family and other informal and voluntary supports, and self-help and mutual aid societies and groups. Additionally, there are numerous combinations of public and private arrangements in such areas as funding, administration, third-party contracts, provision of services, regulation, and so on. However, privatization during the Reagan years was used as a strategy to dismantle the welfare state. This is discussed further in Chapter 6 and the Epilogue.

5. Public assistance policy (welfare) disproportionately affects women and children and its gender, class, and racial implications must be recognized. A more detailed discussion of this topic can be found in a paper by Julius Newman, et al. (1991).

2

Critical Issues in the 1960s and 1980s

It is elusive to try to account for all of the factors that led to the civil rights movement in the 1960s. I have suggested, however, that the movement provided the impetus for the social programs of the decade. It is possible to identify factors associated with the progressive events of the era, and to contrast these events with regressive conditions in the 1980s, in order to understand both decades more fully.

The critical issues of the economy; the status of race, social class, and gender; the role of government and privatization; and the moral imperatives in the society—these are some of the factors that provide the context for understanding the differences between the 1960s and 1980s. These issues are among the most intransigent in society. While many positive adjustments and modifications in social and economic conditions occurred in the 1960s, much remains to be done because of backsliding and because basic social change rarely occurs in the United States, even in the most progressive times. Addressing the critical issues and the political, economic, and social context of public policy should be helpful for understanding and facilitating the process of social change. I am interested in how the civil rights movement and other conditions of the 1960s led to expansive social legislation and what happened to that legislation in the last twenty years.

THE ECONOMY

The post–World War II economic boom in the United States, with some periods of recession, lasted until around 1970. Thus, the 1960s was a time of prosperity in the nation. The decade is even sometimes referred to as the "Golden Age of American Capitalism" (Henwood, 1991) in recognition of the economic growth that occurred and the steadily increasing standard of living that many Americans enjoyed. The decade also marked the beginning of public awareness of the contrasts between the rich and the poor, along with an awareness that, even in times of prosperity, some Americans continued to be poor. Indeed, it became increasingly evident that poverty was not randomly distributed within society but fell much more heavily on specific groups, such as women, people of color and ethnicity, and the elderly.

It is understandable, although ironic, that a by-product of successful capitalism was the infusion of resources into the welfare state in the 1960s. During times of economic growth when government support may be less needed, the government can afford to be generous, possibly because the distribution of power and the "cost of doing business" is less threatened during periods of prosperity. Indeed, issues of social justice may be considered a luxury to be enjoyed during periods of abundance. In contrast, in times of economic decline, as witnessed in the 1980s and now in the early years of the 1990s, when the need is greater, government is most stingy. Thus, the state of the economy is clearly a factor to be reckoned with in understanding periods of progressivism and conservatism. The economy cannot be considered a neutral player in accounting for political and social conditions. The use of unemployment to control inflation is an example of a frequent monetary and business practice that affects workers most adversely. Economists note that the United States is likely to lay off workers when there are slowdowns in the economy, while Japan, for example, is more apt to dip into shareholder profits which is less likely to lead the economy into further decline.

By the 1970s, the economy had ceased to grow (Bluestone and Harrison, 1982). The "oil crisis", led by the OPEC nations in the mid-1970s, was an ominous turning point in the comfort and standard of living of many Americans. However, when Jimmy Carter, campaigning for the presidency in 1976 and 1980, warned of the declining economy, he was dismissed as the voice of gloom and doom. By the beginning of the 1980s, however, the United States had already lost more than 30 million jobs as a result of private disinvestment in American business. This loss mainly occurred, and continues to occur, in the manufacturing sector of the economy. The slide from U.S. economic preeminence in a global marketplace is well known to every American who has bought an automobile, television set, videocassette recorder, or calculator in the last fifteen years. In 1986, amid general prosperity, the New England region alone lost 56,000 manufacturing jobs. In Connecticut, between 1989 and 1991, 79,200 jobs were lost, and, since 1985, a total of more than 90,000 manufacturing jobs have been lost. By 1991, the recession in Connecticut had claimed more jobs than any economic downturn since World War II, and manufacturing employment had fallen to its lowest level since 1940. One reason for this economic disarray in Connecticut is that money from other states, from manufacturing and insurance, for instance, is lost when these industries falter (Campbell, 1991). And Connecticut is certainly not alone. California lost 380,000 jobs in the first half of 1991—including 112,000 in construction and 99,000 in aerospace. Despite a substantial tax increase, California had a $3 billion budget deficit in 1991. As a result of the recession and weaknesses in the safety net, the poverty rate was 13.5 percent of the population in 1991.

In a *New York Times*/CBS News national survey of 1,280 adults, taken in October 1991, 20 percent of respondents rated the economy as very bad, and 46 percent said it was fairly bad. Only 1 percent thought it was very good.

When Ronald Reagan became president in 1980, he immediately cut domestic spending by $50 billion (or 21 percent of the total domestic program). He then cut income taxes, primarily for the rich, 25 percent, phased in over three years. Then he increased military spending, allegedly to make up for laxness in this area under the Carter administration. All of this created enormous budget deficits. The federal government piled up more debt during the 1980s than in the previous 205 years. Throughout his administration, Reagan deregulated business and commerce, ignored antitrust laws, and permitted unlimited mergers and acquisitions. The philosophy of less government intervention also contributes to the do-nothing attitude in domestic affairs of the current leadership. The current national recession, which began in February 1989, is considered a direct result of these actions. And a long list of social programs have never recovered from cutbacks that began in the 1980s. There is speculation from some sources that this is no ordinary recession—a cyclical downturn that will in time cure itself—but the legacy of a decade of reckless and self-indulgent economic policy.

The "deindustrialization of America" (Bluestone and Harrison, 1982)[1] and growth in the global economy have also been accompanied by continued decline in trade unionism in the nation. Almost immediately after his election to the presidency in 1980, Reagan set the negative tone for trade unionism by breaking the strike of the air traffic controllers. The threats of industries and companies that they will close and move elsewhere seeking "a more favorable business climate" has been actualized many times in recent years, and world capital and the international marketplace facilitate this movement. Today, management uses highly sophisticated union-busting strategies and tactics; when jobs are scarce, many workers view trade unions with fear and trepidation, rather than as a source of protection from capricious business practices.

Barry Bluestone and Bennett Harrison (1982) agree with such writers as Piven and Cloward that cutbacks in social spending and destruction of unionism intimidate the poor and working class and thereby help keep wages low. As Piven and Cloward frequently point out (1971, 1977, 1983), unions, welfare benefits, and other public services help the poor and working class resist the exploitations of the business community.

As unionism and the manufacturing sector of the economy declined, the resulting economy has become more bifurcated. Growth in the unstable, low-skill, low-pay retail and service sectors of the economy on one end of the continuum and the development of high-technology, high-skill jobs, unavailable and unsuited for many people in the society, on the other have become the norm. Thus, the blue-collar worker has suffered greatly as structural change has occurred in the economy. The position of the middle-class has also become more tenuous and precarious as the value of real wages has declined. The income of men has been falling since the 1980s, especially in the last five years. The average wages of workers are below 1979 levels, but family incomes have been maintained by wives going to work. In 1960, 30 percent of wives with children under 18 worked; by 1987, 65 percent did. Women are now earning 71 percent of what men earn, primarily because the earnings of men have declined. The creation of new jobs in any geographic region has not kept pace with the number of jobs lost, and thousand of workers, after they lose their jobs, spend long periods of time unemployed. If and when they return to work, often it is for much lower wages, at temporary or part-time work, without fringe benefits (particularly health insurance and pensions) and perhaps relocated to a different part of the country. Further, while many more jobs were created on the lower end of the spectrum than the upper end, and the blue-collar worker is the hardest hit, both manufacturing and service sectors of the economy have experienced the calamities of the recent recession. In addition to financial ruin, these changes in the economy also have major political and social ramifications.

At the present time, the economy of the United States is cause for alarm. A boost in federal spending, using the peace dividend, for health, education, employment, social programs, and infrastructure—rather than further retraction—is absolutely crucial. The current protracted recession has resulted in the unemployment of thousands of individuals (and the loss of as many jobs), with only the dimmest hint of imminent recovery. Retrenchment in major industries, such as the loss of 74,000 General Motors jobs in the next four years and restructuring of such corporations as IBM, suggest a permanent downsizing in U.S. industries unless major reinvestment and growth occurs.

The bifurcation of the economy, which appears to be more entrenched, needs to be restructured. In the 1980s, Connecticut's service sector employment passed that of manufacturing. There is a need for diversification in employment. While Robert Reich (1991) points out that high technology is the growth sector of the future, others note the need for small businesses (New York City has 195,000 small businesses, which mainly employ recent immigrants); a return to manufacturing (New York City alone has lost more than 750,000 manufacturing jobs in the last two decades); and the revitalization of shipping and rail freight, in addition to the trucking industry. There is a moral, as well as an economic imperative, to educate and train the citizens of this nation to occupy jobs at all levels of the economy, and it is a responsibility of government planning and policy to assure a wide mix of employment opportunities. This is necessary for the well-being of individuals and the nation.

THE STATUS OF RACE

In the early part of the 1960s, there was substantial sympathy and support for black Americans who were struggling for their constitutional rights. Media coverage of peaceful black protesters and marchers being hosed by local police and attacked by German shepherds evoked cries of horror and indignation among most TV viewers. Many whites were moved to join with blacks in the righteousness of their efforts, and both whites and blacks shared in the dangers and excitement of the movement. The voice of Martin Luther King, Jr., urging peaceful coexistence and racial integration, had a soothing and reassuring effect.

By the latter part of the 1960s, the civil rights movement had lost Reverend King, and many blacks, particularly in the North, had lost their goodwill and patience toward unyielding whites. As violence erupted in Northern cities across the nation and as the rhetoric of hate, separatism, and Black Power became more dominant, blacks and the civil rights movement appeared less sympathetic to many whites. Concurrently, antipoverty programs were undermined by accusations of waste and fraud, and the government was placed on the defensive about succumbing to the demands of minorities and providing preferential treatment for special interest groups.

At the present time, affirmative action—a successful program of the civil rights movement—is under heavy attack, and racial attitudes are extremely contentious.

Affirmative Action

Affirmative action in employment and education, where minorities and women have made the most gains since the civil rights movement, has been subjected to some of the toughest challenges in the courts and in legislation. By the 1970s, accompanied by a decline in the economy, a full-scale backlash against the black community (and against women) had began to develop. The Reagan administration, in the 1980s, capitalized on racial tensions and divisiveness, and racial conflicts have increased into the 1990s as a part of the Reagan legacy, inherited and perpetuated by

President Bush. Currently, one of the most controversial aspects of race relations is affirmative action, which has been used by conservatives in the 1980s and 1990s to alienate and estrange whites and blacks from each other, and which has recently become the subject of controversy within the black community as well. In fact, whites continue to enjoy preferential treatment in the job market, and disparities in income between whites and blacks have increased rather than abated. A recent study conducted by the Urban Institute found that when equally qualified black and white candidates applied for the same job, the black candidates had worse outcomes 20 percent of the time. In 1991, blacks accounted for about 7,500 of the 127,000 students enrolled in law school in the United States; only 3 percent of doctors are black. Nevertheless, great antagonism to the implementation of affirmative action policies continues.

On almost all indicators blacks did more poorly than whites during the 1980s. The gap between black and white median family income was $14,586 in 1986, higher than at any point in the 1970s, and there has been a consistent pattern of widening income inequality between blacks and whites since 1980 (Phillips, 1990). A 1989 study by the National Research Council of the National Academy of Sciences and Engineering found declines in the 1980s in the quality of life of blacks in all areas: For example, black life expectancy declined, with murder the leading cause of death among young, black men, and infant mortality in the black community is higher than in many third-world countries. Although blacks are only 12.1 percent of the population, 40 percent of prisoners awaiting death penalties are black, and blacks who killed whites are four times as likely to get death sentences as are those who killed black victims. A lagging economy, poor lawyers, and racial discrimination are incriminated in these findings. A recent government report indicates that within the same income group, blacks are twice as likely as whites to be rejected for home ownership mortgages. (Quint, 1991; Flynn, 1991).

Blacks in every income strata, from the poorest to the most affluent, lost ground and had less disposable income in 1984 than in 1980, after adjusting for inflation. Nearly 36 percent of the black population are living in poverty. This is the highest black poverty rate since the Census Bureau began collecting these data in 1968 (U.S. Census Bureau, 1989). In 1985, the Urban League reported that in virtually every area of life that counts, black people made strong progress in the 1960s, peaked in the 1970s, and have been sliding back ever since. In 1975, black unemployment was 14.1 percent, with white unemployment at 7.6 percent. At the end of 1984, black unemployment was 16 percent, with whites at 6.5 percent. Blacks consist of 10 percent of the labor force, but account for 20 percent of the jobless. In 1960, nearly 75 percent of all black men included in the Census data were working; today, only 55 percent are working. In 1986, the median black family had 56 cents to spend for every one dollar white families had to spend, which was two cents less than they had in 1980 and almost six cents less than they had in 1970 (Bell, 1987).

The wealth (i.e., the lifetime accumulation of property and other assets) of affluent people grew substantially in the 1980s, while the assets of other Americans barely kept pace with inflation, as reported by the Census Bureau in 1990 (Pear, 1991a). During the current recession, the rich have gotten richer. White households typically have over ten times more wealth than black households have. While the median net worth of a white family was $43,280, for a black family it was $4,170, and for Hispanics it was $5,520. Thus, economic disparities in wealth would continue even if black and white income were the same. However, the nation's income (i.e., one year's earnings) distribution is also becoming more unequal, with a bigger gap between people of high and low incomes.[2]

Although affirmative action policies and programs have opened opportunities for many educated blacks, other blacks living in inner-city ghettoes have barely been touched by these programs. According to William Julius Wilson (1987) these urban dwellers only represent about 10 percent of individuals living below the poverty level, but they reflect a disproportionate incidence of social problems. Conditions in the Watts neighborhood in Los Angeles, for example, are considered worse today than in 1965, with 18 percent unemployment, more young black males in prison than graduating from high school, inadequate housing, and drug-related gang violence (Volgenau, 1990).

Samuel Myers (1990), writing about the ascendancy of black leaders in electoral politics, raises some gnawing questions:

We need to know why the rise in black political power has not translated into economic improvements for those blacks concentrated at the lowest rungs of American society. We need to know why our brand of democracy allows some blacks to become Supreme Court justices, governors, mayors and states' attorneys, while others remain poor. We need to know why many of our cities that have blossomed into powerhouses of black political talent are sinking under the weight of the black masses' economic distress. . . . It will take a careful introspective look among blacks. It will require a long-term dialogue between blacks and whites about economic inequality. This inequality remains the sore point between blacks and whites.

For all blacks, racism is pervasive. For most middle-class blacks, however, the current agenda is economic empowerment, without affirmative action programs, if possible, but with affirmative action, if necessary. For the poor, it is good jobs and decent housing, with housing too often ignored.[3] With blacks and whites on the right and left challenging affirmative action policies and programs, there is heightened disagreement and antagonism about how to achieve these goals. It is hoped that perhaps the growth in black political leadership will help blacks enter the mainstream of economic opportunity in larger numbers, but that remains to be seen (Applebome, 1990).

In assessing black progress, it is probably fair to say that the civil rights movement helped achieve, first, antidiscrimination legislation and personal empowerment for many blacks; second, voting rights and political leadership goals; and, third, some economic changes and structural changes in society's institutions along with some positive changes in black/white relations. The movement, such as it is currently, continues to seek increased black empowerment in all areas of American life, especially in the economic sphere. In addition to unfinished business for blacks and other people of color and ethnicity, women, children, the elderly, the physically disabled and mentally retarded and mentally ill, are some of the many groups with legitimate civil rights and social justice claims.

Racial Attitudes

In interviews conducted in 1978 and 1979, Bob Blauner (1989) notes the wide discrepancies between whites and blacks in their perception of racial progress, with many whites believing that the dream of Martin Luther King, Jr. for a racially just and integrated society had already occurred, and blacks believing that little progress had been made. After almost a decade of the Reagan administration, in 1988 and 1989, new interest emerged in assessing the status of race relations in the United States.

In 1988, Louis Harris and Associates conducted a survey on American racial attitudes (NAACP Legal Defense and Educational Fund, 1989). The findings indicated that 89 percent of blacks and 79 percent of whites agreed that the rich are getting richer and the poor are getting poorer; 78 percent of blacks and 73 percent of whites favored affirmative action job programs for blacks, provided there are no rigid quotas; and over 90 percent of blacks and whites favored federal programs, business incentives, and early intervention school programs to help low-income, inner-city black youth and young adults. However, there was considerably more disagreement on other subjects. On the question "How are blacks treated by the justice system," 80 percent of blacks and 35 percent of whites believe that blacks are treated less equally. Blacks, substantially more than whites, also believe that blacks have been kept down by the U. S. Supreme Court, Congress, local police, and public schools. There were also large discrepancies between whites and blacks in attitudes toward employment, with many more whites believing that blacks receive equal pay for equal work, that blacks are promoted as rapidly as whites, and that blacks have equal opportunity to join a skilled craft union. In 1988, some 28 percent of blacks and 55 percent of whites opposed busing to achieve racial balance in the schools; in 1967, some 78 percent of whites opposed busing.

A study in 1989 by the University of Connecticut Institute for Social Inquiry also confirms general support for affirmative action, but opposition to specific measures for its implementation, such as "quotas" (Williams & Bixby, 1989). In addition, a report by the National Research Council in 1989 entitled *A Common Destiny: Blacks and American Society* (Shapiro, 1989), states that "blacks and whites share a substantial consensus, in the abstract, on the broad goal of achieving an integrated and egalitarian society" (p. 15). In the University of Connecticut poll mentioned above, questions about integration in friendships, neighborhoods, the workplace, and church or synagogue remind the reader that blacks experience interaction with whites much more fully than whites with blacks in their daily lives and therefore must accommodate more to whites. There is also information that neither blacks nor whites are enthusiastic about the likely outcomes of school integration. Blacks believe their children receive a somewhat worse education than whites, but they do not think integration of public schools would make much difference. This appears to be related to general skepticism about how much racial integration actually improves race relations (Williams and Bixby, 1989). Findings from the National Research Council Study also refute myths that affirmative action has provided equal economic status for whites and blacks. In 1984, the average yearly earnings of black male college graduates was 74 percent of their white counterparts. The report concludes that U. S. society is not likely to move in the direction of greater racial integration and equality without government leadership and policy emanating from the highest levels (Shapiro, 1989).

These findings indicate both areas of agreement and areas where differences in perceptions exist and that an overwhelming majority of Americans, both white and black, agree that the national agenda on civil rights remains unfinished (NAACP League Defense and Educational Fund, 1989). S. M. Miller (1986) reminds us that we are not concerned only about improving the standard of living of people, although this is a major goal, particularly for the poor; we are also concerned about transforming economic and social arrangements throughout society. Blauner (1989) points out that reform continues to occur, but without the passion and conviction that existed previously, as blacks take a more measured view of the possibilities of change and as whites continue to resist racial equality. Bell (1987) goes further; he asserts that "progress in American race relations is largely a mirage, obscuring the fact that whites continue, consciously or unconsciously, to do all in their power to ensure their dominion and maintain their control" (p. 159).

Bell (1987) argues that the issues of race in this country can never be fully resolved through judicial and legislative actions because ambiguities and contradictions around race relations are built into the U. S. Constitution. This begins with protecting property rights over human rights and considering slaves as property and continues in such areas as voting rights, affirmative action, equal protection under the law, and desegregation of schools. Bell believes that even court actions that have been highly touted as helping blacks have really helped whites and "the civil rights decisions of the Warren Court were profoundly conservative and protected the economic and political status quo" (p. 61). This can be seen most vividly in the many frustrations that have resulted from lack of enforcement and restraints on major judicial and legislative actions. On the other hand, after considering other options, including violence and separatism, Bell concludes that the hope for whites and blacks in this country for a just society rests on struggling to uphold Constitutional rights. In seeking a restructured society, he believes that future civil rights campaigns "while seeking relief in traditional forms, should emphasize the chasm between the existing social order and the nation's ideals" (p. 255). Using metaphor, Bell advises that it is prudent to be aware of the hazards of a leaking ship and try to fix the leaks, but not to abandon ship if you have no alternatives.

At the present time, a great deal of attention is paid to issues of race, but in much different ways than in the 1960s. Racial tensions pervade neighborhoods, and black and white murders surround issues of territoriality. Minorities are still disproportionately represented in school dropouts, unemployment, and the criminal justice system, and racial conflicts on college campuses reflect racism and the regressive attitudes of many young people. Destructive and hostile conflict in the North and South between whites and blacks—in neighborhoods, on the street, on college campuses—without any constructive ideological base or social protest movement, has increased. And, although the struggle for civil rights continues, there is no organized protest movement. Thus, blacks and whites lash out in anger and frustration, and there is no grass-roots or government leadership to channel anger into progressive programs or policies.

There is a crisis in our cities once again with social problems that disproportionately victimize people of color. Although crime, drugs, and alienation are not new phenomena, there are no ready solutions—not even constructive proposals for solutions at the present time. Cities and states are financially bankrupt, and the federal government continues its campaigns of sloganism and disinformation and its policies of immoral neglect. Currently, racial discrimination and hostile encounters are as overt and as dangerous throughout the nation as they were in the days of Jim Crow in the South.

THE STATUS OF SOCIAL CLASS

The concept of social class was rediscovered in the 1960s as the civil rights movement provided the impetus and stimulus for rediscovering poverty. As social change occurs within the family structure and in the workplace, with more women and minorities striving for independence, career mobility, and economic security, the issues of social class and changes in status quo and power relations become increasingly salient. Thus, writers such as Wilson (1987) believe that social class may be surpassing race as a more divisive and conflictual aspect of this society.

Certainly the growing gap between the rich and the poor, as documented by Phillips (1990) and others, is chilling. Although issues of social justice and equality are tied to race, gender, and class, conservatives disdain to talk about class because they consider it "divisive." It is considered "unpatriotic" to suggest that reducing the capital gains tax is a give-away to the rich. The myth of the classless society in the United States is as powerful as the melting pot concept, but the former belief may be even more insidious because it so obviously affects social justice, equality, and economic debates. Barbara Ehrenreich (1989) points out that denial of class differences is precisely the way class differences are maintained. Unless these differences are acknowledged, there is no chance of addressing issues of equality and inequality in this society.

Despite economic growth, the widening gap in income between the rich and the poor has become glaring enough to generate popular media attention. The Census Bureau estimates that in the last seven years the poorest one-fifth of U.S. families received 4.6 percent of the total income—the lowest percentage since 1954. By contrast, the wealthiest one-fifth of families accounted for 44 percent of the income—the highest share ever recorded by the Census Bureau. The percentage of families living below the poverty level reached 15.2 percent in 1983 and was 13.5 percent in 1990:

The official overall poverty rate declined markedly from above 20% in the early 1960s, when it first became a focus of attention, to 11% in the early 1970s, with the gain widely shared by all demographic groups. . . . The antipoverty effectiveness of the various public transfer programs is often understated. . . . If all in-kind benefits were counted as income at their cost to the government, the poverty rate by 1979 would have been less than 7% rather than the official rate of 11.7% (Palmer et al., 1988, p. 9).

American workers are earning less after inflation than they did a decade ago. As a result, living standards are lower, and most families have more members working longer hours just to stay even. Despite economic need, however, women continue to be criticized for working outside the home. Upper-income groups, particularly the richest 1 percent saw their incomes grow substantially in the 1980s. Outrage is being expressed in the popular press about the income of CEOs in major corporations. For example, it is reported that since 1988 Reebok's CEO received $40.9 million; in 1990

Disney's CEO made more in a day than the average Disney employee made in a year; and while United Airline's profits fell 71 percent in 1990, United's CEO received $18.3 million in salary, bonuses, and a stock-based incentive plan. Changes in federal, state, and local taxes since 1977 have shifted the tax burden more to the middle class and the poor, while giving large tax cuts to the richest 1 percent of the population. Distribution of the nation's wealth became more concentrated among the richest families, while more lower-income families slipped below the poverty level (Phillips, 1990). Even with the poverty line considered too low, 13.5 percent of the population were in poverty in 1987. This figure fell from a high of 22.2 percent in 1960 when government began to pay attention to the poor to 11.1 percent in 1973, 11.4 percent in 1978, 15.2 percent in 1983, and 13.5 percent in 1987 (Bureau of the Census, 1987).

There is significant interaction between class and race, with people of color disproportionately poor. Although the economic situation for the unskilled black worker has worsened, housing and employment opportunities for educated blacks with skills have increased. In the past thirty years, the black middle class has grown from 10 percent to more than one-third of the black population. Bell (1987) tells us, however, that "affirmative action programs are not designed to deal with the problem of the disproportionate concentration of blacks in the low-wage labor market. . . . [There is a] deepening economic schism . . . developing in the black community, with the black poor falling further and further behind middle- and upper-income blacks" (p. 48). It is important, however, to try to understand the intransigent poverty of many urban blacks before accepting explanations that implicate middle-class blacks.[4] Sociologists such as Wilson (1987), legal scholars such as Bell (1987), and policy analysts such as Gil (1976) point out the economic and sociological ramifications of affirmative action policies that have divided the black community. But they also point out the economic and social conditions in society that cause and perpetuate poverty conditions. Affirmative action policies are also implicated in divisions between the white and black working and middle classes. Attacks on affirmative action policies, generated by conservative forces in society, fuel racial animosities. However, not unlike welfare, trade unionism, and other imperfect systems, the intentions and goals of affirmative action are far more positive than negative in protecting disenfranchised groups and individuals from economic and social oppression.

Gil (1976) points out that racism, ageism, and sexism are not discrete phenomena but, rather, intrinsic aspects of an exploitative, competitive, hierarchically structured class society. He notes that "competition and discrimination are often encouraged overtly and covertly within capitalist systems, so as to counter the emergence of solidarity and class-consciousness among workers, a prerequisite toward socialist transformation" (p. 208).

A class consciousness is basic to a progressive agenda that deals with issues of social justice and equality:

It may be possible for the middle class to rediscover the "lower classes" . . . as allies in a struggle to curb the inordinate and growing power of wealth. This is, in fact, almost the defining dream of the American left: that discontented members of the middle class might join the working-class majority in a political effort to redistribute both power and wealth downward, to those who need them most. . . . The point of discussing class is ultimately to abolish it (Ehrenreich, 1989, p. 256).

It is encouraging to remember that social and economic policies that polarize citizens and erect barriers to equality are changeable and changing all the time, but not without a struggle. And that affirmative action policies, despite their limitations, need to be protected because they have helped women and minorities begin to break out of the oppressive status quo in power relations within this society.

THE STATUS OF GENDER

The feminization of poverty means both that most poor people are women and that the growth of families headed by women is the main source of the rapidly rising poverty among women and children (Piven and Cloward, 1987).

In 1987, the Census Bureau calculated that the overall poverty rate in America was 13.5 percent, increasing for children under 18 to 20 percent, or one out of five children living below the poverty level, including two in every five Hispanic children and 49 percent of all black children. Forty-three percent of mother-only families are poor. At the present time, 51 percent of all poor families in this country are headed by women, 40 percent of whom are employed outside the home, often working for wages below the poverty level.

The *National NOW Times*, February–March 1989, reports the following:

In 1986, 4.5 million women were in the workforce yet lived in poverty. Over half of these poor women had children. The median income for full-time working mothers was a mere $7,056, placing them well below the poverty line for a family of three of $9,056. Almost half of these women have high school diplomas, which have not translated into more than a subsistence level lifestyle. Indeed, thousands of female-headed families in poverty are headed by woman college graduates (Women in Peril, 1989, p. 5).

Regarding equal pay for comparable work, in 1986, the median income for full-time working women with a high school education was $15,947, while male high school graduates received $24,701:

If women and minorities were compensated on the basis of education and experience at the same rate as white men, pay for white women would increase 30%, pay for Hispanic women would rise by 35.6% and pay for black women would go up 37.8%. The segregation of women into low-paying jobs remains a glaring problem . . . and minority women are even more segregated into low-paying jobs than white women (p. 5).

Gertrude Goldberg and Eleanor Kremen (1987) identify four factors that contribute to the feminization of poverty—i.e., the increase in the number of women living below the poverty level: (1) labor market factors, such as gender differences in wages and occupational segregation; (2) the scope and adequacy of government income transfers; (3) the extent of policies to promote economic equality, such as equal pay legislation or affirmative action; and (4) demographic factors, such as rates of divorce and single and teenage motherhood. In their comparison of the feminization of poverty across five European countries and Japan and Canada, these authors find a "ubiquitous and continuing concentration of women in low-wage work and the related substantial wage gaps between men and women" (p. 11). However, there are marked differences in the extent of female poverty in the seven countries:

Sweden, for example, has a family allowance, a housing allowance, universal health care, public assistance, unemployment insurance, and extensive public works and job training programs. Childbirth leave is available to either parent for a total of 12 months; during the first nine months, 90% of earnings are replaced. Parents also get paid leave when their children are ill. Child support payments are guaranteed by the government in case of parental default. France provides a similar array of benefits and services (p. 5).

Comparison of the adequacy of transfer payments indicates that:

In Sweden, a single mother with two children who does not work is assured benefits that equal 94% of the Average Production Worker's Wage (APWW). If the woman has a low-paying job, her combined income from earnings and transfers equals 123% of the APWW. In France, the comparable figures are 79 and 88%. . . . In New York, which has one of the most generous AFDC programs, these benefits plus the cash value of Food Stamps came to about three-fourths of the poverty level for a four-person family with no earned income in 1985 (p. 6).

In the United States, the median income of families with a female householder was only 48 percent of the median income in 1984; in Canada, this figure was half that of families headed by men; and in Japan, the median income of families headed by single women is about 45 percent of the median for all families. In Sweden, the median income for single-mother families was approximately equal to the median for the country

(Goldberg and Kremen, 1987). Thus, given the wage inequities between men and women across all the countries that were studied, it is evident that it is the social policies and social welfare programs that make the significant difference in the feminization of poverty.

The feminization of poverty usually involves the poverty of children, as well. More than 75 percent of the poor are women and children; the poverty rate for children living in female-headed households in 1984 was 54 percent. Accompanying the issues of poverty for children is infant mortality, child physical and sexual abuse, poor education resulting in dropping out of school, and lack of sufficient, adequate child care facilities. The recent World Summit for Children held at the United Nations gave an international perspective to the problem, but President Bush proposed cuts to children's health services in the fiscal year 1992 budget.

The Center on Budget and Policy Priorities reports that in 1987 over 5 million families with children were living in poverty in the United States, an increase of 35 percent since 1979. Only one out of ten families was lifted out of poverty in 1987 by government cash programs such as Social Security, unemployment insurance, or public assistance. In 1979, the same programs helped one out of five families to escape poverty. The decline in effectiveness of government programs is even greater when noncash benefits are also taken into account. Reductions in benefit programs, economic changes that have reduced the earnings of poor families, and changes in the composition of the poverty population, including an increase in single-parent families, are some of the factors associated with increases in poverty.

In our predilection for invidious comparisons and choosing sides, we are now pitting the elderly against children and extending the abortion debate on the rights of women versus children to include punishment for women who allegedly abuse their fetuses through drug and alcohol abuse (Pollitt, 1990). And this is extended to the child welfare system where lack of treatment facilities for women who are substance abusers puts them at risk of losing their children:

Most women prosecuted for using illegal drugs while pregnant have been poor members of racial minorities, even though drug use in pregnancy is equally prevalent in white middle-class women. . . . The American Civil Liberties Union has begun keeping track of races and economic classes of women who are prosecuted for using drugs while pregnant. . . . Eighty percent of the women were black, Hispanic or members of other minorities (Kolata, 1990).

Middle-aged and elderly women are particularly at risk for poverty conditions. The middle-aged woman who has not worked out of the home and whose children are grown is probably not eligible for AFDC or Social Security benefits. The Older Women's League notes that women receive only two-thirds of the Social Security benefits men receive, and only 23.5 percent of retired women receive pension income, at an average of $394 a month. Only 43 percent of women working full-time are covered by employer-financed pension plans. Nearly 75 percent of the elderly poor are women, and in 1989, the median income for women over age 65 was only $7,300 per year (Kleiman, 1991).

Despite awareness that women are among the poorest citizens, the concept of the "family ethic" as explanatory has only recently gained ascendancy through the work of Mimi Abramovitz (1988), who states:

As a dominant social norm, the family ethic articulates the terms of women's work and family roles. According to its rules, proper women marry and have children while being supported by and subordinated to a male breadwinner. . . . [In social welfare policies,] compliance with the family ethic became the basis for distinguishing between deserving and undeserving women (p. 3).

Although the feminization of poverty is still blamed by conservatives on "family breakdown" as its root cause, writers such as Wilson (1987) have documented economic conditions and black male unemployment as decisive factors in poverty for single-parent households.

The major welfare program for women in U. S. society—Aid to Families with Dependent Children (AFDC)—maintains women in conditions of poverty. The Family Support Act of 1988, "welfare reform," has been touted as a major change and improvement in social policy. In fact, the new legislation incorporates myths about the poor that uphold traditional beliefs about the work ethic, the family ethic, and the so-called culture of poverty. As far back as history records welfare practices, there has been an emphasis on the work ethic, almost always defined in righteous terms, usually without reference to labor market conditions. Similarly, an entrenched family ethic has "kept women in their place" (Abramovitz, 1988a). It is also alleged that social programs have created a "culture of poverty" that considers welfare dependency as normative behavior. The Family Support Act of 1988 perpetuates these beliefs and is therefore destined to repeat the welfare failures of the past (Newman et al., 1991). Perhaps most importantly, there is a finality in the recent legislation that cuts off further debate.

Abramovitz (1988) contends that current welfare reform is the latest assault on women. Suggesting that welfare policy has failed to preserve the status quo in upholding traditional women's roles within a patriarchal structure, she argues that the provisions of the Family Support Act of 1988 are an attempt to reinstate the regulatory functions of welfare. This is particularly true in relation to provisions that change AFDC from an income support program, which protected the rights of women to remain at home and care for their children, to a mandatory work program that imposes the work ethic and punishes welfare recipients for violating work ethic and family ethic codes.

We have noted that even a vigorous economy, due to ageism, racism, and sexism, will not necessarily lift all groups out of poverty. But there is evidence that a universalistic, full-employment policy is attainable and would be cost efficient if there were the political will to implement such a program and if women had a right to choose to work at home or in the marketplace. At the present time, means-tested, mandated education and employment training, without job creation, and without an increase in the minimum wage, will not lift AFDC recipients out of poverty conditions, and welfare provides options that insecure, low-paid work does not. In order for women of all ages to achieve economic self-sufficiency, there is the need for adequate income, universal national health insurance, subsidized child care, transportation, and scattered-site, low-income housing.

Without job creation, the current economy cannot absorb additions to the labor force. Thus, once again, there is discrepancy between ideology and reality. Poor women will be harassed to meet the requirements of welfare eligibility, but a shortage of jobs will continue and the jobs that do exist will not lift poor women out of poverty conditions. It remains to be seen if educational efforts, within the current welfare system, can successfully move impoverished women out of welfare into permanent, secure, well-paying jobs.

More attention is currently being given to the relationships between race, class, and gender in the poverty literature (Wilson, 1987). Those who criticize welfare as "colonizing" blacks need to be sensitive to the plight of poor women—black and white. Today, 43 percent of black children are born poor, and two-thirds of black babies are born to unmarried mothers. These figures cry out for more knowledge and understanding. It is a conceptual and research challenge to pursue these issues in relation to social justice and egalitarianism in our society.[5]

THE ROLE OF GOVERNMENT AND PRIVATIZATION

During the 1960s, the American people were still reveling in the glories of the post–World War II era, psychologically as well as economically. They were having babies, buying houses and moving to the suburbs, driving on superhighways, and enrolling in higher education, thanks to the largesse of the federal government. There was confidence that government could be called on to intervene effectively to help other nations on a global level and to help "deserving" citizens within this nation. There was also a willingness to correct social ills, as everyone was benefiting from the federal government's generosity. Trade unionism was strong, and the Democratic party still stood for the rights of the blue-collar worker and the downtrodden in the nation.

Antipoverty programs were sharing power between the federal government as funder and newly created, local, nonprofit community action agencies as purveyor of social programs. The role of the traditional municipal government was changing, as local nontraditional control with "maximum feasible participation" of the poor in planning, decision making, and program operations was growing. Although the role of the private, nonprofit (largely sectarian) social agency has a long history in the United States in human services, the 1960s marked the development and growth of new non-profit, community-based organizations to an unprecedented degree.

The expanding economy, confidence in the government, a moral imperative from the leadership of the country that reinforced democratic ideals, demands from the black community for equal access to the goods and services of society, and empowerment of minorities—all converged to enhance the role of government as a source of social justice in public policy.

By the 1970s, all of this began to unravel. The federal government began to respond negatively to the alleged excesses of the 1960s in social spending and preferential treatment for minority groups. Empowerment of previously oppressed groups and the potential for redistribution of power within the society were quietly squelched. The 1970s can be viewed as the "age of accountability" in government spending. The business practices of the corporate sector were revered as the model for the operation of public human services, and program evaluation, cost-benefit analysis, and efficiency became government buzzwords for curbing spending on social programs. The 1970s also marked the beginning of New Federalism, with a shift from federal to state and local responsibility for the delivery of social services and an increase in privatization (for example, third-party contracts and other kinds of arrangements with for-profit agencies and organizations) as a presumed way to achieve greater efficiency and cost-effectiveness in providing these services. The Vietnam war and the Watergate scandals were crowning blows to confidence in the federal government. Along with a declining economy, the events of the 1970s set the stage for future government retreat from human services in the next decade.

The major government events of the 1980s, mentioned earlier, were initiated and maintained by the Reagan administration. These included massive tax cuts for corporations and the rich; a gigantic military buildup, which was allegedly needed to overcome negligence in this area during the Carter administration; cuts in spending for social programs, which were purported to be needed to improve the morality of the poor and to reduce inflation; and a reduction in the role of the federal government, ostensibly to enhance individual choice in the free market by deregulating business and encouraging privatization of human services.

Tax cuts to the rich and to corporations, increased defense spending, and a declining economy are major factors associated with the dramatic federal budget deficit that grew during the 1980s and which now manifests itself in the 1990s in the economic recession and in state and municipal budget deficits.[6] Deregulation of business, rather than increasing competition and lowering prices, resulted in an unprecedented era of mergers and acquisitions, failed banks and savings and loan associations, and unscrupulous business practices throughout the investment community. Today, it is noted that the federal budget deficit is a subsidy program for the rich (internationally, as well as within the United States), who benefit greatly from interest gained on the purchase of federal bonds (Henwood, 1991).

John Kenneth Galbraith is quoted as saying, "The present recession is not an autonomous, self-correcting economic drama. It is a wholly predictable response to the speculative extravagances and insanities—and the specific Government policies—of the 1980s. We are paying for the mergers-and-acquisitions mania which left around one third of our large corporations with a heavy, sometimes crucifying, burden of debt. We are experiencing the consequences of an extreme and often mindless speculation in urban real estate; of the junk-bond miasma; and of legislative and regulative measures that, in effect, put Government funds—guaranteed bank and S&L deposits—at the disposal of some of the fiscally most extravagant and felonious entrepreneurs since John Law and the South Sea Bubble" (Ivins, 1992).

As a bottom line, a crucial difference between the 1960s and 1980s is the relationship between the public and private sectors in all spheres of American life. Simply put, during the 1960s, the government was viewed as the solver of social problems caused by economic and other societal dislocations. Newly created community-based organizations, with grassroots support, forged a true partnership with the public sector, and a "mixed economy" of private, nonprofit agencies operating with public funding blurred the distinctions between the private and public sectors of service delivery. Although two tracts of public and private service delivery—separate and unequal—continued, never again would the sharp distinctions between public and private services be the same.

In the 1980s, government was not only considered the problem, but it was the private, for-profit sector that was looked to as the redeemer and problem solver. The movement toward privatization with for-profit organizations, which has infiltrated all levels of government, is basically anti-union, anti-affirmative action, and unaccountable to citizens in its use of public funds. The balance between the private and public sectors of our society is currently tipped decidedly in the direction of the private sector. Similar to the balance of power between the federal government and the states, there is a ubiquitous tug and pull in these relations. The direction of this strain reflects the dominance of progressive or regressive forces in the society.

SOCIETY'S MORAL IMPERATIVES

The United States in one of the most moralistic countries in the Western world. Highly religious and prone to righteousness and nationalism, the American people hold ideals and realities that are some of the most contradictory in the world. Going back to the Protestant ethic, a cornerstone of belief among Americans is the alleged link between wealth and power and virtue. This is particularly disturbing because it suggests that if the rich are virtuous, the poor are not. Herein lies the basis for beliefs that the poor are lazy, indolent, and immoral. As Katz (1989) has reiterated, it is the basis for distinctions between the deserving and undeserving poor.

During the 1950s, the moral agenda focused attention on individual shortcomings, expressed in the psychiatric belief that individual rehabilitative services would prevent and ameliorate conditions of poverty. The Social Security amendments of 1962 emphasized family preservation and self-sufficiency and incorporated rehabilitative services into welfare practices to achieve these goals. Despite rehabilitative social services, however, welfare rolls increased during the 1960s as the civil rights movement brought about changes in legislation and public attitudes toward rights and entitlements. While there was continued ambivalence in public policy around women's place in the home or in the workplace (Abramovitz, 1988a), AFDC recipients became empowered and found outlets for their voices in such places as the National Welfare Rights Organization. But as the women's movement began to take shape and poor women were increasingly empowered, backlash against women, particularly poor women, increased. By the 1970s, pressure began to mount to punish and oppress newly empowered groups, and people of color and women became targets for the resurgence of social Darwinism and neoconservatism in the 1980s.

The 1980s can be characterized by a general mean-spiritedness toward the poor. Impatience and resentment toward the homeless with no solutions in sight for the desperately poor, neglect and moral indignation against people with AIDS, and disdain for civil rights and the decline of the standard of living for most Americans—these are some of the domestic problems that have been ignored by the Reagan and Bush administrations.

The decade of the 1950s, which is remembered as one of conformity, repression, and protection of traditional values, is reported by C. Wright Mills (1956) as a time of immorality among the very rich. Similarly, the decade of the 1980s, again characterized by reification of traditional values, will also be remembered for the excesses of greed and materialism of the privileged classes. Thus, it appears that dogmatic support for traditional values is associated with indulgence of the rich. Within this value system, the social justice functions of redistribution are an anathema, and it is considered an entitlement of the rich to benefit most from the capitalist system.

It is clear that belief in less government, a free market economy, and individualism in social arrangements are all associated with maintenance of the status quo and conservative politics. In contrast, confidence in government and belief in social justice and economic and social equality are associated with progressive politics and public policies. The latter conditions are reinforced by ideology and values located in democratic institutions and constitutional ideals. Thus, there is convergence between civil rights and progressive social programs and curtailment of civil rights and regressive social policies and legislation.

A review of selected differences between the 1960s and 1980s helps provide the context for understanding differences in social programs and social legislation in the two decades. These include changes in the economy, in racial attitudes and race relations, in attitudes toward women and the feminization of poverty, in class consciousness and class structure, in the role of government and the growth of the private for-profit sector in human services, and in marked differences in morality and moral definitions and judgments. In considering a return to a progressive agenda, analyzing and updating 1960 conditions to meet the challenges of the 1990s could have a productive outcome.

NOTES

1. Bluestone and Harrison (1982) define deindustrialization as "widespread, systematic disinvestment in the nation's basic productive capacity. . . . The essential problem with the U. S. economy can be traced to the way capital—in the forms of financial resources and of real plant and equipment—has been diverted from productive investment in our basic national industries into unproductive speculation, mergers and acquisitions, and foreign investment. Left behind are shuttered factories, displaced workers, and a newly emerging group of ghost towns" (p. 6).

2. Although I have emphasized blacks in discussions of racial and economic inequalities, other minority groups also suffer greatly from social and economic injustices. In the northeast, Puerto Ricans, particularly, are disproportionately represented among the poor, and in the southwest and west, the same can be said for Mexican-Americans. Thus, all of the social and economic problems identified with the poor disproportionately affect all people of color. A recent Children's Defense Fund study indicates that the poverty rate among Latino children in the United States is skyrocketing. Although these children are less likely to live in poverty than are black children, their rate of poverty is growing faster than those of most other groups. While 20 percent of all children in the United States were living in poverty in 1989, 33 percent of Latino children were poor. Poverty rates increased for all children in every racial and ethnic group between 1979 and 1989, while the poverty rate for Latino children rose at a faster rate than that of white or black children. Only Puerto Rican children, 50 percent of whom are poor, have a higher poverty rate than Mexican-American children, 33 percent of whom are poor (U. S. Census, 1990).

3. Although homelessness has brought some attention to the lack of available, adequate, low-income housing, less attention is being given to the inadequate housing conditions of the poor, generally. Under the Reagan administration, the federal government cut support for new low-income housing by 76 percent, and we have recently learned of the abuse and mismanagement of the remaining funds administered by the Department of Housing and Urban Development (HUD). The deteriorated, segregated, drug-ridden, dangerous environment of low-income, public housing is a national crisis. The current director of HUD believes that home ownership for the poor should be a federal goal. This, of course, would be highly desirable, but probably a very limited solution. Intense pressure needs to be put on HUD to pay *realistic* attention to the problems of housing for the urban poor. (See Wilson, 1987, and Anderson, 1990 for discussions of the sociology, politics, and economics of ghetto life.) At the present time, there is almost no discussion of the housing crisis or homelessness emanating from the White House.

4. The term "underclass" has been used to describe very poor blacks living in urban ghettoes. Similar to the concept of the "culture of poverty," the term "underclass" is considered perjorative for many reasons: it combines concepts of poverty, race, and behavior—particularly antisocial behavior—as if these concepts were undifferentiated; it places the etiology of poverty within individual and group membership rather than within the social and economic structure of society; and the term implies a hopeless prognosis which then justifies failure to implement effective programs to overcome poverty conditions (Reed, 1991).

5. Because of my emphasis on social policy and the poor, I have not addressed economic or social conditions for upper-middle-class women, although sexism prevails at all socioeconomic levels. Women with four years of college receive about the same salary as men with only a high school diploma. At every education level, women make less money than men (U.S. Census Bureau, 1990). In a study by the Feminist Majority Foundation, it is noted that only 2.6 percent of top corporate officers in Fortune 500 companies are women and 4.5 percent of corporate directorships are held by women. Although women occupy 40 percent of all executive, management, and administrative positions, they remain confined mostly to the middle and lower ranks, with the senior ranks occupied almost exclusively by men. Frustration from lack of job mobility and other issues, such as sexual harassment, lack of pay equity with men, and expensive and inadequate child care, are some of the pressures of employment experienced by professional women.

6. The current mammoth *state* budget deficits are also caused, in part, by tax cuts to the rich in the 1980s and, thus, could be alleviated by increasing income taxes from this group. However, implementation of a truly progressive income tax is always a struggle, and, in the meantime, state and municipal workers lose their jobs and such programs as education, Medicaid, and social services bear the brunt of budget shortfalls (Phillips, 1990). It is also noted that cutbacks in public employment have a particularly devastating effect on minority workers (Orfield, 1991).

3

The Civil Rights Act, 1964

The modern civil rights movement was a product of hundreds of people, organizations, and ideas, and the victories and defeats of the movement must be credited to all of its leaders and all of the people on the grass-roots level who participated in every march, vigil, boycott, protest, sit-in, and voter registration drive. The National Association for the Advancement of Colored People (NAACP), maintaining a low profile but an unstinting tenacity, deserves a good deal of credit for protecting Constitutional principles in the judicial arena, as one of the earliest civil rights strategies prior to 1954. The National Urban League, the Congress of Racial Equality (CORE), and the American Civil Liberties Union (ACLU) also existed at that time and were working quietly on civil rights issues. But it was after World War II, when returning black veterans, confronted with segregation and discrimination at home, could not find jobs that a spark was created, igniting the civil rights movement (Hampton and Fayer, 1990). The kind of encouragement provided by a major victory such as *Brown v. Board of Education* in 1954 thrust the budding movement into its next stage.

FROM 1954 TO 1964

Despite "equal protection under the law" established by the Fourteenth Amendment in 1868, the contradictory doctrine of "separate but equal" had become the law of the land in 1896 in the Supreme Court case of *Plessy v. Ferguson* (163 U. S. 537). This action affirmed what was already extant in accordance with state statutes throughout the South. It wasn't until 1954 in *Brown v. Board of Education of Topeka*, following a long and arduous series of legal battles, that the separate but equal doctrine was overturned.

The desegregation of public schools, established by *Brown v. Board of Education*, began another dualistic chapter of optimism and pain in the history of civil rights in the United States—a recurrent theme born of society's ambivalence on issues of race. Many black people in the South believed that this judicial action was a turning point in their history. However, immediately following passage of the landmark judicial action, the white authorities in Farmville, Virginia, for example, closed the entire public school system for five years rather than compromise the practice of racial segregation (Branch, 1988). (The creation of private schools to avoid public school integration continues to the present time as a well-established pattern in the South and elsewhere.) Within several months after the passage of *Brown v. Board of Education*, when parts of the South simply refused to comply, it became evident that provisions for enforcement had not been included in the judicial action and that the federal government was reluctant to intervene. Most middle-aged and older Americans are familiar with media coverage of President Eisenhower's hesitant use of federal troops to prevent a mob, supported by Governor Orval Faubus of Arkansas, from blocking the admission of black students to Central High School in Little Rock, Arkansas, in 1957; President Kennedy faced the same situation at the University of Mississippi in 1962, and in 1963 Governor George Wallace blocked the admission of black students to the University of Alabama (Cox, 1987; Hampton and Fayer, 1990). In the wake of massive resistance to the Supreme Court decision in the South and only halfhearted acceptance by the federal government, the Ku Klux Klan was granted tacit permission to flourish, and it did, with burnings, bombings, and lynchings of black Americans (Viorst, 1979).

In August 1955, a 14-year-old black child from Chicago, named Emmett Till, was murdered while he was visiting in Mississippi. In December 1955, the defiance of Rosa Parks in refusing to give up her seat on a bus to a white person inspired the bus boycott in Montgomery, Alabama. This action was a first for Southern blacks. The bus boycott, which also included an economic boycott of local businesses, introduced Martin Luther King, Jr., to the civil rights struggle. The boycott lasted twelve months and rallied the support of 50,000 blacks and some whites, especially women.

Following the conclusion of the successful bus boycott in Montgomery, at the end of 1956, Dr. King assessed the progress and status of the black civil rights battle. He analyzed the resistance and open defiance in the South to judicial and congressional actions and planned the strategies and actions that would move the struggle forward. He observed:

[There] is no solid South. . . . There is the South of compliance—Oklahoma, Kentucky, Kansas, Missouri, West Virginia, Delaware, and the District of Columbia. There is the wait-and-see South—Tennessee, Texas, North Carolina, Arkansas, and Florida. And there is the South of resistance—Georgia, Alabama, Mississippi, Louisiana, South Carolina, and Virginia (King, 1958, p. 201).

He noted that "as a result of the failure of the moral forces of the nation [specifically, the president of the United States] to mobilize behind school integration, the forces of defeat were given the chance to organize and crystallize their opposition" (p. 196). And he outlined the tasks and responsibilities of white liberals in the North, white moderates in the South, the clergy in the North and South, labor unions, and black people themselves, if freedom was to be achieved. Referring to civil disobedience, King wrote: "The Negro can take direct action against injustice without waiting for the government to act or a majority to agree with him or a court to rule in his favor. . . . If the Negro is to achieve the goal of integration, he must organize himself into a militant and nonviolent mass movement" (pp. 211, 214). Writing in 1958, Dr. King prematurely believed that "social change can take place without violence" (p. 188). This perception changed somewhat, however, as whites continued to literally beat back black efforts to achieve racial equality.

Because the Montgomery bus boycott was such a major victory, bombings, intimidation, arrests, and murders of children and civil rights leaders intensified. Despite the dangers, The Southern Christian Leadership Conference (SCLC) was formed, and the civil rights movement advanced. Detailed chronicles of hundreds of courageous actions are documented in the histories written about the civil rights movement, but we can mention only a few here (e.g., Branch, 1988; Brooks, 1974; Fager, 1974; Franklin, 1967; Hampton and Fayer, 1990; King, 1964; Morris, 1984; Powledge, 1991; Viorst, 1979; Williams, 1987). It is important, for purposes of social change, to note the many different strategies that were used to accomplish civil rights goals. These included all of the following: economic boycotts; the activist role of the black church in the South; nonviolent student sit-ins at lunch counters beginning in Greensboro, North Carolina, in 1960; interracial Freedom Rides in 1961 through the South to register voters; the March on Washington for Jobs and Freedom in 1963 (the site of King's "I Have a Dream" message, which was the impetus for the Civil Rights Act of 1964); attempts to integrate public schools, which required federal troop intervention; electoral efforts such as the Mississippi Freedom Democratic Party in 1964, which tried to unseat the entrenched Democrats from Mississippi at the national convention; the march from Selma, Alabama, to Montgomery, Alabama, in 1965, which required federal action to overturn a state injunction that prohibited the march (and whose success ultimately led to passage of the Voting Rights Act of 1965, which doubled the number of black registered voters in the South within five years and changed the makeup of American politics); riots in Northern cities, separatism and the Black Power movement; and many other local, grass-roots, unnoticed uprisings and protests.

The civil rights movement was implemented person-by-person, town-by-town, spurred on by cumulative success. In the meantime, organizations such as the Congress of Racial Equality, the Student Non-Violent Coordinating Committee, the Southern Christian Leadership Conference, and the National Urban League had joined with the NAACP in the civil rights struggle and added diversity to the movement. In 1966, the Black Panther Party for Self-Defense was formed in Oakland, California, to begin to move the concept of Black Power into the electoral arena. Overt and covert attempts to destroy this movement by local and federal law enforcement agencies are vividly addressed by Dick Cluster (1979).

Although successes in one geographic area provided incentives and courage to move into other areas, these victories also heightened local resistance to change. Thus, civil rights battles were fought one-by-one throughout the South, often with increasing, rather than decreasing, violence from public officials and white residents.

In 1963, King believed that Birmingham, Alabama, was the most segregated city in America. Four black children were killed by a bombing in 1963 in Birmingham's Sixteenth Street Baptist Church (Sikora, 1991). King contended that Birmingham would be the toughest fight of the civil rights movement, but if the fight were successful, it would break the back of segregation all over the nation. (He was wrong about that.) His faith in the strategy of nonviolent civil disobedience was unshaken at that time, even in countering the violence of the Ku Klux Klan and public officials such as "Bull" Connor, the Birmingham Commissioner of Public Safety (King, 1964, p. 60).

King expected to be arrested in Birmingham for civil disobedience. While he was in jail, he wrote the now-famous and powerful "Letter from a Birmingham Jail." In this letter he reaffirms the principle of nonviolence and justifies the importance of disobeying unjust laws. He also adds two additional insights to our understanding of his perspective of the civil rights movement. First, King explains his impatience and disappointment with "the white moderate, who is more devoted to 'order' than to justice; who constantly says: 'I agree with you in the goal you seek, but I cannot agree with your methods of direct action' . . . and who constantly advises the Negro to wait for a 'more convenient season'" (p. 87). Second, in response to reluctant support from the clergy for his actions, King forcefully clarifies the role of the Birmingham police:

I doubt that you would have so warmly commended the police force if you had seen its dogs sinking their teeth into unarmed, nonviolent Negroes. I doubt that you would so quickly commend the policemen if you were to observe their ugly and inhumane treatment of Negroes here in the city jail; if you were to watch them push and curse old Negro women and young Negro girls; if you were to see them slap and kick old Negro men and young boys; if you were to observe them, as they did on two occasions, refuse to give us food because we wanted to sing our grace together. I cannot join you in your praise of the Birmingham police department (p. 98).

King believed that the victories in Birmingham were a turning point for black Americans. He believed that the spring of 1963 was the end of the old order and the beginning of psychological, as well as social and economic, freedom for blacks. It was auspicious that 1963 was also the 100th anniversary of the Emancipation Proclamation.

The March on Washington for Jobs and Freedom in August 1963 explicitly brought together the moral, economic, and political issues of the civil rights movement. King noted that:

There were two and one-half times as many jobless Negroes as whites in 1963, and their median income was half that of the white man. Many white Americans of good will have never connected bigotry with economic exploitation. They have deplored prejudice, but tolerated or ignored economic injustice. But the Negro knows that these two evils have a malignant kinship. . . . Equality meant dignity and dignity demanded a job that was secure and a pay check that lasted throughout the week (p. 12).

A. Philip Randolph, as chairman of the 1963 March on Washington, also spoke eloquently on this subject:

We are the advance guard of a massive moral revolution for jobs and freedom. . . . We know we have no future in a society in which six million black and white people are unemployed and millions live in poverty. . . . We want a free democratic society dedicated to the political, economic, and social advance of man along moral lines (Brooks, 1974, p. 6).

The civil rights movements in the North and South were very different. Blacks in the urban North generally represented individuals and families who had migrated North looking for job opportunities when they were displaced by technology from their Southern rural lives and livelihood. Nicholas Lemann (1991) reports that in Chicago, for example, the black population increased by 77 percent in the 1940s and another 65 percent in the 1950s. While King cajoled, prayed, mobilized, organized, and hoped that white goodwill would support the movement, other black leaders in the North were less patient and less hopeful.

Among the more influential and militant was Malcolm X. In Harlem and elsewhere, he preached a sermon of separatism from whites as promulgated by the Nation of Islam (or Black Muslims). He also connected the civil rights movement in the United States with struggles against oppression worldwide, indicating that people of color were a majority of the world's population and not a minority, as viewed in the United States.

After his suspension from the Nation of Islam in 1963, and influenced by two pilgrimages to Mecca in 1964 where he learned more about the Muslim religion, Malcom X's beliefs about the demonic qualities of white people began to mellow. In a letter to the *New York Times* in 1964, he wrote, "I totally reject Elijah Muhammad's racist philosophy" (Perry, 1989, p. 115). Although he disagreed strongly with Dr. King's philosophy of nonviolence, and his message to blacks was always one of boldness and defiance (Hampton and Fayer, 1990), Malcolm X later in his life developed a belief in the need for many different strategies to win the civil rights war. He is quoted as saying, "You know, I do not think all white folks are evil now, but some of you are, and I'm going to keep on at it until you, whoever you are, grant us the respect that we're due as fellow human beings." In commenting on Dr. King and his supporters, he said, "Look, if you don't deal with them, you're going to have to deal with me" (Hampton and Fayer, 1990, p. 260). On February 21, 1965, Malcolm X was assassinated at the age of 39, but he left a legacy that had an impact on Martin Luther King, Jr., and was inspirational and empowering to all blacks.

ENACTMENT OF THE CIVIL RIGHTS ACT

The Civil Rights Act of 1964 (P. L. 88–352) speaks to the economic and social, as well as the moral, sides of the civil rights movement. Section 1981 of the U. S. Code was passed by Congress during the Reconstruction Era as a means of forcing former slave owners to treat emancipated blacks as full-fledged employees. After the Fourteenth Amendment was passed, Congress enacted the Civil Rights Act of 1875 to give meaning to the equal protection clause. However, the federal government never enforced the law, and in 1883 the U. S. Supreme Court struck it down on the grounds that the Fourteenth Amendment did not authorize Congress to take action to protect the rights of black people (Franklin, 1976). The much-debated Civil Rights Act of 1964 was the first major legislation, after 1883, that extended these rights to employment. This legal victory, of course, did not come easily. It was the culmination of years of judicial and legislative actions, marches, boycotts, protests, and imprisonments of civil rights heroes and heroines. In the filibuster that occurred in the Senate around the Civil Rights Act of 1964, ostensibly it was the issue of states' rights against the power of the federal government that was the rallying point that brought Southern senators together.

The Civil Rights Act of 1964, legitimized by the interstate commerce provisions of the Constitution, prohibits discrimination based on race, sex, color, religion, or national origin in hotels, restaurants, gasoline stations, and places of amusement and by employers, unions, and employment agencies. (Note that sexual preference, age, and disabilities are not mentioned.) The legislation enforces the rights of all citizens to vote, to use public facilities, to attend public schools, and to seek employment on projects involving federal funds. Title IV authorizes the U. S. Attorney General to bring desegregation suits against school boards or public colleges where segregation is alleged to exist. However, desegregation, as defined in this statute, applies to the assignment of students to public schools without regard to race, color, religion, or national origin, but it does not necessarily mean relocation of students to schools (through busing, for example) to overcome racial imbalance. Title VII created the Equal Employment Opportunity Commission (EEOC), which, under the Reagan administration, did so much damage to reverse the civil rights that citizens had already achieved.

The legislation continued to allow states to set qualifications for voters; places of public accommodation did not have to serve all customers; local school boards were given ample time to adjust school segregation complaints before any federal action would be taken; the authority of the U.S. Commission on Civil Rights was restricted; and mortgages, guarantees of savings, and loan and bank accounts were excluded from the ban on discrimination in "federal financial assistance." The Act did not require hiring of members of minority groups; it merely said that there shall be no discrimination on that basis in the case of otherwise qualified applicants. Small enterprises, with fewer than twenty-five employees, were exempted from the legislation (U. S. Code, 1964).

The Civil Rights Act left issues of affirmative action subject to judicial and legislative interpretation. (The equal protection clause of the Fourteenth Amendment has generally been applied to support the right to affirmative action.) It is also clear that issues such as voting rights, school desegregation, and employment rights were not resolved once and for all. As recently as 1986, Lukas has written vividly of the tortuous attempts to desegregate the public schools through busing in Boston, Massachusetts, in the 1970s. Today, residential segregation has, to a great extent, accomplished what *Brown v. Board of Education* attempted to undo. Although progress has been made, the history of school desegregation and resegregation is a battlefield that repeats itself endlessly as different strategies of white resistance continue throughout the land.

There is no question, however, that the Civil Rights Act of 1964 moved the federal government more squarely into the civil rights domain and moved the country forward in social justice and equality. King notes that after the death of John Kennedy, President Johnson, "set the twin goal of a battle against discrimination within the war against poverty" (King, 1964, p. 161). Thus, the spin-off effects of the civil rights movement went beyond the benefits to the black community as other social legislation was passed. The movement also gave incentives and encouragement to individuals in other minority groups, such as all people who are poor, women, the elderly, and the mentally ill.

CHANGES IN THE CIVIL RIGHTS MOVEMENT

Passage of the Civil Rights Act once again raised expectations, as well as frustrations, as usually occurs when social policy attempts to distribute justice and rights. By 1965, the civil rights movement had a momentum of its own and was no longer only a Southern phenomenon. It had become a more complex amalgam of strategies and outcomes in the North and the South. While King asserted that the movement had to inspire whites to a higher level of morality, there was growing impatience with the non-violent, civil disobedience strategies prevalent since 1954. Different factions within the black community were gaining support, so that violence and nonviolence, voting rights victories and economic defeats, Black Power and Power to the People, and ideologies of integration and separatism began to exist in conflict and in unison, side by side. The voice of Malcom X in the North, delivering a message of separatism, resonated for many blacks alongside the voice of Martin Luther King, Jr., in the South, advocating for racial integration. And while 1967 marked the election of Carl Stokes as Mayor of Cleveland, the first black mayor in the nation, this was also the period of ascendancy of the Black Panther movement and the emergence of more vocal demands for local control of public education in the North.

During the civil rights movement, the nonviolent, civil disobedience of blacks had been met with violence from white law enforcement officials and white citizens throughout the South. The federal government acted reluctantly to enforce the laws of the land and to stop these unilateral attacks. When this violence began to grow in the North, however, and blacks began to retaliate, President Johnson was taken by surprise—he had sincerely believed his policies were helping black Americans. He responded by forming the National Advisory Commission on Civil Disorders (the Kerner Commission) to try to understand why the government's response to the civil rights movement was not working and to investigate the causes, consequences, and remedies for racial conflicts within the nation. This did not happen, however, until after the summer of 1965 when the Watts neighborhood in Los Angeles exploded in riots. From 1964 to 1968, American cities suffered 257 racial uprisings, including Detroit, Washington, and Newark in 1967, Washington and Chicago in 1968, and smaller cities in between (Volgenau, 1990).

The findings of the Kerner Commission established that "virtually every major episode of violence was foreshadowed by an accumulation of unresolved grievances and by widespread dissatisfaction among Negroes with the unwillingness or inability of local government to respond" (*Report on the National Advisory Commission*, 1968, p. 16).

After the many struggles of the civil rights movement and the passage of significant legislation, the findings of the Commission were more than simply discouraging. The ominous words of the report, written in 1968, that "our nation is moving toward two societies, one black, one white— separate and unequal" was a devastating indictment and cast a painful shadow over any euphoria that might have accompanied the earlier achievements of the decade. Fortunately, the report generated some hope, along with some proposals for change, and a number of social programs were implemented to offset its disheartening conclusions. The accusations stood, nonetheless, as bitter reminders of the entrenched racism within our society (*Report on the National Advisory Commission*, 1968).

The year 1968 was a major turning point in the civil rights movement. The antiwar movement and the civil rights movement joined in the violence of 1968. The deaths of Martin Luther King, Jr., and Robert Kennedy, the disappointments of the Poor People's Campaign in Washington, and the violence at the 1968 Democratic Party National Convention in Chicago deprived the movement of leadership and spirit. And, although the struggle continued, momentum lagged.

An enormous amount of violence, in addition to urban riots, bombings, and beatings, accompanied the successes and defeats of the civil rights movement. Not only did leaders such as Medgar Evers, John F. Kennedy, Malcolm X, Martin Luther King, Jr., and Robert Kennedy lose their lives, many less well-known adults and children were also casualties. Attacks against black officials and civil rights activists continue today. The history of social change in the United States is much more violent than most citizens recognize.

During the early 1960s when black nonviolence was met with white violence, there was national sympathy and support for the civil rights movement. However, as riots in the North and demands for Black Power resonated through the black community in the North and South, white fear of social change and backlash became more pronounced. In the 1960s, Black Power and racial integration seemed to be mutually exclusive, but in the 1970s, Black Power was the pride and the pressure that opened mainstream doors to opportunities for blacks. Today, the black community continues to have internal differences around integration and separatist goals. And although group militancy has subsided, and many blacks are more skeptical than ever about achieving true integration and parity with whites, individual self-esteem, pride, and empowerment continues to grow (Blauner, 1989).

King's alleged lack of attention to economic and electoral issues brought him into conflict with more militant sectors of the civil rights movement. However, the Civil Rights Act of 1964 and the Voting Rights Act of 1965 helped clear the way for integration of schools and public accommodations; affirmative action policies in employment and business; one person, one vote; and electoral empowerment of blacks in the political arena. King also believed that black pride, dignity, and self-respect were immeasurable effects of the movement that could not be taken away.

The decade of the 1970s witnessed continuation of war in Southeast Asia, the unsettling events of Watergate, economic recession, and backlash from the events of the 1960s. It was a time when the U. S. Supreme Court, in the case of *The University of California v. Bakke*, upheld the plaintiff's charge of reverse discrimination (Cox, 1987). The enthusiasm of the 1960s for what the federal government could do if it put its mind to correcting inequities waned, but it did not die altogether. *Roe v. Wade*, in 1973, was a high point of this decade. Without any doubt, however, the 1970s were marked by growing negativism toward the federal government and its alleged favoritism toward minority groups in federal legislation. As demands for social justice spread to other groups, it appeared that social change might not be contained. Thus, by the time Reagan ran for presidential office, the country was primed for a message that attacked social change and the gains of the civil rights movement, accentuated the failings of government, and promised to get it off the backs of citizens. This was accompanied by a call for "New Federalism," which was a euphemism for cutbacks in civil rights and social programs and a return to the old values of individualism and states' rights, with deregulation and reinforcement of the powers of the business sector of society.

THE REAGAN ADMINISTRATION AND CIVIL RIGHTS

Piven and Cloward (1983) contend that shifts in power in private spheres helped provoke the contemporary countermobilization of capital and the New Right against the welfare state: "The attack is avowedly intended to restore traditional economic and familial power relations. But if . . . the welfare state poses no challenge to capitalism, why has it become the focus of so concerted an assault by corporate interests and their right-wing allies?" (p. 65).

During the Reagan administration, existing civil rights (for example, abortion rights) and civil rights legislation (for example, the provisions of the Civil Rights Act of 1964) began to unravel. In 1987, Archibald Cox wrote that the Reagan administration was less interested in civil rights and the elimination of racial inequality than any other administration in the past fifty years. Cox noted that the administration pressed for revocation of the executive order requiring government contractors to set targets for increased minority employment. The Department of Justice consistently opposed court decrees giving minority applicants even limited employment preference as a remedy for previous unlawful discrimination unless the beneficiaries could show that they had personally been the victims of specific acts of discrimination. In addition to conservative appointments to the federal courts, the Equal Employment Opportunities Commission, and the Civil Rights Commission[1] and attempts to eliminate the Legal Services Corporation (the federal program of legal help for the poor),

Reagan began to systematically dismantle social programs. He was more successful eliminating some programs than others. Many 1960s programs remained, but all were weakened by a decade of attack.

The political nature of the federal courts reached conservative heights in the 1980s as Reagan used the judiciary to circumvent resistance to his programs from the legislative branch. Arguments against civil rights brought to the courts by the administration included the right to abortion; school prayers; issues of affirmative action as reverse discrimination; the implication of quotas in statistical representation of minorities; states' rights taking precedent over federal intervention; and the charge that alleged discrimination by employers had to be applied to actual discrimination of the individual bringing the charges and not to a generalized class action, such as in institutional racism.

The Civil Rights Act of 1990 was mainly introduced to counteract reversals in civil rights that were brought about by U. S. Supreme Court actions during 1989. In that one year, the following cases were decided:

1. *Ward's Cove Packing Co. v. Atonio*, an unintentional discrimination or "disparate impact" case, placed an increased burden on employees to prove that their employer's policies are discriminatory and not justified by business necessity.

2. *Lorance v. A.T.&T.* established the rule that victims of employment discrimination who bring Title VII suits (under the Civil Rights Act of 1964) must do so within a brief period of time after an employer adopts a potentially discriminatory policy, even though the policy might not adversely affect an employee for many years thereafter.

3. *Price Waterhouse v. Hopkins*, a "mixed motives" case, established that an employer can lawfully engage in some intentional discrimination if the employer can claim it also had a nondiscriminatory motive for its actions.

4. *Patterson v. McLean Credit Union* affected Section 1981 of the U. S. Code, which deals specifically with racial discrimination most directly. The Court held that only the actual making of contracts is covered by Section 1981 and the law does not prohibit racial discrimination that arises after an employee is hired. The proposed 1990 Civil Rights Bill amended Section 1981 to reaffirm that the right to make and enforce contracts covers all facets of contracts, including promotion denials and harassment on the job.

5. *Martin v. Wilks* allowed that court-approved settlements in employment discrimination suits are subject to open-ended, later legal challenge by those claiming reverse discrimination. The proposed 1990 legislation established limits on challenges to consent decrees after a court order is final (People for the American Way, 1990).

6. *Richmond v. Croson* reversed set-asides for minorities in public contracts.

In general, these court actions generally restrict definitions of affirmative action and make it more difficult to prove that racial discrimination exists.

THE CURRENT STATUS OF CIVIL RIGHTS

In vetoing the Civil Rights Act of 1990, President Bush alleged that the proposed legislation promoted employment quotas. But proponents of the legislation believed the administration's intent was to revert to the popular belief that white men are "the best qualified" for any job, to free employers to pursue traditional practices that kept minorities and women out of the better jobs by relieving them of the burden of proving the job-relatedness of their worker-selection criteria, to make it harder to bring civil rights suits forward, to appease conservatives, and to mount political support from white voters. The ACLU noted that supporters of the Civil Rights Act of 1990 sought, not quotas, but the requirement that employers use only job related criteria in making employment decisions, as a way of ensuring minorities and/or women equal access to available jobs. Arthur Fletcher, chairperson of the U. S. Commission on Civil Rights wrote, "Today we are told that the 1990 Civil Rights Act would force employers to resort to reverse discrimination or quotas to avoid suits by minorities and women. But this ignores the fact that the principles set forth in the Act have been applied and tested across the country for 19 years in cases decided by the Circuit Courts of Appeal. The Act would do nothing more than restore the laws as applied by most of those courts in the years between the unanimous U. S. Supreme Court Griggs decision in 1971 (referring to *Griggs v. Duke Power*—a 'disparate impact' case)—which put the burden of proof in employment discrimination suits on employers—and Wards Cove" (Fletcher, 1990, p. 19). The Griggs case ruled that where a pattern of exclusion existed, employers had to show that the criteria they used to select workers actually correlated with the skills needed to perform a job. The ACLU also noted that prior to Griggs, there were few minority and no women firefighters. Factory production lines were almost universally segregated either by race, sex, or both, with the highest paid, most desirable jobs going to white men and the lowest paid, least desirable jobs going to women and minorities. The dirtiest jobs went to minorities.[2]

To complicate matters further, some individuals and groups on the left are also critical of affirmative action, and there is currently criticism against affirmative action emanating from the black community as well. These voices express a variety of points of view, personal and societal. From an individual and personal perspective, affirmative action is considered to be demeaning and creating self-doubt by impugning the competence of beneficiaries. From an institutional and societal perspective, the following arguments are expressed: (1) Affirmative action encourages self-blame for nonminority-group individuals (especially white men) who have not "succeeded" economically and socially within the society and implies that the nation is a true meritocracy, except for discrimination against women and people of color; (2) as long as affirmative action policies and programs are superimposed on otherwise traditional educational and employment practices, society remains structurally unchanged; (3) affirmative action has created deep schisms between poor and middle-class blacks and may be, at least partially, responsible for the entrenchment of poverty among inner-city blacks; and (4) without White House or Supreme Court support and a tight labor market—and without a compelling moral force—the appearance of reverse discrimination unnecessarily alienates whites at the expense of helping blacks.

On the other hand, arguments in favor of affirmative action policies and programs are at least equally compelling: (1) Educational and employment discrimination continues against women and people of color—for every one woman and minority hired and promoted, there are dozens of white men hired and promoted; (2) although imperfect, affirmative action is all we currently have to help correct *current* inequities (in addition to arguments about past injustices); and (3) rather than lowering educational and employment standards, affirmative action raises these standards, as multiculturalism and diversity benefit all individuals and enrich society.

Most critics of affirmative action, except perhaps for the far right, would prefer to have a true meritocracy in society, with equal access and opportunity for all citizens. However, until universal social justice is achieved, there is general recognition that affirmative action policies and programs are needed and should be protected in the courts and in legislation (Applebome, 1991; Carter, 1991; Boynton, 1991; Brennan, 1991; Wilkerson, 1991). This is not a point of view supported by the Bush administration.[3]

At the end of 1991, however, a compromise Civil Rights Bill was signed by the president. The Republican party strategy of blaming the Democratic party for affirmative action and using race to alienate white voters from Democrats encountered unforeseen snags, at least temporarily. For one thing, David Duke, an avowed leader of the Ku Klux Klan, ran for Governor of Louisiana as a Republican in 1991; this was a major embarrassment for the Republican party. However, given the racial tactics used in the 1988 presidential election and in 1990 by Republican Senator Jesse Helms in North Carolina, the rise of Duke to power should be no surprise. Nonetheless, the dilemma for Republicans is their desire for electoral support from blacks. Further, President Bush is currently under siege because of the stalled economy and his apparent indifference to domestic affairs. Having initially vetoed legislation that would provide extended unemployment benefits to the long-term unemployed, he cannot continue to appear unsympathetic to the working class, including minorities.

The 1991 Civil Rights legislation generally repudiates the 1989 actions of the conservative U. S. Supreme Court. An analysis of the legislation indicates that most of the civil rights actions taken by the Court in 1989 were overturned by Congress, except *Richmond v. Croson*, which deals with set-asides in public contracts and is a Constitutional, rather than a legislative issue (Greenhouse, 1991). (The removal of set-asides has already had negative consequences for minority contractors.) The legislation also places a cap on damages that victims of sexual discrimination and harassment could collect, an obvious compromise measure.

President Bush has also vetoed legislation that would provide family leaves for parenting and illness, and his administration has attempted to rescind scholarships designated for minority students. Although Bush denies any disregard of domestic affairs, his policies waiver between neglect (which is tantamount to negativism, but without the courage to deal with the conflicts that would ensue) and active opposition to civil rights and social programs. As the presidential campaign for 1992 heats up, however, it can be expected that a semblance of interest in civil rights and domestic issues will be forthcoming from the White House.

One of the more positive actions emanating from the Bush administration was passage of the Americans with Disabilities Act of 1989. This legislation protects the disabled from discrimination in employment and emphasizes accessibility in public buildings, public transportation, telecommunications, and public accommodations. An estimated 43 million people, nearly one-fifth of the population, will benefit from this legislation. Opposition based on cost (and prejudice) was expressed, but this was a relatively easy victory for President Bush because the legislation reinforces traditional images of the deserving poor (Katz, 1989). Scrutiny of the legislation by the federal courts is expected. Litigation is inevitable, say some, and the disabled are not yet out of the woods (Benson, 1991). The disabled are also lobbying strongly to have 25 percent of the more than $20 billion paid to nursing home operators under the Medicaid program diverted from nursing homes to help the disabled pay for personal attendants.

Probably the biggest threat to the civil rights of U. S. citizens, because of its long-term implications, is the current and increased likelihood of a conservative majority in both the lower level federal courts and the U. S. Supreme Court. The successful efforts of liberals and progressives to stave off the appointment of Robert Bork to the Court was only a temporary reprieve, and Clarence Thomas was confirmed as Justice in late 1991. Although predominately conservative, as indicated by the affirmative action rulings cited above, the decisions of the Supreme Court in 1990 were mixed, as the following examples illustrate:

1. *Metro Broadcasting v. FCC* upheld two Federal Communications Commission programs aimed at increasing minority ownership of broadcast licenses. The Court ruled that the Constitution gives the federal government more leeway than state or local governments to undertake "benign race-conscious measures."

2. *U. of Penna. v. EEOC* spelled victory for the EEOC by rejecting the university's assertions that the secrecy of the tenure process protected academic freedom.

3. In *Missouri v. Jenkins* the Court ruled that federal judges may order local governments to increase taxes to remedy constitutional violations such as school desegregation.

4. In *U. S. v. Eichman* the Court overturned a new federal law, making it a crime to burn or deface the U. S. flag.

5. *Cruzan v. Missouri* recognized a Constitutional right to the discontinuance of life-sustaining treatment, based on the Fourteenth Amendment's guarantee of due process.

6. In *Hodgson v. Minnesota* the Court upheld state laws prohibiting teenage girls from obtaining abortions without first notifying their parents.

7. In three separate cases, the Court upheld aspects of death penalty laws.

8. In *Austin v. Michigan Chamber of Commerce* the Court upheld the power of both federal and state governments to restrict corporate involvements in political campaigns, ruling that corporations may be prohibited from spending their own funds on behalf of political candidates.

At the close of the term, one observer is quoted as saying that "on a range of fundamental issues—free speech, abortion rights, civil rights—we are one vote from devastation" (Greenhouse, 1990). With Justice Clarence Thomas on board, this one vote may be secured.

With respect to abortion rights after the Supreme Court's decisions in *Webster v. Reproductive Health Services* in July 1989 and *Rust v. Sullivan* in 1990, pro-choice activists, no longer able to depend on the federal courts, have been forced to turn their attention to state courts and state legislatures:

While the U. S. Supreme Court has been pulling back from the Warren Court's liberal legacy, state court judges increasingly have been looking to state constitutions to preserve civil rights. In these little-read state constitutions they have found greater civil liberties than their brethren in Washington have located in the U. S. Constitution (Spivack, 1990).

Thus, it appears that the right to abortion will be fought on a state-by-state basis. Although there is public support for abortion rights, there is no certainty about how legislators or state courts will vote on this issue.

The common characteristic among people of color and ethnicity, women, children, the elderly, the disabled, and gay men and lesbian women is their lack of power in a white, middle-class, materialistic, patriarchal society. Their issues are freedom from harassment and oppression, the basic rights and entitlements to equality, access to the goods and services of society, and choice, which is empowerment. Although budget deficits are invoked to justify cutbacks in services to the poor, the issues are political and ideological. Instead of using social policy as a tool to promote justice, as occurred in the 1960s, social policies are now used as an instrument to promote and maintain inequality. We are definitely at a crossroads with respect to social justice. Crime, drugs, dangerously inadequate housing, and increasing unemployment can continue to plague a large portion of the American people. We can continue to foster racial conflict and encourage citizens through government actions to impugn the honesty, integrity, and dignity of the poor, particularly the minority poor, and thereby justify withholding decent housing, income, education, and health care. Or we can try to end racial disharmony, unify the poor and working class politically and ideologically, stabilize the middle-class, and take pride in a decent quality of life for all citizens, which is not beyond the will and pocketbooks of Americans. If current leadership has the power to undermine the social obligations of government, then new, emerging leadership can resurrect the social justice roles of government and the democratic ideals embodied in Constitutional rights.

NOTES

1. The U. S. Commission on Civil Rights was once an active player in enforcing civil rights. Today, this agency is a shadow of its former self, outside of the mainstream of civil rights activity. Holmes (1991) suggests that the Commission's history mirrors that of the nation's approach to civil rights: bipartisan support in the 1960s and 1970s, polarization in the 1980s, and paralysis today. Commissioner Arthur Fletcher (1990) notes that with its staff down to 77 from nearly 300 in the 1980s, and its budget now at $7 million from $11.6 million five years ago, the Commission is in a no-win situation. Anti–civil rights actions such as opposing busing to achieve school integration and opposition to set-asides in federal contracts for minorities and women are examples of recent Commission actions.

2. "No organization in the United States has activated more 'reverse discrimination' suits than the International Association of Fire Fighters (IAFF). It was the union that helped finance the litigation for white firefighters in Birmingham, Alabama, an action that led to the Supreme Court's stunning decision in *Martin v. Wilks* on June 12, opening court-approved consent decrees to challenge. After the Rehnquist Five's declaration of open season on affirmative action, the IAFF Executive Board sent out a directional memorandum encouraging its white-run locals to try to overturn consent decrees in their respective cities. It is now common practice for the IAFF to collect dues from its membership, including minorities, to finance lawsuits and campaigns against minority programs" (Rockwell, 1989, p. 715).

3. Anthony Lewis (and others) reported that a group of executives from about 200 leading corporations had been meeting to work out a compromise for a new Civil Rights Bill. However, advisors for the Bush administration telephoned the executives and asked that the negotiations be terminated. Lewis suggests that President Bush wants an issue, not a bill: "They want the Democrats in Congress

to pass the legislation again, so that the President can veto it and Republicans can run as protectors of the white working man. Business support for a compromise bill would spoil that strategy" (Lewis, 1991). The President's intervention successfully ended the meetings, albeit temporarily.

4

The Economic Opportunity Act, 1964

The Civil Rights Act of 1964 was signed into law on July 2, 1964; the Economic Opportunity Act (EOA) of 1964 was enacted less than two months later. While the civil rights legislation was a major achievement of the civil rights movement, the cornerstone of the Great Society programs was the EOA—the set of social programs most directly identified with repercussions from the civil rights movement. As Bayard Rustin wrote in *Commentary* in February 1965: "It seems reasonably clear that the Civil Rights Movement, directly and through the resurgence of the social conscience it kindled, did more to initiate the War on Poverty than any other single force" (p. 27). In facing inequality, civil rights leaders recognized that, although many black people were poor, not all poor people were black. In the struggle for equality, the plight of the poor and the devastating conditions of poverty were highlighted. The nation began to focus its attention not only on the racial inequality that existed, but also on the economically disadvantaged throughout the country. Thus, a class consciousness was aroused.

The stated purpose of the EOA was "to strengthen, supplement, and coordinate efforts in furtherance of . . . the policy of the U. S. to eliminate the paradox of poverty in the midst of plenty in this nation by opening to everyone the opportunity for education and training, the opportunity to work, and the opportunity to live in decency and dignity" (U. S. Code, 1964). Thus, the social justice premises of the legislation were established.

The EOA was the most unique social program of the 1960s in all ways—staffing, funding, administration, and structure. Two provisions of the EOA were most controversial: (1) the creation of new nonprofit community action agencies (CAAs) that would receive funds directly from the federal government, circumventing established local and state governments; and (2) the expectation that the self-sufficiency of the poor could best be achieved through "maximum feasible participation" of residents of the areas and members of the groups served to meet their own needs. The title of the program, emphasizing "economic opportunity," linked civil rights with economic issues, although, as it turned out, the goals of economic redistribution were achieved in only limited ways. Although major changes in the legislation have occurred, the mission of the EOA survives today as CAAs continue to provide unique services for the poor.

COMMUNITY ACTION AGENCIES

The Economic Opportunity Act (P. L. 88–452 created the Office of Economic Opportunity (OEO). Precursors to the EOA were the Ford Foundation Grey Areas Project and the President's Committee on Juvenile Delinquency and Youth Crime, which funded such programs as Mobilization for Youth and Harlem Youth Opportunities Unlimited (HARYOU). The opportunity strategies of these programs were prototypes for the OEO (Cloward and Ohlin, 1960; Marris and Rein, 1969; Clark and Hopkins, 1969).

Rather than becoming part of an existing government agency, the OEO became an independent agency within the executive branch of government. This action officially marked the beginning of the federal government's "War on Poverty." In his message to Congress on March 16, 1964, President Johnson called for a national war on poverty. The objective was total victory over poverty with legislation that was meant to strike at the causes (and not just the consequences) of being poor. However, the budget for the first year of the program was only $970 million, or 1 percent of the national budget, and CAAs had to add 10 percent in local contributions (Meissner, 1973).

From its inception, the program was a source of hope, a target for criticism, and an arena for controversy. Not only did the legislation have the ambitious goal of eliminating poverty nationally, it hoped to achieve this goal through provisions, programs, and structures that were relatively untested. Although the legislation passed with relatively little opposition, once it was implemented, conflict began to mount almost immediately, precipitated primarily by the mayors of several large cities who anticipated major changes in the power structure and status quo within their communities (Levitan, 1967, 1969; O'Brien, 1975; National Association for Community Development, 1970). As the nation struggled with the civil rights movement and urban unrest, the EOA was attacked from both the political right and left.

Moynihan (1969), for example, believed that economic growth and full employment would eliminate poverty (see also Gallaway and Vedder,

1985). However, a report by the Council of Economic Advisors (CEA) in 1963 (cited in Plotnick and Skidmore, 1975) observed that even if the economy were to reach full employment, large numbers of the poor (predominantly the aged, the disabled, and families headed by women) would still remain poor. Labor Secretary Wirtz originally favored a job creation program, but this was rejected by President Johnson. The CEA favored antipoverty policies that supported the opportunity strategy (Katz, 1989). These sentiments continued to be supported by the National Advisory Council on Economic Opportunity even in 1980. Others believed that the legislation was underfunded and designed to fail. David O'Brien (1975) and Robert Plotnick and Felicity Skidmore (1975) believed that the lack of attempts to alter power within the federal system and the lack of a comprehensive set of redistributive policies were major flaws in the legislation. Kenneth Pollinger and Annette Pollinger (1972) were particularly concerned about the poor being socially controlled. In 1969, Kenneth Clark and Jeannette Hopkins wrote:

The campaign for maximum feasible participation by the poor in the antipoverty program must now be seen as a charade. . . . It seems apparent that canny political leadership, national and city, never intended fundamental social reorganization. The political participation by the poor in their own affairs was not to be a serious sharing of power at all (p. vi).

Piven and Cloward (1971) generally concurred that the program was another form of manipulation and social control of the poor, particularly the militant poor, but these authors also thought some positive change had occurred. Some positive change was also observed by Sar Levitan (1969) and Arnold (1974).

The CAAs were designed to mobilize resources and deliver services to poor people with community control of these resources and services. The agencies were expected to coordinate the provision of various services in poverty areas, to deliver new services to the poor or old services in new ways, and to produce social change by social action strategies and having the poor share in decision making (Plotnick and Skidmore, 1975). This self-help strategy was based on the principles of opportunity and competition for the goods and services of society. Thus, from the beginning, CAAs were expected to combine social service and social action perspectives. Although not explicitly stated, urban blacks were encouraged to challenge the existing power structure and demand resources that had previously been denied. Even though local governments wanted to curb community unrest and cities needed the federal dollars that were available, the loss of established power was an unwelcome possibility. Thus, a relatively small amount of money created enormous conflict because community control and the potential for redistribution of power on the local level were involved (Piven, 1970).

Almost every year after the passage of the EOA there were amendments to the legislation (Spar, 1980). Programs were added and later dispersed to other federal agencies, reflecting the competition among government bureaucracies and negative attitudes toward the OEO. The CAAs were expected to initiate demonstration projects and hand them off to other established agencies, thereby limiting the long-term power and control of CAAs. The size of municipal contributions to the program underwent several changes. Although the second-year budget for the OEO was nearly twice that of the first year, by 1967 federal debate was so fierce that it looked as if the EOA would have been killed if a viable alternative had been available at the time (NACD, 1970; O'Brien, 1975; Plotnick and Skidmore, 1975). Instead, a compromise, the so-called Green amendment, was passed.

Edith Green, a Democratic representative from Oregon, formed an anti-OEO coalition with Republicans to sponsor legislation that would further reduce the autonomy of CAAs and limit community control (NACD, 1970). The legislation required that CAAs be designated by state or local government, gave state and local elected officials the authority to prevent a CAA from operating within their political boundaries, and enabled local communities and states to operate CAAs. However, Levitan (1969) notes that "within 8 months after the Green amendment became law, 792 of the 1,018 affected state, county, or city governments took action, and 96.7% elected to continue the existing CAAs without change" (p. 67). Additionally, the Green amendment mandated that CAAs establish a tripartite board of directors, composed as follows: one-third were to be local elected officials or their representatives; at least one-third were to be democratically elected representatives of the poor in the areas served; and the remainder were to be representatives of labor, religious, business, or other major organizations in the community. This board structure continues today. While this provision of the legislation provided an opportunity for different sectors of the community to begin to communicate with each other, community control was again undermined.

Although a General Accounting Office (GAO) study in 1969 was only mildly critical of the OEO, horror stories about waste and fraud in the agency flourished. (In fact, the GAO study found CAAs to be successful advocates for the poor and indicated that job training programs were helpful.) "National emphasis" programs were introduced by the central office of OEO without local initiative, and the war in Vietnam was costing billions of dollars and detracting from the War on Poverty (Blackburn, 1966). Nonetheless, Congress appropriated almost $2 billion for all OEO programs in fiscal year 1969, representing the highest appropriation in the history of the program up until that time (Donovan, 1973).

In 1971, the OEO was funded by a continuing resolution following President Nixon's veto of the Economic Opportunity amendments. After his landslide victory in 1972, Nixon made clear his intention to dismantle the OEO when he requested no further funding for the agency in his fiscal year 1974 budget message to Congress. After several lawsuits protecting the OEO were won, the agency continued to exist, but at drastically reduced funding levels.[1] VISTA and thirteen additional programs were transferred out of OEO and placed in other federal agencies. Finally, on January 4, 1975, the OEO was abolished and was replaced with a new independent agency, the Community Services Administration (CSA). This transition officially shifted the emphasis of CAAs from social action to the provision of social services. At the local level, CAAs were becoming an integral part of their communities. Low-income people received training, served on boards, provided essential services, and advocated for their community, and the agencies became significant local employers.

Between 1975 and 1980, there were a series of congressional investigations and General Accounting Office reports about the effectiveness and efficiency of the CSA. Then, in 1981, after the election of President Reagan and passage of the Omnibus Budget Reconciliation Act (OBRA) of 1981 (P. L. 97–35), the CSA was abolished as a separate federal agency. The Office of Community Services took its place within the Department of Health and Human Services (HHS). Consistent with the intent of "New Federalism" CAAs were funded through the newly created Community Services Block Grant (CSBG) allocated to each state. This marked the end of a federal anti-poverty agency and marked the end of direct federal funding of CAAs. Except for Title II (which funded CAAs and was included in the CSBG) and Titles VIII and X, OBRA repealed the remainder of the EOA.

As a result of the Reagan administration's desire to curtail the role of the federal government in social programs and its concurrent cutbacks in funds and negative attitudes toward the poor (for example, President Reagan proposed to merge the CSBG with the Social Service Block Grant), CAAs throughout the country began to develop strategies to stabilize their existence on the state level. In a number of states, CAAs strongly lobbied their state governments for financial support. On May 6, 1982, the governor of Connecticut, for example, signed into law an Act Concerning Community Action Agencies (P. A. 82–84); other states quickly followed suit. These legislative actions on the state level were crucial to the survival of the CAAs (*State Plan of Action*, 1982). The state legislation largely adopted the language of the preexisting federal legislation, and CAAs remained relatively intact.

At the present time, there are over 900 CAAs operating throughout the country, but there is little publicity, either adverse or laudatory; in 1989, CAAs celebrated their twenty-fifth anniversary. Quite a few other EOA programs also still exist, such as Head Start, Energy Assistance, Surplus Commodities, and Job Corps. Although there was a great deal written about the EOA during the 1960s and 1970s, relatively little has been written about the legislation and its programs during the current decades. In the last decades of conservatism in government, CAAs received little public attention. This may be due to a general decline in consciousness about the poor, or it may be because progressives have tended to be somewhat gun-shy in writing about the poor (Wilson, 1985). Additionally, because of the many changes that have occurred in the original OEO legislation, CAAs no longer pose the threat to established power that was once envisioned. Nonetheless, CAAs continue to exist and are an important source of social services for the poor. In fact, the EOA is one of the few federal programs specifically mandated to help poor people become self-sufficient. Although this has been true since 1964, recent developments in CAAs have particularly emphasized client self-sufficiency.[2] For many CAAs, state financial support has provided stability and growth. Many have large budgets from a variety of sources, large staffs, and many volunteers, and they provide a wide variety of programs that serve thousands of low-income clients, in urban, small-town, and rural communities. We are particularly interested in how the agencies have survived and the contribution they continue to make to social justice and empowerment goals for the poor.[3]

Funding

The reduction in federal funding that occurred in 1975 continued its downward spiral into 1981. However, the introduction of the Low-Income Home Energy Assistance Program, which was funded at $1.8 billion in the first year, provided additional income for the CAAs. Because this program quickly became the largest funding source for the agencies, it is important that the energy program was a federal, rather than a local, initiative: As a federal initiative, it represented a major shift in CAA programs and activities. Under the Omnibus Budget Reconciliation Act of 1981, the community CSBG received $389 million and funding for Head Start was authorized at $950 million, which also provided additional funding for most CAAs (U. S. Code, 1981). The Human Services Reauthorization Act of 1984 (P. L. 98–558) continued CSBG funding at slightly above the 1981 level, and the 1986 amendments to this legislation (P. L. 99–425) extended Head Start, Low-Income Home Energy Assistance, and the CSBG through 1990. The Office of Community Services was placed under the Family Support Administration within HHS. During this period, many CAAs also received additional funding from the Social Services Block Grant (SSBG) and the state, particularly for supplementary energy assistance and child care programs. Since 1987, additional funds are awarded to CAAs to operate shelters and other services for the homeless through the Stewart B. McKinney Homeless Assistance Act.

The funding pattern for CAAs shows a major decrease in core federal funding after 1972. However, special allocations for such programs as

Head Start and Low-Income Home Energy Assistance provide additional revenues for most of the agencies. In a mixed economy of state and other public and private funding, the Office of Community Services is still the largest funding source. Not all CAAs have grown at the same rate or in the same direction, and growth has depended on the initiative of agency directors and the political and economic environment in which CAAs operate. Those agency directors that depend most on federal funds from CSBG feel discouraged about the lack of discretionary funding, the rigidity of programming, and the lack of sufficient funds for administrative purposes. However, others who are more entrepreneurial have expanded into revenue-producing operations and receive funding from a large number of public agencies, as well as the United Way and other private donors. This gives directors more flexibility for program development and spending. Many agencies engage in energy conservation programs, some of which generate profit, such as weatherization, and other economic development activities, which generate little profit (Bok, 1989). In general, directors who depend most exclusively on federal CSBG funds have fewer innovative programs and options and less local participation than directors who have a variety of funding sources and programs, many of which are local initiatives.

At its start, the OEO was providing 90 percent of funding for CAAs nationally. By fiscal year 1975, federal funds represented only 52 percent of total CAA funds in Connecticut, for example, of which only 21 percent came from the CSA (Community Services Administration, 1976). In 1986, federal funding (including CSBG but excluding the Social Services Block Grant) accounted for 69 percent of CAA funds in Connecticut, with a range from 62.3 to 87.5 percent of total funding. CSA funds increased from $16.5 million in 1975 to $56.9 million in 1986 in Connecticut. Currently, the smallest CAA in Connecticut has a budget of $2.1 million and the largest has a budget of $13.6 million from a variety of funding sources.

On the national level in 1989, the average annual CAA income was over $4.6 million. The federal share was 65.6 percent (similar to the 1986 rate for Connecticut), of which CSBG accounted for only 8.1 percent. While there has been a decline in CSBG funding in proportion to other funding, overall funding has not declined. The agencies receive an average of over $2.6 million from federal funding other than CSBG, over $900,000 from the state, $240,000 from county and local sources, and an average of $305,000 from the private sector. CSBG is still considered core funding and provides the flexibility without which other programs would not be possible. CAAs are not dependent on a limited funding source; they received funds from an average of nineteen sources in 1989 (Bok, 1990).

Staff and Volunteers

CAAs have always trained and provided employment for indigenous staff who live in proximity to agency clients and share the culture of the client population. These training and employment opportunities have provided the groundwork for the development of economic, social, and political leadership in the minority community. Traditional social workers, who tended to be white and middle class and used intrapsychic theories to explain human behavior, were likely to be alien to poor urban and rural communities. CAAs have been able to maintain a diverse staff throughout their history.

By the mid-1970s, over 185,000 persons were employed by CAAs nationwide. In 1989, each CAA had an average of 86 full-time and 37 part-time employees and an average of 673 volunteers. The total number of CAA staff has fluctuated greatly as programs have been phased in and out and transferred to other agencies. Generally, CAAs now manage with fewer staff than earlier, although they operate more programs. Staff perform different functions as programs change. Although CAA staff are likely to be more racially mixed than previously, the agencies have consistently provided opportunity for employment of minorities. Today, however, there is an emphasis on professionalism within CAAs, possibly to counteract earlier criticisms of inefficiency and lack of experience in management, and agency directors generally seek staff with formal educational credentials, especially for management-level positions. While there is continued employment of local residents, and for some CAAs this is a priority, the diverse nature of CAA clientele broadens the concept of indigenous worker.

The tripartite system of board composition that was initiated in 1967 with the Green amendment continues; with a minimum of fifteen, a maximum of fifty-one, and an average of twenty-one board members. CAAs also have an average of thirty-nine advisory board members. Agency boards generally operate within a committee structure and perform traditional policy-setting and fund-raising activities. Some CAAs receive help from the corporate community in fund-raising and in establishing efficient financial procedures. There is variation in community interest in board membership, and some CAAs have had declining interest, whereas others have had some increased activism and minority participation as political climate and issues change.

Services and Programs

Over 75 percent of the CAAs continue to operate as private nonprofit agencies; the remainder are operated as parts of government units. Most CAAs serve county or regional geographic areas. The agencies provide an extremely large number and wide array of programs and work closely with federal, state, county, and local governments and the private sector.

The core programs of the OEO at its inception were education and employment. However, most of these programs were later transferred to the Comprehensive Employment and Training Act (CETA) and in the 1980s to the Job Training Partnership Administration (JTPA) within the Department of Labor. Programs such as Head Start, Upward Bound, VISTA, Job Corps, Legal Services, neighborhood family planning and health clinics, and alcohol and drug counseling are some of the programs that have been moved around as the political climate of the nation changed. Some programs have been completely eliminated or separated from CAAs. Others have become delegate agencies—that is, independent agencies who contract with the CAAs for funds.

Today, almost all agencies receive federal Low-Income Home Energy Assistance funds. In Connecticut, this program accounts for 32 percent of the total CAA budget. Many agencies also receive some additional energy assistance funds from the state. Other programs operated by almost all CAAs include weatherization, which is federally and state funded; the surplus commodities program, which is federally funded; Head Start, which is primarily federally funded and comprises 13 percent of the Connecticut budget; both the Summer Youth Employment and Community Neighborhood Service programs; child day-care programs, in addition to Head Start; and nutrition programs for the elderly. In Connecticut, these nine programs constituted more than 77 percent of the CAA budget in 1987 (Connecticut Association for Community Action, 1986).[4]

Almost 75 percent of the agencies are engaged in economic development activities to expand their constituent services and to generate additional revenues. These activities often involve working with the business community and public officials in different ways, involving new and innovative private-public financial and administrative partnerships.[5] Eighty percent of the CAAs are engaged in welfare reform and client self-sufficiency programs; 38 percent focus on substance abuse; 69 percent emphasize housing for the homeless; 45 percent are involved in educational programs; and 26 percent provide services to clients in public housing. CAAs operate an average of over sixteen programs annually.

Target Populations

At the beginning, the major focus of the OEO was on black, inner-city youth and impoverished rural individuals and families. Today, most CAAs have county or regional responsibilities and operate out of several locations. There are more rural than urban CAAs. The largest group of clients are white (over 70 percent); 18 percent are African-American; 7 percent are Latinos; and 5 percent are Asian, Native American, and other. Over

25 percent of all clients are preschool or school-age children (to age 18), reflecting youth employment, Head Start, and other child care and youth components, and 14 percent are elderly, reflecting many programs for this age group. Thus, there is considerable diversity in client characteristics, which is reflected in the diversity in programs.

CAAs continue to serve low-income clients primarily. A recognition that poverty levels in the nation are set too low has resulted in the relaxation of eligibility requirements for most services, so that currently a larger number of poor and near-poor people are served (National Advisory Council, 1980). Although the proportion of inner-city minorities is lower compared to the total number of people served, this diversity in service delivery has increased the political base of CAAs and made the programs of the agencies more universal and acceptable to public officials and the general community.

Unemployed males and youth continue to receive educational and employment services, but many funds for these services have been reduced or transferred to other agencies. Women who are single parents, either employed or receiving welfare, have emerged as a growing target group, particularly in relation to child care, employment and training, and self-sufficiency goals; and educational and vocational programs for other minorities, such as Latinos, has been increasing to some degree. All CAA clients experience hardships with downturns in the economy, and the number of homeless people and the shortage of affordable, adequate housing are recognized service needs.

Social Action

A majority of CAAs continue to engage in some social action on the community level through neighborhood centers that were originally the hub of activism, but to a limited degree (Thomas, 1986). Today there are fewer neighborhood centers because there is less money available for this purpose, and those centers that do remain primarily provide social services and serve as advocates for clients on an individual basis. But neighborhood centers tend to employ indigenous staff, and they are closest geographically and ideologically to the sentiments of the affected populations.

The shift from social action to social services is evident. It was brought about by design from mainstream political forces on the local, state, and federal levels. Shifting from local initiative programs to federally initiated and funded programs is one strategy that was used. Energy assistance, in particular, is singled out as a program over which a CAA has little discretion or control and where the agency functions primarily as a conduit for funds. Although there is little community initiative in this program, energy assistance plays an important role in providing supplementary income for clients. While some agency directors lament the passage of greater possibilities for social change, others find confrontational social action unnecessary since "public officials are not antagonistic." Many CAAs hold annual public meetings and conduct community needs assessment to receive grass-roots input for program development. But this is a far cry from the militancy of an earlier era.

Instead of social action, CAAs engage in strategic planning and adapting to changing conditions and the shifting needs of client populations. While this can be interpreted as "opportunistic," these actions can also be viewed as protecting the mission of the agency because serving the poor is never a popular cause. Similarly, CAAs have developed organizations on the state and national level for lobbying purposes. These activities are considered costly but necessary for the ongoing viability of the agencies.

IMPLICATIONS FOR THE FUTURE

CAAs have maintained their mission of helping the poor become economically and socially self-sufficient and empowered. But this happens mainly as individuals are helped through the network of social services that the agencies deliver. Currently, the emphasis is on case management and a comprehensive, coordinated wholistic family approach to self-sufficiency, consistent with the goals of welfare reform. CAAs are different from other nonprofit agencies in their size; the multifaceted and comprehensive nature of programs; outreach, involvement, and advocacy in the community; and availability at all hours and in all kinds of crisis situations.

There is general sentiment that CAAs have achieved relative stability because they are needed by local and state governments and by the business community to serve the poor. Indeed, some CAAs with the most assets feel that they are not dependent on the federal government and could survive and continue to help the poor even if federal funding were curtailed. Many CAAs are exploring new revenue-generating programs and moving, with some limited success, into profit-making ventures. The area of housing describes the current strategy of some of the agencies: "Poor people can be helped through collaboration with local officials and the business community, while profit can be realized at the same time." Obviously, there are trade-offs in the poverty business, and CAAs are survivors in a buyers market.

Three themes distinguished CAAs when they were established and can be used to evaluate CAAs today: The goal is to (1) eliminate poverty at its roots, (2) through an opportunity strategy, (3) with maximum participation of the affected populations.

What one believes about the impact of the EOA on poverty depends on one's position about spending money on the poor. There are those who believe that the program had no impact on the poor, so it is useless to continue wasting money in this way. Others believe that the antipoverty programs increased poverty and economic dependence, so that continued funding will simply exacerbate the problem. A third group of people believe that, with low unemployment (prior to the current recession), poverty no longer exists or that when the affluent are fulfilled so are the poor, so that continued funding for poverty programs is unnecessary (e.g., Murray, 1984). While it is true that everyone benefits when the economy is vigorous, there is serious disagreement about how to achieve a vibrant economic condition. And even in times of economic upturn, as in the 1960s and early 1970s, there is still a group of people, at least 11 percent of the population (about 27 million people), who live below the poverty level. This occurs even when there is generosity in income transfer and in-kind social programs.

Most people sympathetic to the poor would agree that the antipoverty programs have not eliminated poverty, nor have economic power and resources been redistributed in society. However, the opportunity strategy of the War on Poverty cannot be written off as totally ineffective. CAAs have played a major role in providing access to jobs and social and economic mobility and in developing political leadership for many urban blacks and the rural poor. Although the service orientation of CAAs focuses on individual rather than group accomplishments, the CAAs represent a network of social agencies that bring attention to and advocate for the poor. In Congress and in state legislatures, CAAs and their supporters puncture the consciousness and conscience of citizens, particularly when appropriations are discussed. In addition, the agencies augment other poverty efforts, such as income and employment programs, and CAAs are credited, in part, with reductions in poverty that occurred prior to the Reagan administration.

Part of the opportunity provided by the EOA was in "maximum participation" of the poor in the planning, decision making, and utilization of antipoverty funds and other resources. Translated into local control, or self-help, these principles, if they had been allowed to flourish, had the greatest potential for creating social change. But because of the potential for redistribution of power that was involved, this principle was curbed almost immediately. By 1967, the Green amendment changed the board structure of CAAs, leaving only one-third representation to the poor, and made CAAs beholden to established local and state governments who could veto or approve their existence. The mandated tripartite board effectively eliminated community control from the CAAs. Today, agency boards generally reflect the power structure of their communities, and this provides the opportunity for communication among individuals who represent different interests. For some, this is a positive change. In addition, local control is stifled when programs are initiated by state or federal government, thereby denying citizens the opportunity for empowerment that comes with local-level decision making. Currently, state government is the locus of control of the CAAs. The withdrawal of the federal government from direct funding is a strategy that reduces the likelihood that CAAs can influence power and redistributive policies on the federal level.

It is also believed by some writers that even if local control were effective, it could not solve national problems. In 1973, John Donovan challenged the self-help strategy of the antipoverty programs when he wrote that "it seems most unlikely that very many of the basic social and economic problems plaguing American society in the 1970s will be solved from a neighborhood base" (p. 179). And in 1980, the National Advisory Council on Economic Opportunity wrote: "The evidence shows that poverty is not only still with us, but that it is also increasingly immune to the remedies of the past" (p. 704). Individuals sympathetic to the poor recognize that the original provisions of the EOA were eliminated many years ago. Thus, it might be said that the original legislation was never fully tested; or, conversely, it can be argued that the legislation was tested and came up short as a strategy for eliminating poverty at its roots.

In 1968, S. M. Miller and Frank Riessman observed that CAAs had the distinctive function of linking the needs of the poor with the programs of traditional social service agencies, while changing traditional agencies in the process. In fact, the antipoverty programs reinforced, through social legislation, the opportunity principles of the civil rights movement. Thus, CAAs were viewed as organizations that functioned inside the established service system (because they were federally funded), but with special relationships to poverty populations. This role was considered a limitation to, as well as an opportunity for, influencing change. This analysis of the role of CAAs continues to be relevant today, but the agencies' role in social change is now more diminished. Clearly, the legislation was enough of a threat to the status quo that it was cut down in its infancy. Although it has survived, it is at the expense of affecting larger social change. In fact, it can be argued that CAAs might not have survived at all if the agencies had not retreated from attacking the established power structures in their communities (Arnold, 1974).

As we have noted throughout this book, the EOA is an example of progressive legislation with civil rights and social justice values. But even within the radical change efforts that occurred in the 1960s, the EOA represents a social reformist model in service delivery. It seems disingenuous now to think that opportunity alone could eliminate poverty, or that individuals and groups in positions of power would willingly allow the poor to become empowered through decision making, or that unlimited resources would be made available to accomplish antipoverty goals (Lemann, 1988 and 1989).

One of the lessons of the 1960s is that more than one strategy is needed to affect change. In reality, today CAAs combine local, self-help strategies with federal and state initiatives, mainly in-kind with some limited-income programs (such as energy assistance) and universal programs for the elderly, as well as programs designed specifically for the inner-city and rural poor. The agencies receive funding from federal, state, local, and private sources. However, most of the resources of CAAs are not currently available to help the original targets of antipoverty efforts, such as inner-city black youth with educational and employment needs. Instead, CAA programs have changed and spread from urban and rural to small-town communities with more elderly, more women and children, homeless people, different ethnic groups, the working poor, and the physically and mentally disabled in their clientele. The agencies are serving a wider variety of poverty populations in different ways, mainly with in-kind services. It can be argued, however, that regionalization and the universal nature of programs has extended the political base of the agencies and helped them survive in what otherwise might be hostile environments.

In his recent work, Wilson (1987) examines the broader issues of social and economic policy and poverty. Many of the questions he raises are pertinent to the arguments about the War on Poverty. He challenges the localism of self-help strategies and emphasizes the need for economic growth and full employment, the need for national redistributive policies and programs, the advantages of universal social policy over policies and programs targeted specifically for the poor, the need for education and job training to enhance the employability of inner-city black males, and the need for support services to enhance the self-sufficiency of single-parent, female-headed households. This comprehensive view requires many more changes and is, in fact, far more radical and difficult to accomplish than the original self-help, opportunity strategy of the War on Poverty.

CAAs now help the poor to achieve self-sufficiency by negotiating with, rather than confronting, the mainstream power structure. Today, relations with state and city governments continue to be mutually beneficial. Public officials call on CAAs to help them buffer problems with the poor. (For example, CAAs have been called on to provide social services and operate shelters for the homeless.) This results in an active and stable community role for the agencies. The CAAs have survived primarily because their continued strategies of advocacy and service for the poor have made them important and dependable in the communities in which they operate; and because there is little that is adversarial in the relationship between CAAs, local government, and other elements of the power structure in cities and states.

In conclusion, CAAs are very different now than when they were established, and three major changes can be identified: (1) there is less citizen participation, a reduction in militancy, and social action is limited; there is an increase in professionalism in staff and accountability to funding sources; (2) while local activities continue in a limited way depending on the initiative of agency administrators and boards, federal and state program initiatives represent the largest source of funds; and (3) the agencies provide more programs, for many different groups, as well as programs designed specifically for inner-city minorities and the rural poor.

While their tactics have changed, particularly in implementing explicit self-sufficiency programs through case management, the mission of CAAs has remained intact. The original intention of the EOA to eliminate poverty occurs primarily as individuals are helped, rather than on the community level, and maximum participation of the poor is not a pressing issue, although CAAs maintain close ties to their communities. No one envisions the demise of CAAs, probably because no one really expects poverty to go away in the near future and because CAAs are survivors in a mutually beneficial relationship between government, the business community, and the poor.

Contrary to conservative beliefs that poverty increased as a result of the War on Poverty, poverty actually decreased during the 1960s.[6] However, while poverty generally decreased and there was growth in the middle-class, minority community, and as CAAs began to service a broader constituency, poverty conditions in urban ghettos have worsened and become more entrenched. The intransigence of pockets of poverty in major cities is one of the major challenges that confront social action and political leadership today. The need for more adequate public assistance and public education, job creation, job training and employment, and decent, affordable, scattered-site housing points clearly to current priorities for the poor. Poverty strategies must include community action, community economic development, racial desegregation of education and housing, creation of public service jobs, a higher minimum wage, and reduction of unemployment through national labor and monetary policies. The impact of drugs, the shift away from manufacturing jobs to a service economy with limited opportunities, and the increase in the number of women who are single breadwinners and heads of households are some of the major differences between the 1960s and today. In the 1960s there was government and public desire to fulfill societal obligations. This must be the basis for any beginning reconsideration of social change.

NOTES

1. Funding for the OEO started at $970 million in 1964 and went to $1.78 billion in 1965 and nearly $2 billion in 1969. But in 1972, core funding was at $900 million and declined to $440 million in 1975. However, funds for Head Start in 1975 were at $485 million and this provided additional revenues for some CAAs (U. S. Code, 1965, 1972, 1974).

2. The 1962 service amendments to the Social Security Act and the Family Support Act of 1988 are examples of efforts in public assistance to help individuals and families to achieve self-sufficiency. However, by and large, AFDC and other public assistance programs have done little to help individuals or families become financially independent from welfare. In these conservative times, public agencies and other agencies, such as CAAs, feel particularly pressured to emphasize self-sufficiency goals.

3. Much of the information contained in the remainder of the chapter is derived from several research projects conducted by this author in Connecticut and nationally on Community Action Agencies from 1987 to 1990.

4. Major CAA programs include (1) housing, such as preservation, rehabilitation, rental assistance, and home ownership; (2) emergency, transitional, and permanent shelter and social services for the homeless; (3) employment and training, including adult basic education, English as a Second Language, general equivalency degree, youth, adult, elderly, dislocated workers, and displaced homemakers employment services, and Job Corps; (4) senior citizen services, including transportation, employment, adult day care, and nutrition; (5) emergency fuel banks and energy outreach, energy assistance and weatherization, both federal, state, and local or private; (6) Head Start and other child care and child development programs; and (7) nutrition, including commodities, food pantries, meals-on-wheels, and on-site feeding programs. Additional programs are (8) substance abuse, including drugs and alcohol prevention and treatment; (9) domestic violence, both child and spouse abuse; (10) crime prevention and victim restitution; (11) rape crisis services; (12) Foster Grandparents; (13) economic development, both small business development and job creation; (14) WIC, the Women, Infants, and Children Nutrition Program; (15) family planning and other health services; (16) adolescent pregnancy prevention and care; (17) legal services; (18) child support enforcement; (19) mental health services; (20) Hispanic Affairs; and (21) programs for the developmentally disabled and handicapped.

5. Economic development activities include, for example (in order of frequency): weatherization; housing rehabilitation; job creation; transportation; business development; training; technical assistance; revolving loans; property management; new housing construction; consulting; and industrial/commercial ownership. These ventures involve relationships and partnerships with, for example: community colleges; city/state government; local contractors; Chamber of Commerce; local banks; JTPA/PIC; public utilities/power company; HUD; and the Department of Labor. Very few ventures are profit making. Those that are include recycling, property management, transportation, and landscaping.

6. Data elsewhere indicate that the number of poor people was reduced in the 1960s and that these improvements were due, at least in part, to income transfer and antipoverty programs (Danziger and Weinberg, 1986). Cutbacks in income maintenance and social services during the Reagan administration resulted in new poverty, such as the poverty of women and children and homelessness (Block et al., 1987). Economic conditions have also been changing in the United States in the last fifteen years so that substantial data point to a new class of underemployed and unemployed individuals, which has developed as the low-paid sector of the service economy expands and as skilled manufacturing jobs decline (Bluestone and Harrison, 1982). As this book is written, the country has been in an economic

recession for more than two years. The chronically poor, the working poor, and the middle class are now all experiencing unemployment and extant or impending poverty. President Bush has reluctantly extended unemployment benefits while stating that such legislation reneged on promises not to increase the budget deficit.

5

Project Head Start, 1965

Head Start is not, strictly speaking, a social program. Its purpose lies more directly in the realm of preschool, compensatory education. However, the program has been both a complex social and an educational experiment. Head Start has social policy attributes and social program components; it is an exemplar in the War on Poverty; and it meets the criteria of striving for social justice and equality established in this volume for social programs, including redistributive and social reform goals. It has always been located in human services, rather than education, on the federal level and in many localities as well. Head Start grew out of the Economic Opportunity Act. It is, thus, a natural extension of this book to consider its history and characteristics.

HEAD START LEGISLATION

Most of the policies and programs of the War on Poverty were based on very little information or evidence that affirmed their effectiveness. As mentioned earlier, poverty was just being discovered in the early 1960s, and there was little experience on which to base antipoverty efforts (Harrington, 1962). The opportunity strategy of the Economic Opportunity Act (EOA) was based, somewhat, on the experiences of Cloward and Ohlin (1960) working with juvenile delinquents. But a great deal of program planning and development was founded on ideology, politics, and a limited amount of theory and empirical research. Head Start fits this prototype: "Because the program emphasized parent and community involvement, Head Start developed a grassroots political constituency dedicated to its survival" (Zigler and Valentine, 1979, p. 4).

Head Start was not even established by legislative fiat. Rather, it was derived from Title II of the EOA, which established Community Action Agencies (CAAs). This legislation gave the Office of Economic Opportunity (OEO) flexibility in developing and funding CAAs, with an emphasis on implementing programs with educational and employment opportunities, rather than income maintenance (*Congress and the Nation*, 1965). Thus, there were no restrictions on how Head Start should be operated, in the first year there were no limits on funds, and most bureaucratic regulations were suspended, at least temporarily. However, this unusual political climate, which provided the freedom to experiment, was relatively short-lived.

Head Start was conceived in December 1964, just four months after enactment of the EOA, as a summer program to be implemented in 1965. An interdisciplinary committee, composed of child development experts, was assembled to plan the program. The OEO was already experiencing opposition, and there was need for a visible, noncontroversial, effective program to counteract growing resentment and concern about community action.

Head Start became established as a "National Emphasis Program" within the OEO. As such, the program was initiated in Washington, but administered at the local level, usually through CAAs. Although federal initiatives generally tend to undermine local empowerment, Head Start, because it was innovative and designed for community participation, invoked the involvement of hundreds of volunteers and staff who worked to plan, develop, and implement the initial effort in local communities.[1] The nationwide response to the program was so enthusiastic that by July 1965, $70 million from OEO funds had been committed to Head Start. The first summer program enrolled 561,359 preschool (3–5-year-old) children, five times as many as had been anticipated, in 13,344 centers, based on 2,398 separate grants.

Because it reached into so many geographic areas, rural and urban, fit into the prevailing opportunity ideology, and served so many "deserving poor"(i.e., low-income children), Head Start was very popular with legislators. On August 31, 1965, President Johnson announced a substantial expansion of the program, including establishment of year-round centers, with field trips and home visits included.

In 1966, the OEO issued tentative guidelines intended to operationalize "maximum feasible participation" by the poor in Head Start. These guidelines established Policy Advisory Committees (PACs) composed of parents, staff, and community representatives. Most controversial were the guidelines that permitted PACs to veto staff hiring and firing and urged their involvement in budgetary decisions. Amid torrents of protest against these provisions, in 1967 the OEO withdrew the PACs' right to veto school-board decisions, but the issue was not resolved. PACs maintained their adversarial role in relation to established units of government, and in 1970, the right of PACs to approve or disapprove the appointment of Head Start directors and staff was firmly reestablished. The 1975 guidelines to Head Start policy continued to recognize the educational and political definitions of parent involvement, but the tilt toward parent education and away from parent activism was becoming more apparent (Valentine and Stark, 1979). Just as the EOA had moved away from social action to the delivery of social services, parental involvement in Head Start moved away from empowerment and distributive justice in favor of education as social service. Eventually, parent education became the dominant theme in parent involvement, and change occurred as individuals and families, rather than groups, were empowered.

In the meantime, Congress was increasing funding for Head Start. In fiscal year 1967, Congress earmarked money for Head Start (this had not been done previously) and increased funds for the program to $352 million, while they decreased the allocation of funds to CAAs and the Job Corps, both of which were receiving close scrutiny and opposition. In fiscal year 1968, the Follow Through program was established as an extension of Head Start into the early school years. Follow Through was expected to finance special small-group instruction, language-development classes, cultural-enrichment opportunities, parent activities, staff development, and an array of services that were ancillary to the mainstream curriculum in kindergarten and the first grade (Egbert, 1968).

Congress eliminated the earmarking of funds, which was highly controversial, but ordered that Follow Through be administered by the Department of Health, Education and Welfare (HEW) instead of the OEO. It enumerated eight "special programs" that could be funded through Title II of the EOA. In 1969, the administration of Head Start was also transferred to HEW. Since then, Head Start programs have often been operated by CAAs, but the program has been administered separately on the federal level. To attain some semblance of racial and social class integration, the provision that children who were not low-income could participate in Head Start by paying a fee was added in fiscal year 1970; in 1972, procedures were established to include a minimum of 10 percent handicapped children.

Funding for Head Start increased from $398 million in 1970 to $578 million in 1971, with matching funds of 20 percent from nonfederal sources. Between 1965 and 1975, funds for specific Head Start programs were allocated solely at the discretion of the OEO and later HEW. This resulted in about twenty-five Southern states receiving the largest share of funds. By 1978, however, a formula was worked out that equalized distribution of funding, based primarily on the extent of poverty in respective states (*Congress and the Nation*, 1973).

Although there are seven areas that Head Start was expected to include—health, social service, early childhood education, parent involvement, a volunteer effort, community participation in the governance of the program, and a career ladder and in-service training for staff—implementation of programs was flexible, and a great deal of variation among programs existed. In 1975, performance standards were adopted to ensure that every Head Start program provided the seven core services deemed necessary to meet program goals, but each program continued to reflect all of the variations of region, population, and need.

After 1969, when Head Start was transferred to the Office of Child Development in HEW, innovative, demonstration programs were introduced. These included, for example, Parent and Child Centers for children from birth to age 3 and their families; Home Start, which trained parents to work with their children in their own homes; the Child Development Associate Program, which trained workers in Head Start and day-care centers to achieve professional status in the child care field; and Education for Parenthood, which helps young parents learn child development and parenting skills.

During the expansion of federal initiatives in the 1960s, there were many new programs established in education.[2] By 1981, when the first Omnibus Budget Reconciliation Act (OBRA) was enacted, massive cuts were made in social programs. Head Start, however, probably the most popular legacy from the War on Poverty, experienced increased funding to $820 million in 1981 and $950 million in 1982. In 1981, about 375,000 children were enrolled in 1,262 Head Start programs nationwide. Head Start continues to receive increased funding in 1992.

THE PRINCIPLES UNDERLYING HEAD START

Probably the most important principle underlying Head Start is environmentalism. This was a major step forward from the belief that intelligence and IQ were determined by heredity and therefore immutable to change. Although it did not deal directly with children from poverty, there was some beginning work in child development that was suggestive and helpful in planning Project Head Start, as it was originally called. J. McVicker Hunt (1961) emphasized the power of a child's environment, and Benjamin Bloom's (1964) work emphasized the importance of the preschool years in intellectual development. Susan Gray, working with mentally retarded children at Peabody Teachers College in Nashville was influential, as were Martin Deutsch at the Institute for Developmental Studies at New York Medical College and Jerome Bruner at Harvard University, in relation to understanding the environmental basis of intellectual development in children (Hellmuth, 1967–1970; Zigler and Valentine, 1979).

Cultural Deprivation

The environmental perspective took a unique turn in dealing with low-income children, and new concepts began to emerge. A "cycle of poverty" was discovered and was attributed to social and intellectual deficits in children. This translated into alleged poor parenting, as well as other environmental limitations, such as joblessness and poor schooling. Although poverty was not only a minority problem or an urban problem, black youth were known to be one-half year behind national norms in kindergarten, one year behind in the third grade, and as much as three years behind in the twelfth grade. The failure of the poor to acquire middle-class attitudes and middle-class incomes was attributed to academic failure. Thus, an education program that would prevent school failure was politically and pragmatically very attractive. An emphasis on early education, with parent involvement, as a deterrent to poverty was particularly appealing.

As the "cycle of poverty" further solidified as an ideology and a concept and was used to explain more aspects of poverty, a "culture of poverty" concept was introduced, which was even more inclusive. All aspects of individual, family, and community life could be accounted for, and the concept had social, psychological, behavioral, language, intellectual, political, and sexual ramifications. As Frank Riessman (1962) describes it, the underprivileged were considered to be generally anti-intellectual, suspicious of new ideas, traditional and old-fashioned in many ways, inflexible, and patriarchal. The culturally deprived individual feels alienated, is apathetic about politics, holds the world, rather than himself, responsible for his misfortunes, and is a poor candidate for psychotherapy. The family may be prematurely broken by divorce, desertion, and death; both parents frequently work, and thus the children may be neglected. This litany goes on. However, Riessman also discusses how these seemingly negative attributes contribute to the strengths and coping mechanisms of the poor in a hostile environment.

Today we disparage the "culture of poverty" as an explanatory concept—for its conjecture and lack of empirical verification, for its ethnocentricism, and because it blames the victim for being poor and locates the need for social policy in the deficiencies of individuals and groups (Katz, 1989). In the early 1960s, however, the movement away from nature and belief in the inherited basis of IQ and intelligence was a major social reform, and the popularity of the concept of cultural deprivation led to important advances in child development theories and child development programs, such as Head Start (Hellmuth, 1967–1970).

If the "culture of poverty" had such all-encompassing implications, then comprehensive programming was needed. If children were, indeed, "culturally deprived," they needed cultural enrichment; they needed to be motivated by success; there was a need for parent and community involvement to reinforce school efforts; and there was a need for physical health and nutrition to foster social and intellectual development. Thus, Head Start included all of the elements mentioned: cultural enrichment, intellectual stimulation, social development, parent and community involvement, and a health and nutrition component—in short, health, social services, and education. Head Start pioneers were unabashed in their convictions that inculcating middle-class culture would lead to academic and vocational success for poor children and that academic success would lead to a middle-class way of life. Edward Zigler and Karen Anderson (1979) state:

The failure of the poor to acquire middle-class attitudes and middle-class incomes was attributed to a lack of education. Education, it was believed, could compensate for the "cultural deprivation" and allow the poor to break out of the "cycle" of poverty. According to this reasoning, once the poor were skilled and educated for employment, they could achieve middle-class economic and social status (p. 5).

The family, rather than the school, continued to be identified as the ultimate source of a child's values and behavior, and therefore was the primary target for change. The task force planning the program wanted Head Start centers built in connection with every low-income public housing project as part of the public school system in all underprivileged areas (Zigler and Valentine, 1979).

Parent Involvement

In the culture of poverty jargon, lack of parent involvement and apathy about his or her child's education is considered an intrinsic trait. Even those programs that professed to encourage parental involvement had often been unsuccessful. It was believed that low-income parents were alienated from the educational process. Head Start was able to turn this perception around.

Head Start pioneered in advocating the involvement of parents in all aspects of the program. However, from its inception, there was disagreement among Head Start planners about the proper role of parents. As it turned out, Head Start was one of the most important sources of minority empowerment, particularly for "welfare moms," in the War on Poverty—but not without a struggle; moreover, Head Start marked the beginning of a movement to develop a variety of programs and theoretical approaches to preschool, compensatory education. Parental involvement, which began as an attempt to educate parents to middle-class ways, brought a sense of reality to Head Start that could not have been accomplished solely through white, middle-class, professional expertise. As parents and indigenous paraprofessionals entered the school system, it became apparent that this was not simply an innocuous excursion of parent and community involvement in the education of children. What started as a parent education mandate from the federal government gradually became an empowerment issue for the poor. It became evident that participation and control were vastly different concepts. As such, the federal government began to retreat from parent involvement as it had in the larger War on Poverty.[3]

Parents were encouraged to engage in Head Start in two ways: by providing direct services, such as serving as classroom aides and volunteers, and by acting as decision makers on policy boards, task forces, and committees. In the latter roles, where sharing and/or giving up power were involved, there were not always harmonious relations between local officials and educators and the "newcomers." Parents sat on Head Start boards and parent policy committees. While they served as teacher aides in the classroom, they also participated in budget and personnel deliberations. Parents were also given career opportunities and in-service training. Not only were parents and children changed by the special experience of Head Start, the encouragement of parent and community involvement was the beginning of the local control movement in education. The carry-over of social change from Head Start into the mainstream elementary school system, however, continued to be an elusive goal, and, as was noted earlier, the activism of parents gradually diminished and parent education became a dominant theme.

EVALUATION OF HEAD START

One of the differences between Head Start and other social programs is that Head Start was always being evaluated. This is much more in the tradition of education than social service. While valid and reliable evaluations can contribute greatly to our understanding of educational and social programs and are essential in planning and program development, the following discussion provides insights into some of the difficulties encountered in trying to measure the results of Head Start.

The initial evaluations of Head Start were disheartening because little improvement in intellectual functioning was revealed. In fact, Sheldon White (1970) notes that the summer program showed no effects and the full-year programs had some effects, but there were too few children included to know where the positive results were coming from. Preliminary findings, however, indicated that it was the urban, black children who seemed to be benefiting the most from the program.

In measuring the effects of Head Start, two kinds of comparisons are made: those that compare Head Start participants to other matched samples of children, and those that compare Head Start participants with the noneconomically disadvantaged. In the first instance, the comparisons directly measure the effects of Head Start; in the latter case, the comparisons measure the sustained impact of Head Start into elementary school because intellectual differences in socioeconomic status had already been demonstrated for preschoolers. If measures were reliable and valid and Head Start were totally effective in achieving intellectual goals, Head Start children should exceed their matched peers in intellectual performance immediately upon completion of Head Start and be almost equal or more advanced then their more advantaged counterparts in elementary school.

In commenting on the highly publicized and often quoted National Impact Study of Head Start conducted by a joint effort of the Westinghouse Learning Corporation and the Ohio State University from June 1968 to June 1969 (Westinghouse Learning Corp., 1969), Urie Bronfenbrenner 1979) states:

The proposed design was an overly mechanical and mindless plan for massive computer analysis of data regarding changes in intellectual development of Head Start children, obtained from noncomparable groups of children [through supposedly matched samples] under noncomparable program conditions. [Although broad guidelines for Head Start programs existed, each program reflected the distinct characteristics of its leaders, locale, children, etc.] . . . This evaluation was based upon the results of objective measures primarily restricted to the domain of cognitive development, without regard to other goals of Head Start in the areas of health, motivation, and social development. Nor was any attention being paid to the children's parents or the communities in which the parents lived (p. 87).

Even in the area of cognitive development, which was measured, controversy on research methodology was never resolved (e.g., White, 1970). In fact, the issues of culture-free testing were first recognized around efforts to evaluate Head Start.

Despite criticism of the research methodology and the prematurity of the nationwide evaluation effort (too few children in the third grade, for example), because of political reasons, these findings almost resulted in the demise of Head Start. On the positive side, however, the findings were jolting and led to important questions about the program and its assumptions, goals, methods of evaluation, and future directions for compensatory education for low-income children. Doxey Wilkerson (1970), for example, identifies such questions as the etiology of academic deficits in low-income children, the reversibility of these deficits, the kind of curriculum reform that is needed, and the evaluation methodology that is most appropriate. She notes that questions concerning the relative emphasis to be placed on different evaluative criteria, such as community and parent involvement and social values, and the appropriateness of standard instruments and norms are important in the appraisal of compensatory programs. Wilkerson also challenges, on statistical grounds, the findings of the influential "Coleman Report" that socioeconomic factors account for more variability in school performance than school influences (Coleman, 1966).

The findings of slight cognitive benefits of Head Start only in the first grade suggested that long-range change cannot be expected from the limited intervention of Head Start. On the other hand, perhaps the children might have done much more poorly without Head Start. The limited long-range achievement of the Head Start children is also an indictment of the schools. Robert Egbert (1968) notes that one summer or one year of Head Start should not be expected to overcome the cumulative effects of deprivation in the early years. But he goes on to say that "the desire to learn dies because it is unfed." In a New York City evaluation of Head Start, findings indicated that Head Start children do better than their classmates when both have good teachers. But these youngsters do worse and are more damaged by poor kindergarten teaching than their classmates: "More damage is done to the child who looks forward eagerly to an educational program he has learned to enjoy than to the child who has no previous knowledge of what to expect, if the later school experience is poor" (Egbert, 1968, p. 573). Using a learning theory approach, Donald Campbell and Peter Frey (1970) suggest that the fade-out of gains from preschool compensatory education can be understood from the socioeconomic "learning opportunity" environments of different children. Thus, in discussing vocabulary, these authors conclude that:

When the enrichment program is discontinued and the Head Start children return to their normal word environment, the benefits of the enrichment program dissipate. . . . At age 12, the vocabulary of the Head Start group is quite similar to that of the disadvantaged children who did not participate in the enrichment program. . . . The only condition not entailing a fade-out is a situation in which the compensatory input is maintained throughout the educational years (p. 462).

This includes home and school environments.

A later longitudinal study conducted by Yale University suggested that Head Start children often demonstrated a "sleeper effect." As they moved through school, Head Start children showed no difference from a control group in the third grade, but they did show superiority over the control group in three out of five academic measures by the end of the fifth grade. A study conducted by Kirschner Associates in 1970 documented approximately 1,500 instances in which health and educational services for poor children were improved in Head Start communities (Richmond et al., 1979).

After the initial, and probably premature, Westinghouse/Ohio evaluation findings, numerous other studies documented more conclusive results.

The major conclusions from these studies is that the Head Start experience has a substantial immediate effect on participants. Long-term effects are less reliably found, and even when they are statistically different from comparison groups, the findings "are still not high enough to offer much encouragement for regarding Head Start as a powerful way to equalize educational achievement" (Datta, 1979, p. 407). In summarizing twelve years of evaluation studies, Lois-Ellin Datta concludes that:

Numerous studies have confirmed that Head Start graduates enter primary school close at or at national norms on measures of school readiness. This advantage seems to be maintained during the first year of school. In the second and third grade, however, only a few on-site studies show substantially better performance for Head Start graduates versus non–Head Start participants. . . . Final levels of test performance for both groups are troublingly far below adequate levels of competence (p. 417).

These findings are analogous to the early experiments in deinstitutionalization. Attempts to intervene in the hospital environment with "milieu therapy" helped patients leave the hospital. But without a supportive environment after discharge, community tenure was often short-lived. Similarly, lack of a supportive academic environment after Head Start—particularly the school environment—is apt to negate Head Start accomplishments.

In 1967, Jonathan Kozol commented that the "standardized condescension" that existed in the Boston pubic schools was designed to maintain the status quo and reinforce the existing authority within the schools. He wrote:

The way the threat [to authority] is handled is by a continual and standardized underrating of the children: They can't do it, couldn't do it, wouldn't like it, don't deserve it. . . . In such manner, many children are tragically and unjustifiably held back from a great many of the good things that they might come to like or admire and are pinned down instead to books the teacher knows and to easy tastes that she can handle (p. 188).

Kozol is referring primarily, but not totally, to the exclusion of multiethnic, multiracial, pluralistic content from the school curriculum. These observations are confirmed in a Conference in Community Control of Schools sponsored by the Brookings Institution in 1970: "The choice of textbooks and curriculum can rarely be modified by a teacher no matter how useless or deleterious they may be to the pupils. . . . Attempts to introduce relevant activities were criticized as violations of the 'required' curriculum" (Levin, 1970, p. 277). Experiences such as these are among the major arguments in support of school decentralization in order to increase the responsiveness and accountability of schools to the population they serve. Most recently, Kozol (1991) has written about the inequities in education between the rich and poor and challenged the use of local property taxes as the main source of revenues for public schools.

Today, school systems are finally beginning to go beyond lip service to acknowledge their role in school failures. But it will require a massive shift in public priorities and attitudes to change the entrenched public education system in the United States.

In evaluating Head Start, we are reminded by Mendelsohn (1970) that this program, and other antipoverty efforts, are means and not ends. The ends are the elimination of poverty or at least getting individual families out of poverty. Thus, Robert Mendelsohn suggests that evaluation should not concentrate on measuring changes in children but, rather, on determining institutional change and change in the economic and social conditions of families. To others, the goals of Head Start are to improve the academic performance of children in elementary school, to help children cope better with school, to improve their health, to increase parent participation in their child's education, and to provide employment and training opportunities for paraprofessionals in the child care field (White, 1970; Richmond et al., 1979). There are disagreements among professional educators about the goals of Head Start, and there are conflicts and power struggles between professionals and nonprofessionals on policies, curriculum, staff qualifications and training, as well as goals. These discrepancies in program direction and grandiose expectations provide insights into some of the difficulties in assessing all of the antipoverty efforts of the Great Society. Today, the goals of Head Start are more modest than formerly, and there appears to be agreement that the program is expected to bring about a greater degree of social competence in children of low-income families—but that is as far as agreement seems to go (U.S. Department of Health and Human Services, 1989).

CURRENT STATUS OF HEAD START

Head Start is now a program within the Administration for Children, Youth and Families at the Department of Health and Human Services. Since 1965, the program has served over 11.9 million children and their families. From an initial financial investment of $96.4 million in 1965, Head Start received an allocation of $1.95 billion from the federal government in 1991. The program is currently administered by 1,290 community-based nonprofit organizations and school systems, serving 540,930 children. A minimum local financial contribution of 20 percent continues to be mandated.

In 1990, 38 percent of children in Head Start were black; 33 percent were white; 22 percent were Latino; 4 percent were Native American;

and 3 percent were Asian. Four-year-olds constituted 63 percent of the total. Twenty-seven percent of all 4-year-olds in Head Start were in foster care, and 33 percent of all 4-year-old AFDC children were in foster care. Children with disabilities accounted for 13.9 percent of Head Start's total enrollment. In 1990, 68,000 children with disabilities were served (Project Head Start Statistical Fact Sheet, January, 1991).

The Administration for Children, Youth and Families, in 1988, undertook a thorough examination of performance standards for Services for Children with Handicaps in Head Start programs. This effort reflected the positive, as well as the negative, aspects of identifying children as handicapped in the preschool years. Head Start has now become the largest provider of services in a mainstream setting, in the nation, for preschool children with handicapping conditions. Although legislation permits up to 10 percent of enrollment to be filled with over-income children, in 1987–88, only 5 percent were over-income, and, of that 5 percent, 2 percent were children with disabilities (USDHHS, 1989).

Thirty-five percent of staff are parents of current or former Head Start children. Over 484,000 parents have been volunteers in their local programs. Fifty-four percent of Head Start families are headed by a single parent, and 51 percent have income below $6,000 per year. To coincide with passage of the Family Support Act of 1988, Head Start considered 1989 the "Year of Social Services" in recognition of the extent to which social services play a part in Head Start programming. Although preparation for economic self-sufficiency is one component, the initiative reflected the comprehensive intentions of Head Start and included, for example, programs in positive parenting, work with refugee families, and assisting dysfunctional families and those at risk of homelessness to become stabilized. It is a basic tenet of the program that a partnership between staff and parents is critical to empowering parents in the areas of self-determination and education for their children (USDHHS, 1989). Ninety-five percent of families currently receive social services from Head Start and/or referrals to other agencies (USDHHS, 1991).

Head Start is particularly proud of its health program. About 96 to 99 percent of program children complete medical screening, including all appropriate tests, receive treatment for identified medical problems, complete necessary dental work, and have received required immunizations. Recent data indicate the 54 percent of Head Start children are enrolled in the Medicaid/Early Periodic Screening Diagnosis and Treatment (EPSDT) program that pays for their medical and dental services. Changes in the law in 1989 expanded the income eligibility requirements of the EPSDT so that almost all Head Start children are now eligible for this program.

Staff development and training has remained an important component of Head Start. The Child Development Associate (CDA) program gives professionals and nonprofessionals an opportunity to obtain credentials to work in the child care field. Since 1975, over 30,000 CDAs in the nation have earned a CDA credential, including some with a bilingual specialization. The CDA credential is now also available for Family Day Care providers. Parent and Child Centers (PCCs) are operating in thirty-eight centers.

Although Head Start has been the least controversial of all Great Society programs, it, too, has needed political support to exist. Because the program emphasized parent and community involvement, Head Start developed a strong constituent base. During the 1960s, Head Start mothers could be counted on to advocate and lobby for Head Start, as well as for welfare rights and other service provisions.

Overpromising and raising unfulfilled expectations obviously leads to frustration and bitterness. This is true in accepting the rhetoric that the War on Poverty would eliminate poverty or that Head Start would compensate for all the educational and social problems brought about by poverty conditions. I have noted how programs designed specifically for the poor have not resulted in integrating the poor into mainstream society. This includes health care under Medicaid, the deinstitutionalization movement, and civil rights such as affirmative action and quality education in the schools.

It is equally unjustified, however, to write off programs such as Head Start as failures because they do not achieve all that was unrealistically promised. The tendency to discredit all social programs because of limited achievements is prevalent. Head Start, because of its complexity and uneven implementation, is a good example of the need for balance in appraising program accomplishments.

The concept of "compensatory eduction" has a checkered history. There are those who fervently believe that compensatory education maintains the status quo as minority children continue to be labeled "inadequate" in skills and therefore justifiably isolated from the mainstream of education, without change in the mainstream. As James Winschel (1970) angrily states: "The problem, of course, is that compensatory education has attempted to solve the problem of racial and social class isolation in schools which are themselves isolated by race and class, staffed by teachers who have been systematically steeped in the passive acceptance of discrimination and underachievement" (p. 7). Today, arguments center on mainstream and multicultural curricula, the advantages and disadvantages of integrated versus segregated schools (such as alternative schools) for special education groups, bilingual education, English as a second language, and the English-only movement. These arguments continue to reflect some of the unresolved issues in this area and indicate the political nature of the debate.

Head Start is an early example of affirmative action. Sargent Shriver, the first director of the OEO, observed:

A lot of poor kids arrive at the first grade beaten or at least handicapped before they start. . . . They don't get a fair, equal start with everybody else when they come to school at age six. So we said, "What can we do to help these youngsters? How can we help them to arrive at the starting line even with other children?" (Zigler and Valentine, 1979, p. 51).

These words have the now familiar ring of social justice and equality. Thus, the goal of Head Start was to put all children on an even footing as they entered elementary school. We know now that Head Start did its job, but the elementary schools did not, nor did the rest of society.

Thus, a great deal has been learned from the Head Start experience. The program began as an effort to inculcate middle-class values into lower-class children and families. It evolved into a program that recognized the fallacies of such an approach and tried to empower individuals and families. However, there has been much resistance to this latter perspective. It is a lot easier to articulate the principles of pluralism and a democratic society than it is to implement and sustain these ideas in reality. Strategies for social change, the goals of social change, and the criteria that need to be applied to evaluate social change are known. A commitment to democratic principles and processes is the first step toward the achievement of empowerment and equality for people who are currently disadvantaged, disenfranchised, and dispossessed.

NOTES

1. There were CAAs that refused to operate Head Start because it was a service program. These organizations were committed to community action and empowerment, and they saw service programs as antithetical to these goals.

2. The most important education programs of the 1960s included the Elementary and Secondary Education Act of 1965, which provided financial assistance to local educational agencies for the education of children of low-income families, including preschool programs, to help meet the special education needs of "educationally deprived" children; the Higher Education Act of 1965, which provided educational opportunity grants for students with "exceptional financial need"; and the Handicapped Children's Early Education Assistance Act of 1968, which provided funds for preschool and early education for children with handicapping conditions.

3. A classic example of this conflict is illustrated by the Head Start program operated in Mississippi by the Child Development Group of Mississippi (CDGM). Serving more than 6,000 children in eighty-four centers throughout the state, the project emphasized the fullest participation of the indigenous poor. CDGM actively challenged the white supremist political and social structure in Mississippi. Sargent Shriver, the first director of OEO, recalls that CDGM was repeatedly warned about mismanagement of funds, then defunded, and ultimately refunded after it was reorganized. Shriver believed that if CDGM had not been stopped, the whole War on Poverty might have been destroyed. This is often said about CAAs, as well (e.g., Zigler and Valentine, 1979, chapters 3 and 12).

6

Medicare and Medicaid, 1965

Gleaming palaces of modern science, replete with the most advanced specialty services, now stood next to neighborhoods that had been medically abandoned, that had no doctors for everyday needs, and where the most elementary public health and preventive care was frequently unavailable. In the 1960s many began to observe that abundance and scarcity in medicine were side by side. After World War II, medicine had been a metaphor for progress, but to many it was now becoming a symbol of the continuing inequities and irrationalities of American life" (Paul Starr, 1982, p. 363).

Rather than a partnership between the public and private sectors, according to Starr, health care reflects the politics of accommodation, with government losing the battle and the private sector making all of the gains: "While government expanded its redistributive efforts, it continually sought to reassure private interests that it would make no effort to control them" (Starr, 1982, p. 377).

Medicare and Medicaid are examples of redistributive efforts by government in the 1960s, within the limits of social reform, to make health care available to large segments of the population. But health care is unique among human services because there is an interdependent and often adversarial relationship between citizens and the health care system, including physicians, hospitals, pharmaceutical companies, and the private insurance industry. From the beginning, Medicare and Medicaid reflected the many conflicting strands of the health care debate, including a universal, social insurance component for the elderly; a voluntary component, also for the elderly, but more of a hardship for lower-income individuals; and a means-tested welfare program for the poor. With working class and middle-income individuals presumably protected by employer-paid health benefits, it appeared that all sectors of society were being taken care of.

The growth of health insurance as a fringe benefit of employment and the rise of real income in the 1940s and 1950s made it possible for working-class families to enjoy greater access to medical services than they had before the war. But a crisis in confidence was looming, mainly attributable to inflationary health care costs, lack of regulation, uneven access, and a self-aggrandizing attitude of physicians toward patients and patient care. In looking at health care in this country, Starr (1982) applies a historical approach and identifies three developmental phases: expansion, equity, and cost containment. He notes that the unparalleled growth of medicine in the United States, without conflict and without concerns for distribution, broke down in the 1960s. In the 1960s, growth continued, accompanied by distribution concerns, but without reorganization; in the 1970s, the emphasis became the need for reorganization to stop growth. During the 1980s many different approaches to regulation were considered and a few were implemented. Perhaps the 1990s will reveal a willingness, based on demand, to make a commitment to a more equitable, more effective health care system.

This chapter includes many of the ideas promulgated by Starr, discusses the debates around Medicare and Medicaid, and describes the provisions of the legislation as they relate to issues of access and availability, including equity, cost and financing, and quality of care. There is considerable overlap between these categories, as the reader will see. The role of the public and private sectors is interwoven throughout. As indicated in earlier chapters, Medicare and Medicaid are examples of the kind of social policy that developed during the 1960s that attempted to meet the social obligations of government to its citizens and the social justice goals of society.

NATIONAL HEALTH CARE—'60s STYLE

After prolonged debate and intense opposition by the American Medical Association and private insurance companies, the enacted Social Security Amendments of 1965 (P. L. 89–97) contained two new components with major implications for American society and health care in the future: Title XVIII—Health Insurance for the Aged (Medicare) and Title XIX (Medicaid), which provides Grants to States for a Medical Assistance Program for the medically indigent of all ages. Medicare has two parts: Part A is a universal health insurance program for all people aged 65 and older. It is financed through a payroll tax on employees and employers and establishes a federal Hospital Insurance Trust Fund; and Part B which provides Supplementary Insurance Benefits for the Aged. This is a voluntary insurance program that provides nonhospital, medical benefits financed through premium payments by enrollees together with contributions from funds appropriated by the federal government. In 1966, the premium amounted to $3.00 per month for the elderly; today, the premium is $31.80 a month and is increasing all the time.

Medicaid is a means-tested program financed by state and federal general revenues and administered by the states. It is a program of mixed lineage, with both health and welfare components. Because it is means-tested and not an entitlement program, it suffers from the same kind of exigencies as other welfare programs: stigma, discretion, and unevenness across states; inadequate funding; and extreme vulnerability to political and economic conditions. As Stuart Eizenstadt (1991) states: "The dire problems of the Medicaid program reflect the lack of middle-class support for domestic programs for the poor. The solution—becoming part of a universal health-care system in which the middle-class has a stake—can become a model of how to regain the public confidence necessary for further social advances". Currently, and for the first time, President Bush is proposing that Medicare Part B also be linked to income, thus making it, too, means-tested.

Enacting a federal health insurance program, but limiting universal entitlements only to the elderly and including a means-tested component, might be predictable within a social reformist framework. The elderly constitute large and growing numbers, and both in 1965 and today, they are a political force to be reckoned with. They are usually considered to be among the deserving poor, which the younger, allegedly more able-bodied welfare recipient is not (Katz, 1989). Social Security, including Medicare, is financed by a flat payroll tax with a ceiling on taxable wages and includes only wages in its calculations. Thus, it is a regressive tax. However, one of the more redistributive aspects of the program is that, irrespective of the amount of money paid into the system, all elderly are eligible for the same health benefits. (This is not true, of course, with Social Security income benefits.)

When Medicare was debated, there was by no means united Congressional support for a universal health insurance program that covered all elderly, irrespective of income. The mix of principles included in Medicare and Medicaid reflect ongoing issues in the health care debate. Some of these are as follows: (1) Should the program be voluntary only for those who want it in place of private insurance? (2) Should it cover just the elderly, or should all age groups be included? (3) Should it be financed out of general revenues or a special payroll tax? (4) Should it cover physician services, or only hospital costs? (5) Should the state and federal government participate? (6) What about fee-for-service payment or some other payment system? (7) Should it be an entitlement or means-tested? (8) Should acute and/or chronic care be included? (9) What about long-term care? (10) What about preventive care, coverage for children, and infectious diseases?

Among other things, there was concern about damage to the private insurance system because 60 percent of the elderly in 1963 had some form of private health care. Provisions for fiscal intermediaries and private carriers addressed part of that concern. Moreover, inclusion of voluntary Part B, and deductibles and coinsurance provisions in both Parts A and B, which had to be paid for directly by the elderly or paid out of private insurance, provided assurance that personal responsibility and the private initiative of the elderly to protect themselves would not be destroyed. There were some who believed that Medicare did not go far enough to protect the elderly from long-term, catastrophic illness, and there was legitimate concern that costs would accelerate. Some limited attention was given to cost containment in provisions for paying physicians only "reasonable costs," but, as it turned out, the principles of fee-for-service, payment of costs plus a negotiated rate of profit, and emphasis on short-term, hospital-based, acute health care were some of the costliest, and least cost-efficient, components of the legislation.

Although Medicare as a federal program, administered by the federal Health Care Financing Administration (HCFA), has many redistributive features, the legislation contains many provisions that reveal the power of the private sector in its formulation. For example, the freedom of individuals to choose their health care provider was guaranteed: "Any individual entitled to insurance benefits under this title may obtain health services from any institution, agency, or person qualified to participate under this title if such institution, agency, or person undertakes to provide such services" (U. S. Code, 1965). Although this is changing, the strong belief among Americans in this "free-choice" option belies the lack of choice in this area for millions of citizens, but it forms the basis for much opposition to so-called socialized forms of medicine.

Similarly, there is prohibition against any federal interference in the practice of medicine:

Nothing in this title shall be construed to authorize any federal officer or employee to exercise any supervision or control over the practice of medicine or the manner in which medical services are provided, or over the selection, tenure, or compensation of any officer or employee of any institution, agency, or person providing health services; or to exercise any supervision or control over the administration or operation of any such institution, agency, or person (U. S. Code, 1965).

The concepts of "fiscal intermediary" and private carriers are other examples of the federal government relinquishing responsibility for the program by contracting with the private insurance sector for program operations. The emphasis on the controlling role of the private sector in health care is a uniquely U. S. phenomenon, not shared by other Western nations.

Medicaid, in contrast to Medicare, is public assistance and not an insurance program. The legislation was predated by the Kerr-Mills program enacted in 1960. That program was means-tested and involved cost-sharing between states and the federal government, but only the elderly poor were eligible for coverage. The program failed to take hold, however, as very few states acted to take advantage of the federal funds.

In 1990, Medicaid, as a means-tested program, was heavily used by three groups: 11.2 million children at a cost of $9.1 billion; 3.6 million disabled at $23.9 billion; and 3.2 million elderly at a cost of $21.5 billion. The fastest growing Medicaid expenses are for intensive care, nursing facility care, and home health care. Medicaid expenditures over the years have far exceeded the increase in number of persons or services provided (*Gerontology News,* 1991).

In 1980, total Medicaid expenditures nationally were approximately $27.6 billion, of which $15.6 billion were federal funds and $12.0 billion came from the states. In 1991, Medicaid served 27 million people at a cost of $51.5 billion for the federal government and more than $39 billion from the states (Pear, 1991b). States determine the scope of services to be offered and the reimbursement rates, subject to minimum federal requirements. States also determine income eligibility (National Commission on Social Security, 1981). Herein lies much of the unevenness of the program. In Alabama, for example, a family of three must earn less than $1,416 annually to qualify for Medicaid, and the percentage of poor covered by Medicaid has actually dropped from 63 to about 50 percent, compared with 96 percent of the elderly covered by Medicare.

As a public assistance program, Medicaid mandates that recipients deplete almost all of their financial resources in order to meet eligibility requirements. Both Medicare and Medicaid operate on a fee-for-service basis, but there is a ceiling on how much each will pay for services. In Medicaid, the federal government and the states set ceilings on their respective expenditures. Long-term care facilities, other health care providers, and consumers are much more vulnerable to cutbacks in these funds, and state budget shortfalls are likely to affect Medicaid more than Medicare. What Medicare does not cover, the elderly are expected to pay for with private insurance, out-of-pocket expenses, or, if eligible, Medicaid. In 1974, Howard Newman observed: "No single element of my association with Medicaid stands out more clearly or was a greater source of frustration to me than the program's lack of an effectively organized political constituency. . . . There was almost a total lack of political pressure exercised on behalf of the recipients of the program" (p. 23). This is a sad commentary on the powerlessness of the poor.

THE NIXON YEARS

In the early 1970s, with social justice and equity issues still salient, it looked like the nation was moving closer to national health insurance. However, Starr (1982) comments on the shift that occurred later in the 1970s from a redistributive to a regulatory perspective in health care that may not have been consistent with a universal, federal health insurance program. As technology grew, along with costs, access to quality health care diminished for everyone except the most affluent. With higher infant mortality rates and lower life expectancy than most Europeans, there was a growing consensus that:

American medicine was overly specialized, overbuilt and overbedded, and insufficiently attentive to the needs of the poor in inner-city and rural areas. The system needed fewer hospitals, more "primary" care, incentives to get doctors into underserved communities, and better management and organization. And most of all, Americans required national health insurance—not a giveaway to the providers like Medicare, but "rational," "coordinated" programs that would include "tough cost controls" (Starr, 1982, p. 383).

In 1974, Howard Newman, former Commissioner of the Medical Services Administration, was sanguine that "one can hardly pick up a newspaper or a magazine or the *Congressional Record*, for that matter, without gaining the impression that we are barely moments away from national health insurance" (Newman, 1974, p. 21). In the same year, in a statement before the House Committee on Ways and Means discussing national health insurance, Wilbur Cohen said: "The current debate is not whether, but what and how. Thus, the questions to be resolved during your deliberations are those of who will be covered by the program, what the benefit structure will be, how to administer and finance the program, and its role in improving the nation's health services system" (Cohen, 1974, p. 15). It also appeared that long-term care under Medicare might become a reality. Again quoting Cohen:

We are especially pleased [representing the American Public Welfare Association] that the long-term care services program places priority on comprehensive, community-based, in-home or ambulatory services over inpatient institutional services and that full opportunity will be given to the individual and his family to participate in the determination of the plans for and the evaluation of the services received by the individual (p. 18).

But by 1975, Eveline Burns was saying: "It does not take any unusual prophetic skill to assert that there will not be any national health insurance (NHI) legislation in 1975. But I am prepared to risk the charge of being

Cassandra and prophesy that 1976 is unlikely to show a better record" (Burns, 1976, p. 33).

What was occurring during this brief time period? Lack of trust in Nixon and his administration and a general skepticism about the role of government were among some of the obstacles. Economic recession and inflation, the oil crisis, and even more inflation in health care costs were some other factors involved. Ironically, at 8 percent of the Gross National Product, the United States was already outspending most other countries that had comprehensive national health plans. The United States lacked a viable structure for cost containment, and this was a serious hindrance to the enactment of any national health policy: "The U.S. maintained its fragmented, cost-based reimbursement system, while the Canadian provinces controlled costs by setting rates in negotiations with health care providers" (Starr, 1982, p. 412). While Health Maintenance Organizations (HMOs) were slowly developing and showed promise of containing costs, it was too soon to tell how that would work out. Politically, backlash from the 1960s was beginning to take its toll, and the tide was turning away from progressive legislation and toward a more conservative outlook for the nation—away from redistribution and government intervention toward a freer market in health care and the business community. The cause of social justice was once again on the decline and with it any further serious consideration of national health care.

OMNIBUS BUDGET RECONCILIATION ACT OF 1981: P. L. 97-35

The Omnibus Budget Reconciliation Act of 1981 had sweeping effects on social programs as the Reagan administration sought to undo progressive legislation from the 1960s. For example, Medicare reimbursement to hospitals was restricted and cost-sharing by beneficiaries increased, Medicaid payments to states were reduced, and the legislation limited oversight and permitted termination of Professional Standards Review Organization (PSROs) (Davis, 1981). There have been cutbacks of $43 billion in Medicare in the last five years, and President Bush is currently proposing additional cuts.[1]

The OBRA legislation consolidated separate categorical grant programs in health and transferred 75 percent of these funds (25 percent was cut) into two block grants: the Health Services and Facilities Block Grant and the Alcohol, Drug Abuse, and Mental Health Services Block Grant, which consolidated alcohol, drug abuse, and mental health into a single program. The consolidation of programs and block grants to the states—continuing the New Federalism that was started with Nixon—was alleged to provide greater flexibility (through state operations) and coordination of programs, to reduce redundance and duplication, and to counteract uncertainty with respect to funding. In fact, reductions in funding and discretion in using funds (block grant characteristics) have also meant that the poor might not be protected in the so-called safety net at all. Some other Reagan administration proposals, such as eliminating minimum Social Security benefits for individuals with limited eligibility, aspects of the recertification process for the disabled, and additional cutbacks in AFDC, were either not enacted, partially enacted, or overturned by the Congress.

Testimony in Congress in opposition to the president's budget argued that:

The Administration's proposal for health programs reflects a deep indifference to the serious health care needs of the poor. . . . The Administration proposed an across-the-board 25 percent reduction in vital health and prevention programs, including community health centers, mental health, childhood immunizations, alcohol and drug abuse, and family planning . . . fold[ing] all of these programs into two formless block grants with little accountability and no assurance that vital programs will be continued by the states (U. S. Code, 1981, p. 945).

Other Reagan administration proposals included elimination of funding for health planning, which was believed to place a needed brake on capital expenditures; elimination of PSROs, which monitored hospital care; and elimination of the requirement of community involvement on community health and mental health centers' governing boards. Additional testimony in Congress noted that "this requirement is one of the most important and innovative features of these programs. The participation of center users on the board assures that services are responsive to the community's needs and is a key component of the center's success" (U. S. Code, 1981, p. 946).

In evaluating health care, access and equity, cost, and quality of care are major criteria.

ACCESS AND EQUITY

The incentives that favored hospital care promoted the neglect of ambulatory and preventive health services; the incentives that favored specialization also caused primary care to be neglected. Paying doctors according to the fees prevailing in their areas encouraged doctors to settle in wealthy suburbs rather than in rural or inner-city areas (Starr, 1982, p. 387).

With Medicare and Medicaid in place, this left the majority of Americans without any publicly supported health care. And although Medicare and Medicaid resulted in greater access and utilization of services, neither program provided full coverage of health needs for their respective targeted populations. In Medicare, frequent increases in deductibles and coinsurance erode the universalism of the program. Efforts to persuade physicians to accept the approved Medicare payment for their services are being fought in state legislatures. Payment for prescription drugs, which was a feature of the Catastrophic Care Act of 1988 that was later repealed, is not available, nor is dental care, eye care, audiology services, routine physical examinations, immunizations (e.g., flu shots), and many other nonhospital, health, and home care costs. There are also serious limitations on payment for mental health services. The emphasis on acute, in-hospital care is an anomaly for the elderly who suffer from chronic health problems that usually require community care or long-term nursing home care. And Medicare provisions also require the highest level of health care by physicians or registered nurses, which is most expensive, when, in fact, lower level care from home health aides or personal care attendants or chore services are what many elderly need.

A large portion of Medicaid pays for long-term nursing home care of the elderly, many of whom have become poor after paying out-of-pocket expenses for their long-term home and institutional needs.[2] In contrast to Medicare, where individuals either have supplementary insurance or personally pay for costs above Medicare rates, Medicaid pays a fixed amount for physician, hospital, and long-term care services. This has resulted in individuals and families frequently being refused treatment because rates are considered too low, and this situation is getting worse as federal and state governments place tighter reins on Medicaid expenditures. Recent data indicate that, on average, Medicaid pays 69 percent of what Medicare pays for the same service and an even smaller proportion of what private insurers pay, and there is increasing pressure for Medicaid to at least match Medicare payments.[3] A federal advisory commission, dealing with health care since 1986, has vehemently stated that "Medicaid beneficiaries should have access to mainstream medical care and this is almost impossible at current levels of payment under Medicaid" (Pear, 1991b). Additionally, eligibility for Medicaid varies among states, so that many medically needy families are not covered at all. There is concern that if the federal government mandated payment increases for Medicaid, states would limit eligibility or the scope of benefits to offset increased costs (Pear, 1991c).

Back in 1974, Newman noted that Medicaid had responded to many unmet health needs of the poor. But he added that "the program has done little to bring the poor into the mainstream of medical care." He optimistically believed, however, that "it has . . . perpetuated a system of providing health services to the poor which I believe will be unacceptable in the future" (p. 22). Newman concluded that no health program designed specifically for the poor can be successful because of political, economic, and social realities. As indicated earlier, means-tested programs either offer "poor services" or are doomed to budget cuts largely because of resentment of these programs by the middle class.

Issues of access also relate to the supply and distribution of medical personnel. Professional medical associations in the past have not only limited the number of doctors who are trained but also encouraged medical research and medical specialization and the construction of hospital beds without corresponding growth in the availability of primary care. After World War II, instead of training more health care professionals and different types of medical personnel, the solution to demand was to increase the supply of hospital beds. In 1946, the Hill-Burton legislation was passed, which provided primarily for hospital construction. A report from the Commission on Hospital Care at the time recommended the addition of 195,000 hospital beds at a cost of $1.8 billion for construction and an additional $375 million a year for operating expenses. Between 1947 and 1971, $3.7 billion was spent by the federal government, matched by $9.1 billion in local and state funds, primarily for hospital expansion. Although Hill-Burton was modified in 1954 to permit grants to long-term care and ambulatory care facilities, as of 1971, more than three quarters of the money had gone to hospitals (Starr, 1982). Some of this construction occurred in cities, but most was in middle-income communities. The Hill-Burton legislation also included prohibitions on federal intervention in hospital policy. Along with the need to keep hospital beds filled, these hospitals had an insatiable appetite for the highest and most expensive technology, which added to the prestige and status, and therefore the income, of physicians.

Only recently has health care begun to change. The supply of physicians has increased, and other trained personnel, such as physician assistants and nurse practitioners, are available. There has also been some turnaround in the training of medical specialists, and more young physicians are choosing family medicine. But the domination by medical specialists, who are the most costly of all medical personnel, the maldistribution of health care services, with most physicians practicing in more lucrative suburban communities rather than inner cities, and the continuation of fee-for-service programs and discrimination against Medicaid recipients still continue to represent the bulk of health care practices.

Recent articles in *The Journal of the American Medical Association* admit that patients who lack health insurance or who are covered by Medicaid are far less likely to be given common hospital procedures than are patients with private medical coverage. The burden of paying for the treatment of AIDS, for example, is shifting rapidly to Medicaid as people lose their jobs either because of their illness or because of discrimination. This trend is considered ominous because private physicians, who are the preferred choice to handle AIDS, are becoming increasingly reluctant to care for Medicaid patients. Natalie Angier (1990) cites the "growing evidence that patients without insurance have reduced access to private physicians" and acknowledges that "this is the first study we're aware of that deals with what happens to inadequately insured patients after they're admitted to hospitals." Differences in services between insured and uninsured patients strongly suggests that the poor are deprived of services, while the more affluent may be receiving services they do not need.

Although many doctors insist they cannot afford to treat Medicaid patients because payment is too low, other factors, such as prejudice and a shortage of doctors in poor, urban areas, also impede patient access to care. Some physicians freely admit that:

Doctors aren't really interested in seeing Medicaid patients. As a result, they don't lobby their state legislatures for fee increases. Hospitals and nursing homes do lobby to assure they have adequate payment. . . . Even with a dramatic increase in fees, private physicians will pay a very limited role in care of the poor. . . . We should not be so naive as to think that if we raise Medicaid fees . . . we will suddenly get a group of doctors going to practice in the inner city who are of the same caliber as doctors practicing in wealthier locations (Pear, 1991c).

Because of physician reluctance to serve the poor, a two-track system of health care is becoming entrenched. Medicaid patients generally receive their health care through an institutional provider, such as a community health center, a hospital outpatient department, or an emergency room. It is being recommended that increases in Medicaid payments be given to these facilities, rather than to private physicians, many of whom are unwilling to serve the poor at any cost.

The needs of children for adequate health care have also been neglected, perhaps because so many children are poor. These needs are developmental, beginning with prenatal care to prevent at-risk, low-birthweight babies; early childhood care, now helped substantially by the Womens, Infants, and Childrens (WIC) nutrition program; childhood care, now served by Maternal and Child Health Programs and the underutilized Early and Periodic Screening and Diagnosis and Treatment Program (EPSDT) within Medicaid; and adolescent family life education programs to prevent teenage pregnancy and to help teenage parents improve parenting skills. Children's needs are educational, social, and economic, as well as medical, and there is a concern for advocacy and outreach if their needs are to be met. In fact, Eveline Burns (1976) suggests that national health insurance begin with children. Such a program would include a comprehensive range of services, free of any means or income test, with no cost-sharing, utilizing a delivery system that is based on capitation payments, with financing from general revenues. This would be politically acceptable, not very costly, and would test the principles of prevention that have eluded the medical profession for so long.

Long-term care protection for the elderly to countermand the acute-care thrust of Medicare is another recognized need. One of the programs that the now-deceased octogenarian Senator Claude Pepper of Florida advocated for the elderly was such legislation. In fact, the Catastrophic Care Act of 1988 was a result of his efforts. However, no sooner was the legislation passed, and there was greater awareness of its provisions, than the elderly began to object vehemently to its contents. In fact, the legislation did not meet the long-term institutional or home care needs of the elderly where the greatest costs were incurred, but rather only addressed hospital and medical care costs. Despite the legitimacy of elderly complaints, members of Congress were peevish in their judgment that the affluent elderly simply did not want to pay the premiums for the coverage, and henceforth they would not be so generous to the elderly: "Children rather than the ungrateful elderly would receive federal support." The cost, which was to be borne solely by the elderly, was, in fact, excessive. But equally important, while the legislation provided for virtually unlimited days of hospital care, it is estimated that fewer than 500,000 Medicare patients a year (less than 2 percent of the elderly) are hospitalized more than 60 days, and this length of hospital stay was already covered under the old system. With Diagnostic Related Groups (DRGs), which assign hospital payment to specific medical problems and procedures and limit hospital stays, this figure might be even lower. The legislation did pay for some deductibles and coinsurance features, as well as prescription drugs, which is important, but it did not pay for treatment of long-term, chronic illnesses in home care or nursing homes, which the elderly really need. As might be expected, in addition to Congressional petulance about repeal of the legislation, which they felt they had generously proffered, private insurance companies who offer supplementary Medicare coverage raised their rates as much as 41 percent after the legislation was repealed allegedly to fill in the gaps in coverage left by repealing the Catastrophic Care Bill.

In the 1960s, when the authority of physicians first began to be challenged, the right to health care became an expectation, and access to care was a rallying cry. In that decade, in health care, as in many other domestic concerns, government paid attention and appropriated funds for such programs as community health centers, health systems agencies, and Medicare and Medicaid. The women's movement developed a strong self-determination component that resulted in national legalized abortion in 1973. But since that time, as we have seen throughout this book, there has been an erosion of these gains. There are now more than 34 million Americans without any health insurance at all, 80 percent of whom are employed, and employers are adamant that they cannot afford to continue to pay health premiums for their employees as a fringe benefit. There is also an erosion of Medicare entitlements and Medicaid coverage.

Back in 1981, the National Commission on Social Security began to recommend a surtax on individual income for Medicare. An income tax on Social Security income benefits has since been enacted. As of 1991, a higher wage base is being used to compute only the health insurance portion of the Social Security tax (FICA). For Medicaid, the National Commission recommended a more uniform program, with federal standards of eligibility and coverage, rather than state-by-state determinations. The commission recommended Medicaid payments for abortions, which was not approved, and it also recommended that a separate title of the Social Security Act be created to provide services other than acute medical and hospital care to needy persons who require long-term care. U. S. Representative Dan Rostenkowski has recently recommended lowering eligibility for Medicare to age 60. Thus, there are many different models and ways to achieve access to health care for all Americans, but a goal of universal health care has to be established first if access and equity in health care is to be achieved.

COST

Physicians have often blamed the insurance industry, lawyers, the courts, and patients for the high cost of care, implying that litigious patients, greedy lawyers, and an obliging court, along with mercenary malpractice insurance companies, have all conspired to inflate the costs of medical care. There is also a strong tendency to victimize consumers for abuse in the health care system. For example, popular belief is that cost-sharing between employers and employees will help the latter appreciate the cost of care, reduce utilization, and thereby be a cost-containment measure. Recently initiated practices that charge different premiums based on the age and health status of subscribers operate on these principles. Where previously actuarial tables determined costs of insurance for everyone, today there are proposals for different rates for different kinds of people. As a health policy analyst observed: "It used to be that this nation said we're all in this together and the healthy subsidize the sick, the young subsidize the old, and so on. Now we are caving in to an ethic that says sick people should pay higher premiums than healthy people and why should I be forced to subsidize someone who is sick" (Kramon, 1991). This mean-spiritedness is a consequence, and not a cause, of unjust health policies. On the other hand, Newman (1974) observed that "any incentive to overutilize is clearly with the provider who receives the payment for the service" (p. 23). And, as Alain Enthoven (1989) says: "The growth in spending cannot be explained by the usual suspects—an aging population, the threat of malpractice and advancing technology." More fundamental, he suggests, is the system of "cost-unconscious, open-ended demand, in which doctors and hospitals faced no budgetary limits." The fee-for-service system implemented under Medicare and Medicaid provides financial incentives that encourage a higher volume of patient services, whether these are needed or not. There are also incentives to hospitalize patients rather than treat them on an outpatient basis. Visiting patients in the hospital is much more cost efficient than conducting office visits; with house calls the least cost-efficient alternative of all. Fee-for-service systems also provide few physician incentives for patients to get well (Starr, 1982).

Hospital costs have been increasing even more rapidly than physicians' fees, and inflationary pharmaceutical costs, as revealed in the AIDS epidemic, for example, also have few, if any, controls.[4] On the other hand, hospitals in inner-city communities that depend solely or primarily on Medicaid reimbursement for services, where controls are in place, can barely stay in business because Medicaid payments are too low (Pear, 1991d).

From 1950 to 1965 per capita expenditures for general hospital care rose 8 percent annually; after 1965 the rate of growth increased to 14 percent a year. Per capita national health expenditures went from $142 to $198 between 1960 and 1965, then jumped to $336 by 1970. The growth rate for medical care costs was 3.2 percent in the seven years before Medicare and increased to 7.9 percent growth annually in the next five years, while the inflation rate for all other services went from 2.0 to 5.8 percent annually. The rate of government expenditures for health care increased even more rapidly. Health expenditures, as part of the federal budget, went from 4.4 percent in 1965 to 11.3 percent in 1973. In 1975, during a period of inflation, medical care ran about three points ahead of the economy's 6.8 percent inflation rate. Hospital charges in 1977 rose 15.6 percent over those in 1976, compared to an overall inflation rate of 6 percent (Starr, 1982). In 1989, health care spending was nearly 12 percent of the GNP and growing, up from 9.1 percent in 1981. By contrast, Canadians spend 8.6 percent of their GNP on health care and this figure appeared stable (Enthoven, 1989). On a per capita basis, the United States spends 41 percent more than Canada, 85 percent more than France, 131 percent more than Japan, and 171 percent more than Britain—"all countries that provide universal health care at well below 10 percent of their G.N.P." (Gordon, 1991, p. 376).

The Health Maintenance Organization legislation of 1973 empowered the federal government to utilize grants, loans, and other financial incentives to encourage the expansion of organizations which provide a comprehensive range of services in return for a capitation fee (Burns, 1976). HMOs represent a real change in health care structuring away from fee-for-service models. The growth of HMOs in the 1970s and other prepaid and prospective payment health plans appear to provide cost savings mainly because of the emphasis on primary care and avoidance of hospitalization. And, contrary to belief that free choice of physician is a dominant consideration in health care, Americans are becoming more responsive to the HMO model where choice may or may not be available. Additionally, HMOs are a private-sector solution to cost containment for those who oppose a strong government presence in the health care field. With help from the federal government in the form of loans and increased restrictions on enrollments and benefits, HMO subscriptions have steadily increased. Additionally, demonstration programs show promise and have extended HMOs into chronic care for the elderly (Leutz et al., 1988).

For business and the insurance industry, cost containment has become more important than any other considerations in health care. Business health care plans have little to do with equity or accessibility: "The corporate call for national health insurance is less a coherent policy than an ad hoc, almost panicky response to long-term struggles with cost control and short-term problems of labor relations and federal regulation" (Gordon, 1991, p. 376). For example, under the 1989 AT&T contract, employees not using company-designated doctors must assume 20 percent of health care premiums: "In general, contracts signed in 1989 and the first half of 1990 introduced higher deductibles, caps on the employer's share of health care premiums, and cost sharing or 'co-payment' plans previously funded entirely by employers" (p. 378). Many different kinds of public and private regulations have been introduced, such as Diagnostic Related Groups (DRGs). DRGs set a predetermined rate for specific hospital procedures, limit the length of hospital stay, require second opinions for nonemergency surgery, require preadmission screening to prevent inappropriate and unnecessary hospital procedures and admissions to long-term care facilities, and require "managed care," which uses primary care physicians and other health care personnel (who are employed by the insurance company or under contract) as case managers to monitor treatment to be sure only absolutely necessary procedures are employed.

Efforts at regulation are somewhat helpful at cost containment, but as Starr (1982) suggests, nothing short of restructuring is needed. As far back as 1974, Cohen warned that pending legislation based on restrictive benefit structure, purchase of private insurance, and provisions tied to place of employment, which included lapses in coverage as individuals change jobs, was unacceptable. Under the Social Security amendments of 1972, the federal government was given the power to undertake research experiments and demonstration projects in health care reimbursement and financing policy in ten areas, which included prospective payment systems, incentive reimbursement, state rate reimbursement, performance incentives, physician extender services, intermediate care, and homemaker services, among others. Further demonstrations were added by the National Health Planning and Resource Development Act in 1974 and the 1975 amendments to the Public Health Service Act. At that time there were even proposals to use federal training grants to influence the geographic distribution of medical personnel and medical specialization (Burns, 1976). In 1992, President Bush supported a change in Medicare designed to redistribute excessive payments away from medical specialists back to primary care physicians.

Clearly, there is no lack of ideas for public policy, but there is need for political will. For example, the movement toward greater privatization, which was expanded under the Reagan administration, will not contain costs. With current pressure from business and industry some change can be expected, but probably with preference for a strong private-sector component. It is unlikely that change will immediately evolve into a totally unified, universal national health insurance program. Change is more likely to be incremental and pluralistic, involving several different options for different target populations and resulting in all segments of the population included in different ways. A private component will surely continue, but perhaps subdued and less dependent on a fee-for-service reimbursement structure. Presently, President Bush, under great pressure to pay attention to the crisis in health care, is recommending that the medical industry cut costs by curtailing the administrative costs derived from a multitude of private insurers. But how does that help the almost 34 million who are uninsured?

As mentioned above, managed care is currently enjoying popularity among private insurers as an alternative to public programs. But this is simply private regulation replacing public regulation, without structural change. The latter requires such practices as a greatly reduced role for the private sector, unified, universal coverage, incentives for wellness, and fee setting and rate controls, as well as a variety of capitation, prospective payment plans. In 1981, the National Commission on Social Security was still protecting the entrepreneurial rights of physicians and encouraging competition to control costs. And in 1991, Robert O'Brien, President of Cigna Employee Benefits Companies, continued to propose a public-private partnership that

... balances regulations and tax incentives and preserves the best features of the marketplace—consumer choice; competition; efficient, hands-on management; and dedication to high quality.... We will make health care more accessible using competition and free-market incentives, not coercive government controls (O'Brien, 1991).

So far, greater regulation (public or private) has not resulted in major change. However, now that health care is on the public agenda, pressure from many different directions, including consumers, labor unions, public officials, and the insurance industry and business community can make a difference. Once again, as in the 1960s, there are opportunities for progressive change, with redistribution included. Experience with health care in the last two decades suggests that there is desire for change, with cost savings a high priority, but also including access, social justice, and equity goals.

QUALITY OF CARE

An expectation that the health status of Americans and the quality of health care in the United States are related is intuitively sound. However, the medical profession's preoccupation with illness, rather than health, makes data on morbidity and mortality largely irrelevant to quality of care issues. If a patient dies of cancer, is that the physician's fault? There are a few indicators—such as infant mortality and life expectancy—that are applied, and demographic differences in the incidence and prevalence of specific diseases have sociological, as well as medical, significance. But generally, health care in the United States is not evaluated. It is interesting that a number of recent surveys find Americans dissatisfied with the health care they are receiving. These sentiments are likely to be based on issues such as access, cost, and attitudes of health care professionals and less on quality of care.

On the other hand, using a public health model that emphasizes wellness and prevention of disease opens up whole new areas for evaluating the health status of Americans. This model makes it possible to establish goals for health and then measure the achievement of these goals and their consequences. Environmental issues, immunizations, physical fitness, nutrition, smoking, substance abuse, and stress are some factors that can be tested and which are believed to be related to physical health. James Mulvihill (1990) discusses a report released by the Public Health Service called "Healthy People 2000," which announced national health goals for the 1990s. The report particularly emphasizes the health needs of vulnerable populations, such as the poor, minorities, children, and the elderly. The wellness approach also provides direction for actions that the medical profession can take in the areas of prevention and health promotion, as well as health policy. Attitudinal changes that recognize patients' rights and encourage patient self-determination would also improve quality of care. Vernon Smith and Ronald Eggleston (1989) emphasize the importance of a holistic approach to patient needs, with medical care only one part of a much larger picture of social services for all citizens. These authors also recognize the need to change health policies and health care payment systems if such a goal is to be achieved.

EQUITY, COST, AND QUALITY

"Health care transcends all political boundaries. . . . It is taken as an article of faith by Canadians that they are entitled to health care as a basic right" (Freudenheim, 1989). Recent surveys comparing Canadian and American attitudes toward health care provide information that cuts across access, equity, cost, and quality of care issues. Not only is the United States spending more than other Western countries on health care, its citizens are more dissatisfied than most with the care they are receiving. This dissatisfaction extends to those paying the bills, as well as consumers. The Ford Motor Company, for example, is spending the equivalent of $311 a vehicle for health care for its American employees, while in Canada the cost is $49.80. The Canadian system is a federal program, operated on the provincial level, and financed by general taxes. Public policy sets hospital and physician rates, consumers have free choice of provider, and provider earnings are based on volume of care. Canadians are guaranteed care, at no charge. Yet Canada has held health spending to 9 percent of its GNP, while in the United States spending on health care consumes 11.3 percent of the GNP, with incomplete coverage. Costs in Canada are lower because doctor and hospital fees are tightly controlled; administrative costs are higher in the United States because of hundreds of different payment plans; and the purchase of advanced technology in Canada lags well behind that in the United States (see Table 1). The values of equity and access are priorities. By some measures, Canadians not only pay less for health care, they are also healthier: They live longer and their infant mortality rate is 25 percent lower. Even though health care is obviously rationed, shortages and maldistribution of resources also results in rationing in the United States, but in Canada, this is not based on ability to pay (Kirp, 1990). Contrary to expectations of massive bureaucratic inefficiency, Canadian overhead absorbs about 3 percent of health budgets; in the United States, private insurers have overhead costs close to 12 percent.

Table 1: Comparing Canadian and U.S. Health Care Systems: Examples of Differing Investments in Technology

	Canada		United States	
	Units	*Pop. per unit (1,000s)*	*Units*	*Pop. per unit (1,000s)*
Cardiac Catherization Labs: Diagnosis and treatment of cardiovascular disease	31	816	1,500	166
Lithotripters: Pulverize kidney stones and gallstones	4	6,325	228	1,096
Magnetic Resonance Imagers: Diagnosing a wide range of diseases	12	2,108	1,375	182

Source: Canadian Health and Welfare Ministry, U.S. Health Care Financing Administration, 1989.

Not surprisingly, there are delays in receiving nonemergency surgery and special tests in Canada. And at the same time that provincial medical and hospital associates were trying to hold down nurses' salaries, nurses in British Columbia were striking for higher pay. One academic observer notes that the health care system is as political as any other service in Canada or anywhere else: "The rhetoric of underfunding, shortages, excessive waiting lists and so on is an important part of the process by which providers negotiate their share of public resources" (Freudenheim, 1989).

Starr's (1982) concept of restructuring and implementing universal health care includes a return to redistribution of health care as a matter of entitlement. Just as the deinstitutionalization movement in mental health is enhanced by a strong civil rights and social justice component, so are all other areas of health care. This does not preclude cost-containment measures, which are necessary if all citizens are to share equally in health resources, but it emphasizes consumer rights rather than the authority of health professionals.

Citizens have a right to expect access and excellence in health care at affordable prices, with an emphasis on wellness and the prevention of disease and with outreach to children receiving much more attention than currently exists. As Starr suggests, this includes not only access to treatment, but also the rights of patients within treatment to challenge the distribution of power and expertise. These are rights that affect the patient-physician relationship, such as informed consent, the right to refuse treatment, the right to see one's medical records, and the right to participate in therapeutic decisions.

The need for social action cannot be overstated. In commenting on the lack of consumer advocacy for Medicaid in 1974, Newman stated that "it is an accurate account of Medicaid's history to say that when states have felt financial pressure, eligibility levels and maintenance of effort requirements became the prime targets for attack and, conversely, the strongest resistance to a reduction in benefit levels reflected the efforts of organized provider groups" (p. 24). Children need advocates; poor adults need to be encouraged to advocate for themselves; and community and national organizations need to support both. Women's health needs have also been neglected by the health establishment, including their struggle for abortion rights.

The points of view of special interests around health care can be summarized as follows: Representatives of community health centers, labor unions, and community action groups, as well as advocates for the poor, emphasize the need for prevention, primary care, and attention to the needs of pregnant women and children. They note that poor people use emergency rooms for care, which is the most expensive, because they lack primary care physicians, and they lack primary care because an estimated 35 to 50 percent of physicians will not treat Medicaid patients. Consumer advocates also reject employment-based insurance and favor universal coverage, with perhaps greater rationing of services, if necessary, along with the need for publicly mandated fixed rates for hospitals and physicians. These groups do not think piecemeal approaches based on the private sector would achieve the goal of universal coverage, and they doubt that private enterprise can control health care costs, indicating that the public sector can do a better job.

Representatives from the insurance industry support the need for a public-private partnership in which the private sector would regulate itself and the public (state, rather than federal) sector would provide subsidies and incentives to assist the private insurance companies to provide coverage, for example, to small businesses. They are not in favor of a unified approach but are strong advocates of managed care. They believe that the health system has excess capacity and that "managed care" cuts down on costs by limiting utilization. Under managed care a primary care physician or other health care specialist prescribes and monitors the total care a patient receives and ascertains that no unnecessary care is provided. Cost containment is emphasized and access is not discussed. It is believed that cost-sharing between employees and employers would cut down on utilization, as workers would be motivated to contain costs.

Other factors that need to be included in the health care debate are as follows: (1) The training of fewer specialists and more women and minorities; (2) control of the distribution of health care providers, especially physicians, so equal quality and equal access to care is assured; (3) sharing of high-technology resources among a consortium of hospitals; (4) long-term care, including home care and nursing home care and personal care, as well as medical care; (5) reduction in incentives for sickness and emphasis on prevention, health, and wellness for all age groups; (6) elimination of deductibles, coinsurance, and means-tested programs; and (7) uniformity and equity in the provision of and payment for all medical procedures, irrespective of region, population characteristics, or ability to pay. While a well-managed, universal health program will redistribute costs, there is evidence that such a system will not be more costly (in terms of its proportion of the GNP, for example) than the nonsystem that exists today.[5]

NOTES

1. The effects of the massive cuts in social spending, drastically rising health care costs, tax cuts for the rich, and military buildup that accompanied Reagan's election to the presidency in 1980 are still being felt as the country grapples with such domestic problems as the federal budget deficit, an economic depression, homelessness, lack of affordable and adequate low-income housing, crime, and drugs. The opening statement in the Omnibus Budget Reconciliation Act (OBRA) lays the groundwork for these problems:

Spending targets for the fiscal years 1981 to 1984 contained in this resolution will result in a cut of more than one-half in the average annual growth in federal spending in the past five years, while allowing for real growth in spending for the national defense, thus reversing the decline in real defense dollars in the 1970s (U. S. Code, 1981).

2. As the economic recession continues and states continue to experience budget short-falls, Medicaid once again becomes the brunt of anger and resentment. A series of articles in the *Hartford Courant* emphasize a new kind of fraud that the affluent elderly are supposedly perpetuating on the welfare system. It is alleged that elderly needing long-term care, who divest themselves of their assets (by giving gifts to their relatives) in order to qualify for Medicaid, are a major force driving up Medicaid costs (Williams, 1992).

3. In order to contain costs, the federal government is also trying to cut Medicare costs. All of these efforts at cost-containment are "band-aids" that avoid dealing with basic, structural change and further alienate consumers and providers from each other.

4. AIDS generally, and its attendant pharmaceutical issues, is a relevant example of the difference social activism can make. ACT UP, an activist component of the gay community, has been effective in reducing pharmaceutical costs for inordinately expensive AIDS medication; it has helped speed up distribution of needed drugs and kept the pressure on government and private companies to provide additional funds and resources for drug experimentation and care.

5. The National Association of Social Workers (NASW) recently released its plan for national health care. Major provisions include a single-payer comprehensive system, administered by the states under federal guidelines, with cost-sharing based on income (means-tested) "to control excess utilization" and fee-for-service within a negotiated fee structure for physicians and other practitioners. Hospitals would be given a lump sum yearly for operating expenses. Prevention, health education, long-term care, and mental health services are included. The plan would be funded by earmarked federal personal income tax and an employer payroll tax and run by an independent National Health Board, which would set federal guidelines. Consumers would continue to choose their own providers. (NASW, 1991). This plan is briefly outlined here to provide an example of what is probably considered feasible and realistic by the NASW in these ultraconservative times. However, cost-sharing and copayments and fee-for-service are current components of Medicare that tend to discriminate against the poor and provide incentives for increased medical costs, respectively. Thus, the NASW plan can be considered a pro-consumer, progressive proposal for national health insurance within a limited social reform framework.

7

The Community Mental Health Centers Act, 1963

Although the community mental health movement and the process of deinstitutionalization are not totally synonymous, there is a great deal of overlap in the two most important reforms in modern mental health history. Failure to achieve deinstitutionalization goals is certainly related to failures of the community mental health movement, but it is the former that poses the most serious social problems at the present time. It is for this reason that the deinstitutionalization part of the community mental health movement is emphasized in this chapter.

For all practical purposes, the current history of deinstitutionalization begins in post–World War II America, when a variety of civil rights protests gained widespread support. Reaching their peak expression in the 1960s, these initiatives were ideologically committed to the goal of improving the lot of individuals perceived as helpless in gaining access to life's entitlements. Like other civil rights protests of that era, the movement to deinstitutionalize chronic mental patients emphasized the inalienable rights of the mentally ill and their legitimate claims on society. Deinstitutionalization sought to exchange physically isolated treatment settings for services to be provided in patients' home communities, on the assumption that community-based treatment is both more humane and more therapeutic. Since the physical isolation of patients was understood to be inevitably accompanied by an invidious social exclusion that had to be corrected, those who pioneered in deinstitutionalization objected to both the content and the quality of care in large, secluded, mental hospitals (p. 7).

Thus, Leona Bachrach, in 1983, locates the deinstitutionalization movement within the context of social justice in the 1960s.

SOCIAL CLASS AND MENTAL ILLNESS

In their benchmark work on the relationship between social class and mental illness, August Hollingshead and Frederich Redlich (1958) arrived at three important conclusions: The prevalence of mental illness is significantly related to an individual's position within the class structure; the type of psychiatric disorder is significantly correlated with social class; and the type of psychiatric treatment is also significantly associated with social class. At the time, this research was a breakthrough in the field of mental illness and mental hospitalization. And although some of the specific findings of Hollingshead and Redlich are challenged by writers such as S. M. Miller and Elliot Mishler (1964), the general conclusions indicating that mental illness is a sociological, as well as a psychiatric, problem have been upheld over time (French, 1987). Gerald Grob (1983) confirms, for example, that mental hospitals were used for people who were dependent when almshouses were closed, thereby affirming the social class and sociological implications of mental illness and hospitalization. Historically, the use of public psychiatric facilities for custodial care was apparently commonplace, but no one paid much attention. Mental hospitals not only provided custodial care and no treatment, but also isolated people who were poor and dependent from the community.

With the closing of almshouses, responsibility for caring for dependent people, who may or may not have been mentally ill, shifted from local sources to the states. During the 1930s, for example, there were individuals who became socially and psychologically devastated by economic conditions. Many of these people ended up in state psychiatric facilities where they languished for decades with little or no active treatment. In the meantime, their more affluent peers with mental disorders were receiving treatment in private psychiatric facilities.

The history of mental illness and mental hospitalization in the United States is similar to the history of social welfare policy and programs in general. There has always been a group of white, middle- and upper-class people who have received mental health services in private, psychiatric facilities. During the era of so-called moral treatment, these services were likely to be highly individualized and provided through intense personal relationships with a hospital superintendent. These treatments tended to be highly successful, and the length of hospital stay was short (Grob, 1973).

Extensive immigration from Europe in the late nineteenth and early twentieth centuries changed the United States from a homogenous country to an exceedingly heterogeneous society. From the beginning, there was apprehension about newcomers with different languages, cultures, and color and they were treated with skepticism and prejudice, economically and socially. As their numbers grew and they had little claim to local community responsibility, the growth of public state institutions ensued for those who became dependent and manifested unacceptable behavior. Thus, the two-track system of mental health care, with private facilities for the more affluent and public facilities for the poor, mirrored and perpetuated societal expectations and attitudes toward these different socioeconomic groups (Grob, 1973). Mental health workers tend to be clinically oriented and apolitical. But because the events of the 1960s politicized even the most detached observers, it is not surprising that conditions in public psychiatric facilities eventually caught the attention of social reform.

THE MOVEMENT TO DEINSTITUTIONALIZE

Although certainly not for the first time, in the 1960s, people began to pay attention to the mentally ill along with other oppressed groups. Once it became widely acknowledged that psychiatry did not have sole claim on the realm of mental illness, other social science researchers, lawyers, and patient advocates began to challenge and investigate mental illness and mental hospitalization. It was particularly in the latter area that dramatic findings began to emerge.

One of the most important findings was that length of hospitalization was inversely related to the likelihood of hospital discharge. Patients were not getting mentally healthier with longer hospitalization; on the contrary, they were getting worse. In 1959, the average length of stay for schizophrenic patients in state hospitals was eleven years, compared with outpatient clinics or psychiatric wards of general hospitals where seven out of ten schizophrenic patients were discharged within one year of admission and lengths of stay of sixteen days or three weeks were not uncommon (U. S. Code, 1963). This was a serious indictment of the efficacy of "treatment" in state psychiatric hospitals, which led to further questions about conditions in these facilities.

Concurrently, other changes were also taking place. Grob (1983) notes that psychiatrists were losing interest in institutional practice and were aligning themselves with other physicians who were engaged in noninstitutional, private, individual, clinical arrangements. Psychotropic drugs were creating major changes in patient care (Bachrach, 1983). And it was believed that community care was less costly than state hospital care. With the advent of Medicare, Medicaid, and later Supplemental Security Income, the federal government, rather than the states, began to pick up most of the costs of mental health care (Smyer, 1989). Thus, the cost of care for the socially and economically dependent and the mentally ill moved from local almshouses and county farms to state coffers, and then primarily to federal auspices. The two-track system of mental hospital care continued to prevail, separating the poor and dependent from the more affluent mentally ill.

In 1955, in response to questions that were already being raised at the time, Congress approved the Mental Health Study Act (P. L. 84–182), which authorized an intensive, long-range study of the nation's resources for coping with the mental health problem. The legislation also asked for recommendations for a national mental health program (U. S. Code, 1963). A six-year study by the Joint Commission on Mental Illness and Health, published in 1961, identified the following inadequacies in the mental health system: lack of progress in treating the mentally ill; the need for research; the need to train additional mental health personnel; and the need to mobilize treatment resources so that comprehensive mental health services could be made available. The Joint Commission report outlined two major new roles for the federal government: financial participation in patient care (formerly the responsibility of the states), and the establishment and maintenance of standards for the quality of care of the mentally ill (Connery et al., 1968).

By 1960, issues of "right to treatment," defined as the legal right of a patient in a public hospital to adequate medical and psychiatric treatment for his or her mental illness, began to receive wider recognition (Birnbaum, 1960). In 1959, it was noted that there was less than one psychiatrist for 500 patients in state psychiatric facilities. These facilities also lacked sufficient nurses, social workers, and psychologists. Rather than differentiating individuals with or without mental illness, very little, if any, assessment or treatment was offered to anyone. Only a small percentage of the 278 state mental institutions were considered therapeutic and not merely custodial (U. S. Code, 1963).

Up until the 1970s, the philosophy of *parens patriae* continued to prevail; this meant the state was expected to protect mentally ill persons who were unable to care for themselves. Thus, hospitalization of the mentally ill continued to be the norm. During this period, however, a number of landmark judicial and statutory actions were passed, which strengthened a mental patient's right to treatment. Judge Bazelon is credited with first articulating this principle for persons in mental institutions in *Rouse v. Cameron,* 1966. This case established that to deprive a person of his or her freedom by institutionalization for mental illness, and then to fail to provide treatment, is a violation of the due process provision of the Fourteenth Amendment (Alexander, 1989). This court action was followed up five years later in Alabama in the case of *Wyatt v. Stickney,* 1971. In this situation, Judge Johnson ruled that "to deprive any citizen of his or her liberty upon the altruistic theory that the confinement is for humane therapeutic reasons and then fail to provide adequate treatment violates the very fundamentals of due process" (p. 110). In the mid-1970s, in *O'Connor v. Donaldson,* the Supreme Court emphasized the concept of involuntary commitment only if the individual was a danger to society and not for treatment purposes (Brooks, 1988). These court actions have been supported by federal and state statutes, in which rights of the mentally ill charged with crimes, of special offenders in correctional systems (e.g., sex offenders), and of the mentally retarded have also been included.

Writing in 1983, Stephen Rachlin stated: "By now, this concept [right to treatment] is widely recognized as a moral imperative and is a feature of many state mental health laws. My colleagues and I have stated our belief that it is the most fundamental substantive right of mental patients. In courts, however, it had fared less well" (p. 48). In 1988, Alexander Brooks wrote that "the role of law in the mental health system has expanded to where it now influences every aspect of care and treatment, both in the hospital and the community" (p. 62). But Rudolph Alexander (1989) notes that:

While most states recognize a statutory right to treatment, a major problem still exists in transforming this right into meaningful treatment. Advocacy . . . is needed to ensure that mental health services are not slighted in competition with other institutional services and to ensure that the right to treatment is not allowed to exist only on paper (p. 112).

In practice at the present time, there is increased argument for the need for the custodial functions of mental hospitals and a shift back to the *parens patriae* approach for the elderly and the homeless mentally ill. Invidious comparisons are made between state, inpatient facilities and community mental health services that favor the former arrangements for the severe, chronically mentally ill (Grob, 1983). Brooks (1988) notes the conflict between legal and psychiatric professionals, with the former usually favoring libertarianism and the latter often emphasizing the need for hospitalization over "liberty, enforced treatment over autonomy, and a paternalistic and often authoritarian relationship of doctor to mental patient" (p. 62).

In addition to the right to treatment (and the right to refuse treatment, including medication that may have serious side effects), the principles of treatment in the least restrictive alternative and the application of more stringent criteria for involuntary commitment (with an emphasis on due process and the danger the individual poses for society, rather than alleged need for treatment) have been implemented to be supportive and protective of individual rights (Rachlin, 1983). Issues of confidentiality, client access to personal records, and privileged communication are additional individual protections.

Thus, evidence of poor care and lack of treatment in state psychiatric facilities, the retreat of psychiatrists from institutional care, the Joint Commission Report, the seemingly lower cost of community care, the availability of psychotropic drugs, and litigation that upheld the legal rights of patients were some of the factors that converged to form the deinstitutionalization movement for the mentally ill.

Legislation that Made
Deinstitutionalization Possible

In 1963, the Mental Retardation Facilities and Community Mental Health Centers Construction Act (P. L. 88–164) was approved by Congress (the Community Mental Health Centers Act is Title II of this legislation), and the transfer of resources from public, inpatient facilities to community-based treatment was legitimized. Consistent with the tenor of the decade, it was a hopeful time.

Although there seemed to be undue emphasis on providing federal matching funds for construction of mental health centers (reminiscent of Hill-Burton in 1946), the legislation also stipulated the services to be offered in the newly constructed centers. These included the following: an emergency psychiatric unit; inpatient services; outpatient services; day and night care; foster home care; rehabilitation programs; general diagnostic and evaluation services; and consultation and community education. The need for primary prevention was given some recognition (but not enough), and some focusing on environmental conditions in treating mental illness was supported. Services were to be provided where people lived, and administration would occur on the state level. Each community program was expected to have as much local determination as possible, and the use of existing community facilities was encouraged. All states were required to submit a comprehensive plan that set priorities for mental health projects. Federal funding for construction grants was $35 million for fiscal year 1965, $50 million for 1966, and $65 million for 1967. In 1965, additional federal funds were granted to help with initial staffing costs (U. S. Code, 1963, 1965). However, the federal government did not commit itself to long-range funding for community mental health centers, and the local control aspect of the legislation was expected to extend to financing, as well (Connery et al., 1968). The goal of establishing hundreds of community mental health centers throughout the nation was not achieved. In addition, ambiguity and uncertainty about the roles of service and social action and social change were not resolved, and social class issues rapidly emerged. Community mental health centers tended to serve the poor, and the middle class continued to receive mental health services from private therapists or private agencies (Reiff, 1974).

Current Status of the Legislation

What looked like somewhat of an auspicious beginning that was ideologically sound obviously never materialized. The civil rights movement ended, and with it a great deal of progress in freeing oppressed people came to a halt. As noted earlier, not only did the Vietnam war divert resources away from the War On Poverty, there was a political and economic backlash that further reversed progress that had been made. In fact, the condition of the mentally ill may be worse now than before deinstitutionalization. Certainly it is more visible. A research study by the Public Citizen Health Research Group and the National Alliance for the Mentally Ill finds:

Not since the 1820's have so many mentally ill individuals lived untreated in public shelters, on the streets and in jails. More than 250,000 people with schizophrenia or manic-depressive illness are in such a condition. Only about 68,000 people with these conditions are in mental hospitals. . . . There has been a near total breakdown in public psychiatric services in the United States. . . . Of the 250,000 with serious mental illnesses, it is estimated that 100,000 are in jails or prisons. The largest de facto mental hospital in the United States is the Los Angeles County Jail, where there are 3,600 inmates who are seriously mentally ill on an average day, 700 more than the nation's largest hospital (Hilts, 1990).

The report cites similar figures for other major cities in the United States.

The consolidation of mental health and substance abuse legislation and funding into the Alcohol, Drug Abuse, and Mental Health Block Grant in 1981, as a part of President Reagan's New Federalism, signaled abdication of federal responsibility for the mentally ill (U. S. Code, 1981). In addition, Medicaid rules and regulations have not been adapted to the needs of the seriously mentally ill. The deinstitutionalization movement not only channeled the mentally ill out of public inpatient facilities and closed the doors behind them, but also diverted public funds into private non profit, not-for-profit, and for-profit facilities as part of the Reagan administration's privatization efforts (Shadish, 1989). These facilities are not eager to serve the poor who have only limited public funds and no private funds at all. Thus, the poor continued to be dependent on virtually nonexistent public facilities, while the more affluent continued to be served in the private sector. What we have witnessed really is a demise of the community mental health movement not for everyone—just for the poor (Bickman and Dokecki, 1989; Perkey, 1989; Shadish, 1989; Simons, 1989). And as Starr (1982) states, the rights of the mentally ill are abridged in two ways: be repression and by neglect.

Not unexpectedly, some writers hold social workers, the legal profession, individual patients, and the "rights" movement responsible for the failure of deinstitutionalization. Laurence French (1987) and John Belcher (1988), for example, strongly suggest that the quest for the least restrictive environment and patients' rights to refuse treatment are particularly culpable in this regard. Belcher (1988) specifically argues for hospital care of the severely mentally ill, rather than suggesting community alternatives, and indicts social workers for adherence to principles of client self-determination as clients are allegedly neglected and placed at "greater risk of further mental decompensation" (p. 400). Richard Gaskins and Mona Wasow (1979) specifically note that due process laws have been uncritically applied to the mentally ill, thus depriving many individuals of needed care. These statements are good examples of the social control functions of social policy. William Shadish (1984) cites the principles of professionalism, individualism, intolerance toward and stigmatization of deviance, profit-making, and pragmatism as contributing to the movement's lack of success. He also notes that a systems perspective was not used in implementing change:

Mental health systems participate in networks for health reimbursement, social control, welfare, and tax, to name a few. Changing the mental health system potentially changes all these networks, impinging on their ideologies and structures. Moreover, mental health professionals participate not just in mental health networks but also in the others, and they may find these other interests threatened by a mental health change (p. 730).

Deborah Salem et al. (1988) in their excellent article, suggest, among other factors, a lack of political and economic support for deinstitutionalization. As recently as 1980, it was estimated that 70 percent of the funds spent on mental health care were spent for hospitalization. These authors note that the three main sources of federal funding—Medicare, Medicaid, and the Supplementary Security Income program (SSI)—only provide financial support for brief hospitalizations (related to the infamous revolving door in hospital admissions) and "community-based" custodial care, such as nursing homes.

As is true of all social programs, insufficient funds are implicated. Lack of sufficient funding from the federal, state, and local levels makes the likelihood of failure quite predictable. This situation reached dire dimensions during the Reagan administration and continues under President Bush, where neglect of domestic policy is considered an acceptable government posture. Once again, lack of funds and appropriate social policy can only be attributed to low societal priorities based on the social class characteristics of the population that needs to be served. As mentioned earlier, any legislative or judicial actions that give citizens more rights and entitlements also is empowering. Herein lies the essence of social change that is resisted by those who support the status quo. The condition of the elderly and the homeless mentally ill illustrate the plight of these two important constituent groups at the present time.

The Deinstitutionalized Elderly

Between 1969 and 1973, the nursing home resident population aged sixty-five and over with chronic mental disorders increased by more than 100 percent, while the residents in this age group in all types of psychiatric hospitals fell by 30 to

40 percent. . . . In 1974 approximately 85,000 nursing home residents were transferred directly from mental hospitals. Consequently, the resident population of state mental hospitals aged sixty-five and over decreased from 158,000 in 1955 to 39,000 in 1979 (Goldman, 1983, p. 34).

Goldman also points out that of all the organized health care settings, only the nursing home can be demonstrated clearly to have substituted for the long-term custodial care function of the state mental hospital.

In a study of elderly patients discharged from Northampton State Hospital in Massachusetts between 1979 and 1986, Ira Sommers et al. (1988) note that only 15 percent were discharged to nursing homes. This relatively low number may reflect the availability of different types of community facilities for the mentally ill elderly in Massachusetts. There are also additional mentally ill elderly who enter nursing homes from the community or from other facilities, or who develop psychiatric problems as they age in nursing home settings. As Benjamin Liptzin (1984) notes:

For elderly psychiatric patients, deinstitutionalization has really represented transinstitutionalization with movement to a nursing home from the psychiatric hospital. . . . The mentally ill elderly in nursing homes include chronically mentally ill persons who have been discharged from public mental hospitals and those whose behavioral disturbance is new but who can no longer live independently or with their families (p. 176–177).

There is continued documentation of inadequate therapeutic and rehabilitative services available to nursing home patients with psychiatric needs (Kultgen and Habenstein, 1984; Liptzin, 1984). However, the findings of Sommers et al. (1988), cited above, suggest the development of increased community options for elderly mental patients since the beginning of deinstitutionalization.

According to Michael Smyer (1989), two policy initiatives have directly affected the growth of the nursing home industry: the Medicaid program and the deinstitutionalization of mental hospital residents. Together, these policies have had the unintended consequence of providing a basis for the development and funding of an alternative long-term care mental health system, especially for the poor elderly. Thus, custodial care in psychiatric facilities became custodial care in nursing homes. My own study in 1968 indicated that elderly chronic mental patients discharged from long-term public psychiatric hospitalization to a variety of community facilities (such as boarding homes, family arrangements, and independent living) had the lowest return rate to the hospital from nursing home settings. This suggested, at the time, the continuities between long-term hospital psychiatric care and long-term nursing home placement (Bok, 1971).

Following a number of years of attempted reform of the nursing home industry, in December 1987, the Omnibus Budget Reconciliation Act of

1987 (P. L. 100–203) was signed into law by President Reagan. The act requires that states, in order to receive Medicaid reimbursement, must develop a preadmission screening procedure and annual review, among other new provisions, and a process for certifying the type of care that the mentally impaired older adult requires. Residents not in need of nursing home care and in need of active mental health treatment, but who have resided in the facility at least thirty months, must be offered the choice of remaining in the facility, and active treatment must be provided regardless of the resident's choice. Those who have lived in the nursing home thirty months or less must either be placed in alternative care or must receive the mental health treatment in their current facility (American Association of Homes for the Aged, 1988; Newman et al., 1989; Smyer, 1989). The legislation also attempts to upgrade the quality of care in nursing homes by mandating nurses' aide training and certification, and there are explicit provisions for patients' rights that include, for example, the right to participate in one's own assessment and plan of care or changes in care; freedom of choice of physician; the right to privacy and confidentiality; the right to voice grievances and to have such grievances promptly resolved; the right to participate in resident and family groups; and freedom from unnecessary physical and chemical restraints (Omnibus Budget Reconciliation Act, 1988). Extensive violations of the latter provisions, in conflict with the spirit of independence in the legislation, is documented in a recent Yale University School of Medicine study (Megan, 1991). Although some aspects of the legislation are obviously financial, other components speak directly to patients' rights and quality of care issues. Cathy McDermott (1989) for example, describes a campaign for patient rights in a nursing home that "provided an opportunity for residents to reclaim some control over their environment [which] improved their levels of activity, sociability, and motivation. . . . These conditions enhance self-esteem and mental clarity and reduce depression and mortality rates" (p. 156). The patient bill of rights had five categories: access to information, privacy, access to the community, dignified treatment, and independent decision-making.

The OBRA legislation provides an opportunity to apply the principle of "right to treatment" to the elderly with mental problems. This recognizes the dignity and worth of the individual and is a long-awaited, necessary, and laudable goal. It is an attempt to correct abuses of the mentally ill who have continued to receive custodial care even after discharge from custodial psychiatric hospitals and to increase patient choice and self-determination. However, in view of the lack of resources and the intense frustration with the deinstitutionalization movement, staff in nursing homes and others working with the mentally ill tend to reject the principles, as well as the implementation, of deinstitutionalization policies. The mental health treatment provisions of the legislation may be circumvented to a large degree because elderly patients in nursing homes may suffer from physical illnesses that are life threatening. But the legislation is important in the attention it brings to the rights of a group of mentally ill whose oppression has generally not been recognized.

The possibility of utilizing outpatient mental health services to prevent institutionalization of the elderly is a related issue. The underutilization of outpatient mental health services by the elderly is well documented. According to Liptzin (1984), 2 percent of patients seen by private psychiatrists are 65 or older, and 4 percent of patients seen in community mental health centers or outpatient psychiatric facilities are elderly, although the elderly represent 11 percent of the population and their need for these services is not considered less than the need among younger people. In fact, the elderly use mental health services at less than half the rate of the younger populations (McGuire, 1989). While Thomas McGuire identifies many possible reasons for this situation, he also identifies social policy as a relevant issue. For example, he notes that Medicare expenditures for outpatient mental health care amounts to less than 0.1 percent of total Medicare costs. OBRA in 1987 increased the outpatient covered limit to $2,200 but retained the 50 percent coinsurance for beneficiaries. McGuire believes that the 50 percent coinsurance portion is a serious deterrent to elderly utilization of mental health services. He believes that reducing that amount to 20 percent and the limit to $1,000 or $2,000 would result in little or no increase in cost to Medicare and, based on empirical data and projections, would meet the needs of many more elderly than utilize these services today. However, Liptzin (1984) notes that in Canada where health care is a right and is provided at no direct cost to the individual and with no limits, in 1976–77, only 4.5 percent of psychiatric services billed to the Ontario Health Insurance Plan were for people 65 years of age or older, when the elderly are 9 percent of the total population.

Obviously, other considerations are also at stake, but certainly cost of care is a factor to be reckoned with. Some of these other considerations are provider attitudes toward the elderly (Kultgen and Habenstein, 1984), the attitudes of the elderly toward mental health services, and the efficacy and appropriateness of the services provided. If deinstitutionalization of the elderly is to be a reality and if the quality of life of the elderly mentally ill in the community is to be enhanced, a holistic approach is needed and the whole area of community-based mental health services for older citizens needs much more attention than it has thus far received.

The Homeless Mentally Ill

If the older mentally ill often end up in nursing homes, many of the younger deinstitutionalized end up homeless or in the criminal justice system. (French, 1987; Hilts, 1990). In 1959, a total of 559,000 chronically mentally ill individuals were in state hospitals; in 1988, there were fewer than 130,000 individuals in these institutions. In New York State, the number of people in public psychiatric hospitals in 1955 was 94,175; in 1984, it was 23,109; and in January 1990, it was 15,599. With severe budgetary shortages, the state was proposing to close several psychiatric facilities in 1991. However, even these figures fail to reflect the extent of mental illness in the society. It is believed that there are 1.5 million deinstitutionalized chronically mentally ill and that an estimated 30–40 percent of the homeless suffer from mental illness (Surber et al., 1988). In some studies as many as 50 percent of the homeless mentally ill also have a concurrent alcohol or other substance abuse problems (Levine and Rog, 1990). Goldman (1983) points out that there are actually more deinstitutionalized, reinstitutionalized, or never-institutionalized chronic mental patients living outside state mental hospitals, and a sizable portion continue to use state mental hospitals, although they are no longer permanent residents. In fact, the length of stay in these facilities is currently three to four months.

Beginning in 1981, with the initial Omnibus Budget Reconciliation Act, there were cutbacks in mental health funds, and funds for substance abuse and mental illness were consolidated into one block grant (U. S. Code, 1981). Despite the alleged commitment to community-based care, on the average, state mental health agencies spent 66.5 percent of their budgets in state mental hospitals and 29.7 percent in community-based programs in 1985 when inpatient hospital beds were at an all-time low (Brown and Fellin, 1988). Concurrent cutbacks in federal low-income housing funds and an explosion in residential and commercial real estate activity all combined to aggravate the homelessness of the deinstitutionalized mentally ill. About 500,000 low-income housing units disappear annually. From 1970 to 1982, a total of 1.1 million single room units disappeared. In Michigan, the highest possible AFDC shelter allowance was only 45 percent of the fair market value in 1984. Poverty, unemployment, cuts in social programs, and family conflicts and dissolution also contribute to homelessness and mental illness (Brown and Fellin, 1988).

Probably the most important recent federal legislation for the homeless is the Stewart B. McKinney Homeless Assistance Act (P. L. 100–77), which was passed in July 1987. This legislation contains two sections of particular importance to the mentally ill: Section 612, which authorizes a Community Mental Health Services Demonstration Program for Homeless Individuals Who Are Chronically Mentally Ill, and Section 611, which authorizes a noncompetitive Block Grant Program for Services to Homeless Individuals Who Are Chronically Mentally Ill. The latter provides funds to states for outreach, case management, mental health treatment, support and supervisory services in housing for homeless mentally ill persons, and training for service providers (Levine and Rog, 1990).

These services are crucial for community care of the mentally ill, but the need for permanent housing is not addressed.

Thus, there appears to be some effort to help the homeless mentally ill, and certainly there is considerable knowledge about what is needed. For example, the homeless among the severely mentally ill can be characterized by:

> . . . social isolation and diminished social support networks, residential instability, and the significant prevalence of concomitant substance abuse problems. Hence, these and other indicators suggest the need for services of greater intensity, diversity, and flexibility than may be required for severely mentally ill individuals who have a home and support from family, friends, and service providers (Levine and Rog, 1990, p. 966).

But the situation continues to spiral out of control, primarily because of social and political considerations. Peter Rossi (1990) describes the new homeless as much greater in number, younger, poorer, and more likely to be African-American and Latino than the former homeless (see also First et al., 1988). As we know, poor housing, economic recession, and lack of mental health and substance abuse services affect minority populations disproportionally. And the appearance of women (Bachrach, 1984) and women and children among the homeless is a totally new phenomenon.

Kozol's indictment of the homeless situation for families in New York City highlights the ramifications of political rather than social justice considerations in social welfare policy. Although welfare payments for permanent housing in New York City fall way below market levels, it is not unusual for the city to pay anywhere from $1,900 to $3,000 a month to house the homeless in welfare hotels (Kozol, 1988). Kozol cites evidence to indicate that the largest welfare hotel owners in New York City also make substantial contributions to the electoral campaigns of city officials.

It is a pretense to suggest that the right to refuse treatment is a major deterrent to service delivery. In fact, even in San Francisco, which is probably more progressive than many other communities, Surber et al. (1988) note that the service delivery system was functioning at or beyond capacity and was not able to accept many new referrals: "More disconcerting was the fact that most programs, by design or by default, excluded the homeless population" (p. 118) because they were dirty, didn't keep regularly scheduled appointments, smelled of alcohol, or were not completely abstinent from substance abuse. Even if they were a substance abuse program, the program wouldn't accept individuals using psychotropic drugs. Additionally, welfare programs denied services because individuals lacked certain types of identification, and, after insisting on extensive job searches, they rejected applicants who could not find a job. Having no income, the individual could not obtain housing

(Surber et al., 1988). This litany does not exhaust the attitudinal and institutional barriers to service delivery. Kozol (1988) quotes a study by a committee of the New York City Council that illustrates this point:

Present policy bases its programs on the theory that if homelessness is made comfortable, more people will allow themselves to remain or to become homeless. [The reader will recognize similar arguments about welfare.] The Committee found no evidence to support this. . . . On the contrary, the programs providing the best conditions with the best social services have the best placement record. Programs with the worst conditions usually have the longest average length of stay (p. 196). [The reader will also recall similar findings for custodial mental hospitals.]

IMPLICATIONS FOR THE FUTURE

The promises of the deinstitutionalization movement, because they are based on ideological principles that support social justice, found its voice during the 1960s and has almost died for lack of resources and caring in the last two decades. A strong social class component is evident in the mental health events of the last two decades. At the present time, as a response to the alleged failures of deinstitutionalization, there are pressures from mental health workers to return poor people to custodial, institutional care. But deinstitutionalization is not the failure it is professed to be. As Salem et al. (1988) state: "A growing literature indicates that when time, money, and care have been invested in positive programs, they can be equally as effective or more effective than hospitalization" (p. 403). And Brown and Fellin (1988) describe a large number of specialized programs designed to meet the diverse needs of the homeless mentally ill.

What have we learned and accomplished, in addition to the more obvious questions of power and politics, about the mentally ill? First, there is need to differentiate the so-called mentally ill much more carefully so that appropriate services can be provided. There are individuals whose mental illness may cause them to be homeless, and there are individuals who develop symptoms of mental disability from living on the streets. There are also many individuals with varying degrees of dependency—economic and social—who may not be mentally ill at all, but who may need varying degrees of personal care and social support. Many homeless women with children may fit into this group (Johnson and Kreuger, 1989). These services should be provided within the social service system using a wholistic perspective to meet the needs of all members of the family. In addition, there are gender, age, and racial and ethnic differences that must be recognized in mental health assessment and treatment. The importance of differentiating the homeless population so that treatment is matched to individual needs is discussed by Nancy Koroloff and Sandra Anderson (1989) in relation to homeless alcoholics and by Alice Johnson and Larry Kreuger (1989) in relation to women, with and without children.

Second, the deinstitutionalization movement has provided the opportunity to think about mental health treatment in new and different ways. There are now many different kinds of alternative residential facilities—day hospitals, drop-in centers, emergency and transitional programs, and supported living, for example. The importance of concrete services, social support systems, long-term follow-up and aftercare, case management, rehabilitation, outreach, advocacy, consumerism, and political action are being emphasized. Sommers et al. (1988) identify at least four levels of care for the mentally ill elderly: independent living (with or without family; alone or with companions); residential facilities, such as group homes and supported living; and intermediate and intensive care in nursing homes. Brown and Fellin (1988) identify services for the homeless, services for the mentally ill, and services for the homeless mentally ill, as well as services for women, men, and families. Within these groupings, a variety of options exist. What about the role of the family? They have been included in the past as part of the problem in family therapy. Now they are beginning to be recognized as partners in the treatment process (Bachrach, 1983).

What needs further development are the goals of treatment. What is it that the patient, community, or mental health professional want to achieve? Is it reduction or elimination of symptoms, decreased recidivism rates, employment and economic independence, social adjustment, or community living skills? Chronic mental illness is analogous to any other chronic disease: Cure may not be possible, but if the condition is untreated, it will deteriorate. This seemingly simple aphorism has not found a comfortable place in the mental health vernacular, however, and professionals continue to be uncertain and disagree with each other and with patients about quality of life issues for the severely mentally ill. Ira Sommers and Deborah Baskin (1991) emphasize the need to not only normalize the community environment for the deinstitutionalized individual, but to redefine concepts of normality to reduce the social isolation of the mentally ill.

Third, there is the need for consumer choice and client self-determination:

Consumers own preferences are emerging as a powerful determinant of the need for housing and supports. . . . Professionals and consumers hold virtually opposite views about housing and support needs, with professionals favoring transitional, highly staffed residential programs for the great majority of consumers, and consumers expressing preference for normal housing with flexible supports. . . . Most persons preferred to live in their own apartment or house . . . rather than in a mental-health-operated facility, single-room-occupancy hotel (SRO), or community-care (boarding) home, or with their family. . . . People in SROs were least satisfied of all respondents, including those who were in the state hospital or homeless. The most preferred characteristics of living situations were freedom and autonomy, permanence, security, and privacy (Carling, 1990, p. 969).

The Comprehensive Mental Health Services Act of 1986 (P. L. 99–660) mandates consumer involvement in planning mental health services and is thus a vehicle for moving toward greater consumer empowerment. Salem et al. (1988) discuss the successes of mutual help and self-help groups and organizations. This may be a pragmatic, economic response to lack of funds, but, on the positive side, it is a solution that meets the principles of client choice, self-determination, and empowerment.

The homeless mentally ill (and elderly) do not fit the model of the client, motivated for help, who will show up for a scheduled, in-office appointment. As Marcia Cohen (1989) points out, "for this client population, contacts with professionals generally have been associated with involuntary confinement in institutional settings" (p. 505). Thus, there is need for unconventional, nontraditional outreach, engagement, and empowerment strategies in which the client has maximum control over the treatment situation. This includes full participation in identifying needs, determining goals, and setting the terms of the helping process (Cohen, 1989). Brown and Fellin (1988) point out that it is helpful if services are less formally structured, more accessible, and more accepting and if they provide for basic needs, minimize bureaucratic requirements, and "allow opportunities for specialized services at the discretion of and at locations acceptable to clients" (p. 100).

Both political and social actions are needed for advocacy and policy change. Public payment for mental health services is inadequate, and private insurance programs prevent social change and uphold the status quo. Insurance programs take a strictly medical approach to mental health, so that comprehensive, flexible services are not insured. A more socially conscious mental health worker needs to be trained; prevention and childrens' mental health services need greater recognition; and a more egalitarian mental health structure between patients and professionals and between different kinds of professionals needs to be developed to truly serve the poor (Billingsley, 1974; Foley, 1974).

Finally, the rights of the mentally ill remain a controversial issue. We are all familiar with the media interest, which is attendant to coercing individuals off the streets and into shelters and treatment facilities "for their own protection"; we are also familiar with incarceration for the same reasons. Ruta Wilk (1988) discusses the pros and cons of involuntary outpatient commitment, for the protection of the individual, and aggressive case management, in which individuals are mandated to accept treatment. Although it is essential to guard against social control in the guise of treatment, it is also important not to avoid offering treatment on libertarian grounds when, in fact, it is needed. Treatment offered to the mentally ill may be rejected. But this is insufficient justification for withholding treatment or not developing appropriate treatments when there is need.

I have not even touched on forensic psychiatry and the rights of the mentally ill in the criminal justice system. I am aware that many criminals who are mentally ill are placed in prisons, where they receive determinate sentences but little or no treatment, rather than in psychiatric facilities, where they may also receive limited treatment but where sentences are indeterminate. This may be one reason why the population of mentally ill in prisons is exploding, although treatment is desperately needed. The assault on women who abuse drugs, in the name of fetal rights (Pollitt, 1990) and issues of dual diagnosis—that is, the relationship between substance abuse and mental illness—are other serious topics that need attention. We do know, however, that visits by homeless people to the psychiatric emergency rooms in New York City have risen steadily. Those visits, tied to use of crack cocaine, increased from 11 percent in 1987 to an estimated 45 percent in 1989. We also know that many drug treatment centers reject mentally ill people and that mental health programs turn away patients who use drugs. And then there is the role of privatization. The number of beds in for-profit psychiatric hospitals in the United States grew to 37,500 in 1990 from 21,400 in 1984. The total number of such hospitals grew to 440 in 1988 from 220 in 1984. The linkage between the growth of private, psychiatric hospitals and insurance and reimbursement policies is drawn by the *New York Times* in a series of articles in October 1991 (Kerr, 1991). The type of patient care, the length of patient care, and the termination or extension of care based on available third-party payments provides a discouraging picture of failure in mental health treatment.

At the present time, at least twenty states are seeking court action to mandate that mental patients be provided secure housing (not shelters) and treatment when they are deinstitutionalized (Golden, 1990). In the meantime, while there are many issues and many questions, there are also some answers and knowledge that a caring community can pursue, particularly in the areas of individual rights and social justice. We have noted, for example, that client self-determination, however controversial, is a basic right. Constitutional principles and democratic processes apply to social policy in the care and treatment of the mentally ill.

Epilogue

Throughout this book the concept of social justice has been used to mean equality of opportunity, equal access to the goods and services of society, and equality in outcomes; the principles of redistribution in social policy are seen as means to achieve social justice goals. The term "empowerment" has been applied rather loosely to concepts of economic and political power and also extended to include personal enrichment and a sense of personal fulfillment and pride. In the United States, the principles of democracy and the Constitutional rights of individuals are the social, political, and legal processes and structures for achieving social justice and empowerment goals. These moral imperatives are the criteria against which all social policy should be evaluated. These concepts lay the groundwork for understanding and contrasting the achievements and shortcomings of the civil rights movement and the social programs of the 1960s with the more recent occurrences of the 1980s and early 1990s. Social movements may be radical in seeking societal change, but electoral politics are based on bargaining and compromise, so that the social legislation of the 1960s expresses the spirit of social reform.

A review of some of the major 1960s civil rights, antipoverty, health, and mental health policies and programs has attempted to illustrate how many of the programs developed in the 1960s, representing the progressive politics of that era, have evolved into less adequate and less effective social programs in the 1980s and 1990s, and how this backsliding represents the regressive politics of recent years. Having discussed the concepts of civil rights, social justice, and social policy, it is evident how a conservative period impacts on these issues.

The 1990 Civil Rights Bill was vetoed by President Bush (a compromise measure has since been passed). That legislation sought to reestablish civil rights gains that had been overturned in 1989 by the United States Supreme Court. Thus, there are assaults on civil rights from the Court and the White House (which, during this era, both represent the same interests). Antipoverty programs such as the Economic Opportunity Act and Head Start, however effective in many ways, remain outside the mainstream and have not changed the basic structures and institutions of society. The weakening of the EOA illustrates the strength of entrenched political forces, and the limitations of Head Start reflect the entrenchment of the educational system. The auspicious beginnings of universal health care for the elderly as an entitlement have not been extended to the rest of the population and, in fact, the entitlement features of Medicare are threatened. We have also seen how Medicaid has failed to impact mainstream medicine and how Medicaid provisions and the entire health care system in the United States has worsened. The strength of the private, profit sector of medicine has contributed to the withdrawal of Medicare and Medicaid from their original goals. The social justice features of the community mental health movement have not been realized and deinstitutionalization, particularly that illustrated by the homeless and elderly mentally ill, has fallen far short of its aspirations. Lack of housing policies to assist low-income people and the general attack on social programs and social justice for stigmatized groups occurred in the last two decades. However, the basic structure of the 1960s legislation remains intact and can be rebuilt within a progressive agenda. The legacy of the 1960s is best understood by realizing how much conservative effort has gone into undoing the many positive changes that occurred during that era.

Concerns about distributive justice, notably in the economic arena, for example, indicate how disparities in income between the rich and the poor and between middle-class and low-income blacks have grown in the last decade and received media attention. It is a source of grave distress to many Americans to see the economy falter and their own standard of living fall, while the rich get richer. Census data from 1990 indicate that, in the 1980s, the top 1 percent of the population saw average family income grow by 75 percent, from $313,206 in 1980 to $548,970 in 1990, while families falling in the bottom 90 percent saw average earnings grow by 7 percent, from $27,451 to $29,334. Families in the bottom 10 percent saw their average income decline during the 1980s from $4,791 to $4,295. By 1989, one out of seven black families had incomes exceeding $50,000 annually, compared to less than $22,000 for the average black household, and black college-educated married couples currently earn 93 percent of the family income of comparable white couples. But the overwhelming majority of black families experienced deterioration of income in the 1980s (Marable, 1991). Similarly, poverty among women and children increased substantially. What appeared to be an awakening of class consciousness in the 1960s has been submerged—first, by ignoring the needs of the poor; second, by casting aspersion on the integrity of the poor; and, third, by rewarding and admiring the power and virtue of the rich. Many writers point out how the policies of the Reagan administration regarding taxes, wages, unions, deregulation, and social programs produced one of the most dramatic redistributions upward of wealth in the nation's history (Phillips, 1990).

The social policies of the 1980s and 1990s have been those of retrenchment, cutbacks, and undoing earlier accomplishments. The Family Support Act of 1988, welfare reform, emphasizes economic self-sufficiency for AFDC recipients at a time when the economy is in a deep recession. With an economy that appears to be dangerously inert, with a minimum wage that is characteristic of wages in the unskilled, service sector of the economy and does not lift a family of three above the poverty level, with educational programs that train welfare recipients for jobs that underpay or do not exist, and with the growth of part-time and temporary work without any fringe benefits, the goals of client self-sufficiency are a charade (Abramovitz, 1988b). The current health care debate has been addressed by the president in the most limited way, when a major overhaul of the system is needed. Issues of the environment have received only limited or negative attention, such as "studying" the problem of global warming and allowing expanded private-sector development of America's wetlands, and when major educational reform is needed, vouchers are considered the solution. As mentioned earlier, conservative politics that reinforce the current status quo and power relations in the society are associated with regressive legislative and judicial actions and a retreat from the Constitutional rights of citizens.[1]

Knowing something about where we have been and where we are should provide some help in understanding where we are going. The history of the United States suggests that there are alternating cycles of progression and regression, with some speculation about the causes of these cycles. Based on past events, it is possible to speculate about what is needed to implement a progressive agenda. It is considerably more difficult to predict when a progressive era will return, especially in the short run. Thus, these final notes are meant to be more prescriptive than prophetic.

The questions of greatest urgency revolve around the need to alleviate poverty, sexism, and racism in the nation; how to achieve greater economic security and a higher and more stable standard of living for the poor, the working class, and the middle class; and how to achieve social justice and uphold democratic ideals and Constitutional principles for all citizens. A limited number of basic premises are relevant to these goals. These generally can be confined to a discussion of the obligations of government to its citizens and the responsibilities of citizens in a democratic society in relation to grass-roots organizing and electoral politics. It is also noteworthy how closely related these two basic premises are.

THE NEW ROLES OF GOVERNMENT

There are many proposals for the alleviation of poverty in the nation. I have suggested that a wide variety of strategies are needed. As noted earlier, the social programs of the 1960s were primarily in-kind, rather than income, programs. "A hand up rather than a hand-out" was an aphorism of the Johnson administration. The role of means-tested programs only for the poor continues to be controversial, and, for many people, welfare is seen as colonizing the minority community. An emphasis on jobs and full-employment policies is preferred. But I have also noted that public assistance provides some degree of choice, independence, and empowerment for the poor, and that, given the economic structure, with only low-paying, precarious employment available for the poor, a coordinated system of employment and social service (including welfare) benefits is needed.

While job creation and full-employment policies are basic, there is also a need for redistributive tax policies and effective welfare and social service programs. Within the welfare system, provisions such as universal entitlements and citizen control of goods and services would strengthen these programs. Piven and Cloward (1983) argue that with the demise of industrial America, the modes and relations of politics, particularly the welfare state, have gradually superseded the modes and relations of production as the main source of popular power. And for these reasons Robert Fisher (1991) argues that the emphasis on privatization in the last decade is an attempt to undermine the welfare state. In this book, I have emphasized the significance of social welfare programs and the public sector for empowerment purposes.

The controversy about the role of government in relation to the alleviation of poverty divides along conservative and progressive lines. Not only is less government generally a conservative rallying cry, there are implications for specific configurations of government involvement, as well. For example, it is disputed whether government's role should be primarily reactive, to alleviate distress in times of temporary societal disjuncture, as Glazer (1988) argues—or proactive, to provide a decent standard of living and quality of life that is normative for all citizens. It is noted throughout this book that programs for the poor are generally of the former type—marginal and outside the mainstream of society. Programs such as Medicaid and Head Start, for example, no matter how helpful in serving the poor, rarely influence either the health care or the educational system. Thus, the gains made by preschoolers in Head Start are not reinforced in mainstream elementary school. These reactive programs infrequently result in basic societal, institutional change (Kozol, 1991). Marable (1991) suggests that quests for racial integration have had similar effects: "By asking to be integrated into the existing structures of society, rather than demanding basic transformation of the system, blacks became hostage to their own ideological demands" (p. 21).

Proactive programs, on the other hand, in which universal entitlements are involved, have the potential to restructure aspects of society. The current disarray of the health care system and public education in the United States are examples of universal programs gone awry, primarily because the rich and the poor do not use the same health and educational systems and the rich have little or no interest in preserving the systems utilized by the poor. Only as *all* citizens demand quality education and health care will these systems improve. However, this presupposes social justice and equality as moral imperatives, with unified systems of health and education as goals, rather than separate and unequal systems for the rich and poor. One goal of a progressive agenda is to encourage the unity and integration of all citizens in the reestablishment of universal rights, in health and education specifically, but in all areas of life as well.

The conservative press and politicians insist that this country cannot afford entitlements. However, Robert Reich (1991) writes:

Americans are not overtaxed. In 1989 we paid less in taxes as a percentage of GNP (about 30 percent) than the citizens of any other industrialized country. Wealthy Americans, in particular, are not overtaxed. Their marginal income-tax rate is the lowest top tax rate in any industrialized nation. Nor does the U. S. government overspend. If defense spending is excluded, the combined spending of state, local, and federal government accounts for a smaller share of GNP in America than in any other industrialized country, including Japan (p. 51).

However, as the economy declines and workers lose their jobs and the need to raise taxes increases, a working-class and middle-class tax revolt is predictable unless a truly progressive tax is implemented.

Although Reich (1991) believes that the country can afford social programs, he does not favor income programs as an antidote to poverty, even though it has been shown that income transfers are effective in alleviating poverty conditions. His position is more consistent with proponents of vastly improved education and full-employment policies, with government as the employer of last resort. What should government spend money on? Infrastructure, education, training (the private sector spends little on job training and then only for "executive training" of its most skilled employees), and related public endeavors, such as communications and transportation. Reich notes that in the current recession, loosening credit will not be effective, nor will pushing interest rates down or cutting capital gains tax. What is needed, Reich states, is an expanded role for government programs.

Unfortunately, distrust of government at the present time is a barrier to effective public intervention. The crisis of confidence in the public sector is not a recent phenomenon in U.S. history. The fear of strong central government goes back to Revolutionary days. But the current distrust interferes with economic recovery. Many economists agree that tax increases, and not tax cuts, are needed in the long-run to revitalize the economy. Steven Greenhouse (1992) points out that the U.S. is tied for last place with Greece in the amount of taxes it raises as a percentage of its annual economic output. He notes that many Americans hate taxes because they feel little direct benefit from them with so much money going for interest payments, the military, and for perceived benefits to the poor. In Europe, where the public sector covers the costs of health care and higher education, and services are visible, there is greater support for taxes. Even when Americans favor social programs, they tend to believe that government is wasteful.

As the affluent withdraw from the public sector in their private lives, the public sector justifies these moves by apologizing about its own inadequacy. Thus, state governments use private for-profit psychiatric hospitals, and municipal governments contract with private companies for a variety of services. I have suggested how privatization of human services is anti–affirmative action (the public sector is the largest employer of minorities), anti-union (service unions are stronger in the public than the private domain), and largely unaccountable in the use of public funds (reporting requirements are largely pro forma). Privatization produces reduced wages, health benefits, and pensions for workers; it uses part-time help and other cost-saving devices and transfers wealth to the upper classes in society. All this results in a decline in the standard of living for most Americans. This can only lead to greater dissatisfaction in the nation and eventually to social change. Thus, the Reagan-Bush strategies ultimately carry the seeds of their own demise, but this destruction is not imminent.

In relation to privatization, it would be useful to document costs, efficiency, and effectiveness of public versus private service delivery. For example, Massachusetts has hired a Florida firm to provide medical services to the state's 9,300 prison inmates, and the governor is proposing to sell the Massachusetts Turnpike to a private owner who would operate it for the tolls. Towns in Connecticut and elsewhere have contracted to have trash removal by private contractors instead of municipal employees. There are hundreds of examples of privatization of traditional public services. We need to determine the quality and costs of these endeavors. In addition, it is important to confront the ideological dimensions of the private/public controversy. Where it appears that quality and costs may be equal, other factors should be assessed, such as hiring minorities and women, salaries and fringe benefits, and so on.

Probably most important of all to restore confidence is the need to improve government sensitivity and responsiveness to the needs of all citizens. This includes taxation that distributes resources downward rather than upward; increased minimum wage, job creation, full-employment policies, and plant-closing legislation; and reinstatement of business regulation and elimination of greed and disinformation in government. In employment there is the need to restructure the bifurcation of the job market and provide diversity in jobs, from high-technology to service jobs, retail, unskilled and semiskilled manufacturing jobs, and small businesses where entry-level jobs are located. All of this requires public incentives and policies that encourage, rather than discourage, investment in the U. S. economy, and revitalization of trade unions.

The New Federalism of the last two decades deprives citizens of control by reducing the available resources to so low a level that conflict rather than cooperation occurs. Thus, local control, with adequate resources, needs to be forthcoming. As Bluestone and Harrison (1982) state, the reindustrialization of America requires new partnerships, not between business and government but between labor, community groups, community-based development corporations, churches, and municipalities. There is a need for democratic social planning of investment, rather than disinvestment, in urban areas and of worker-ownership and worker-initiated conversion plans from defense to a peace economy.

Samuel Bowles, et al. (1992) believe that liberals and progressives are generally agreed that laissez-faire conservatism has been damaging the economy. These authors support the need for "a wide range of new government initiatives and interventions, including public investments in infrastructure, education, and training; more adequate environmental regulations; and one or another form of national health insurance. Growing numbers further agree that we could finance many of these initiatives, even in the short run, through a combination of military spending cuts and higher tax rates on the wealthy. . . . If we are to promote sustainable long-term improvements in living standards and extend justice and democracy, we need to begin mobilizing now to change the rules of the game in the private sector. . . . We need to start talking about rebuilding the U.S. economy from the bottom up, rather than the top down." (p. 165). These writers believe that democracy is an essential ingredient for a thriving and just economy.

As suggested above, just as the successes of the civil rights movement required multiple strategies, similarly, effective antipoverty outcomes require diverse methods of approach. As long as the economic and social structure perpetuate poverty conditions, a variety of redistributive, education, employment, income transfer, and social service programs have been shown to be effective in counteracting poverty status. Observers of social policy need to be wary of any reform, however, that erodes entitlements and increases means-tested programs, that mandates training and work programs for poor women with young children, especially without adequate income and other long-term supports, and that resists redistribution of power and resources in order to maintain the status quo, such as in New Federalism where there is local responsibility without empowerment.

The need for antipoverty programs continues, and lessons from the War on Poverty and the Economic Opportunity Act still apply. Lemann (1991) points out that conservatives within the Bush administration have written that the War on Poverty committed three crucial errors: Policy-making was centralized in Washington; the idea of "welfare rights" guided many programs; and the War on Poverty assumed that the best way to help people was to send training professionals into communities to help the poor. Lemann correctly observes that none of the charges listed above is true. Policy-making was decentralized in community action agencies and not centralized in Washington; the War on Poverty explicitly rejected welfare as a strategy; and the community action agencies specifically did not hire professional social workers but favored indigenous local staff. The use of disinformation and the need to discredit social programs and people who are poor are some of the more grim tactics of the current power elite. The backbone for democratic government is an informed electorate, and that can only be achieved through pressure at the grass-roots level.

Because poverty falls most heavily on women and minorities, strategies to alleviate poverty must address sexism and racism. In fact, it is nearly impossible to understand poverty in this country without understanding its sexist and racist underpinnings. Issues of affirmative action are part of the current controversy that has blacks divided among themselves and blacks and whites in adversarial roles. Race relations between whites and blacks on the one hand and Asians or Latinos on the other, for example, are inordinately demoralized at the present time. It remains to be seen, however, if the right wing of the Republican party has moved too far right on racial issues for the rank and file of Americans to accept. The civil rights of women, around such issues as abortion and sexual harassment, are currently precariously situated in federal and state courts and legislative bodies. But, as suggested earlier, it is grass-roots protest and mass movements in the United States that can ultimately be expected to move the pendulum at least back to center if the swing is too far to the left or the right.

We live in a time of intense feelings about women and racial issues. As long as women's issues can arouse the kind of vehement reactions generated by sexual harassment and abortion, and as long as racial contentions continue to be debated, the possibility of constructive change is alive. It is when issues such as social class are not discussed that the possibility of constructive action is totally blocked. Thus, when the importance of citizen involvement and open dialogue is negated, there is cause for alarm in a democratic society.

CITIZEN PARTICIPATION AND ELECTORAL POLITICS

There is little doubt that peoples' movements, beginning at the grass-roots level and with new coalitions and partnerships, are needed to turn the current conservatism around. While there is considerable community activism, it tends to be isolated and neither sufficiently well organized nor broadly-based. Single issues of great magnitude, such as abortion rights and environmental issues, and racial antagonisms tend to characterize the dominant forces of activism at the present time. Single-issue activists have been largely unsuccessful in building coalitions with activists from other causes, and anger and resentment need to be channeled into constructive social change. This occurs in two ways: grass-roots organizing and mobilization and electoral politics.

Stewart Burns (1990) defines social movements as organized, nongovernmental efforts of large numbers of people to attain significant social and political change. The essence of social movements is power at the grass-roots level. In the United States, democracy is expressed in two ways: politically, through electoral politics, and in protest movements. Burns believes that grass-roots democracy has had a greater impact on social change than electoral-representative democracy, and anyone who has worked in grass-roots community organizing can attest to the truth of this observation. It is humbling to observe how community activists, once in electoral office, often succumb to the politics of bargaining, compromise, and power-group arm-twisting. Thus it is likely that leadership in the black community will emerge from the bottom up, rather than from elected officials (Anderson, 1989).

Grass-roots democracy, grounded in the principles of activism, moral passion, and commitment to substantive purposes, is the characteristic political expression of social movements. [In the social movements of the 1960s,] presidents, politicians, and the higher leadership circles played lesser roles, responding to and trying to manage change but not initiating it" (Burns, 1990, p. xii). [In fact, Jesse Jackson's career reflects the conflict created when grassroots loyalties and electoral politics collide.]

At the present time, there is growing activism among Americans. Thus, the tendency to passively rely on the leadership of the country to define the public agenda, so prominent in the 1980s, appears to be changing. Although not all of the issues of activism might be considered progressive, such as some citizen tax revolts, initiating and taking control of the public agenda at the grass-roots level is heartening. Thus, the conservative leadership of the last decades, which has shaped the consciousness and conscience of Americans who are ambivalent in their attitudes toward race, social programs, the poor, trade unions, and the role of government, is now being challenged.

Ever since the crusade to abolish slavery, a recurring impetus behind social movements in the U. S. has been the clash between the values of the "American creed" that furnishes a national identity for Americans—liberty, individualism, democracy, constitutionalism, and equality—and social realities, such as oppression of black people and women, that trampled these ideas. . . . "Cultural contradictions" were probably the most decisive cause of the movements of the 1960s (Burns, 1990, p. xv).

Bell (1987) also addresses the contradictions between ideals and reality; and when dealing in the political domain, the gap between rhetoric and reality is glaring.

Thus, it is hopeful that Americans can be moved to action by awareness of contradictions and deceptions in society, although the ability to overcome the power of sloganism, "image," innuendo, and labeling is not an easy task. It is not surprising that recent political campaigns fail to address important issues and prefer to use sound bites and shibboleth to convey their message since a thoughtful electorate leads to social change. So far, Americans are turned off by this sort of political behavior, lose interest, and stay home from the polls. The challenge is to turn disgust and anger away from apathy and violence into constructive action.

Fisher (1991) argues that privatization undercuts the ability of the public sector to address social problems and promote redistributional policy. He believes that grass-roots insurgency, complementing electoral strategies, is necessary to place the needs and demands of the poor on the public sector agenda. Thus, the more privatization, the less potential for local democracy as the removal of decisions from the public arena diminishes individual incentive for community action. Despite the adage that "you can't fight city hall," public officials and public bureaucracies are basically political and are organized into a formal and well-defined system for citizen access, while the private sector is not mandated by public accountability to be responsive to the needs of the citizenry at all:

Current reprivatization strategies to dismantle the welfare state and diminish federal power in social affairs are a last-ditch effort to remove government responsibility for the welfare of citizens and society, so that claims on the government—whether for cleaner air or welfare benefits—are seen as illegitimate and anachronistic. And if such claims are illegitimate, then most community organization is fundamentally undermined (Fisher, 1991, p. 11).

The tactics and strategies of social movements must involve pragmatism and ideology. It is a strongly held belief within community organizing that it is necessary to win battles in order to maintain constituent involvement and engagement in the struggle. But there is also experience from Alinsky-type organizing, for example, that pragmatism without political education and ideology may lose its direction and its reason for being. Both Harry Boyte (1989) and Frances Moore Lappé (1989) emphasize the need to rediscover America's values through participatory democracy. The emphasis on participatory themes and ideology characterizes the writing of Harrington (1988), as well. Single-issue groups often have limited success and are unable to translate localized successes into social change because they often fail to build coalitions, and fail to understand and impact the larger context in which political behavior and moral values play such a significant role. Political education and ideology are the difference between democratic movements with unity as a goal and activism based on concrete, short-range goals. Boyte (1989) particularly emphasizes the limitations of narrowly defined issues, the importance of political education in returning power to the people, and the need to reconnect action and vision in order to achieve long-range goals.

In electoral politics, the formation of progressive third parties on the local level appears to be gaining some success. These political efforts often represent the alternative voices of progressive grassroots movements. However, in no case recently have local political efforts been translated into a progressive national third party. On the national level, neither major political party is effectively meeting the needs of the majority of citizens, but little or no third party activity has emerged. Jesse Jackson has provided effective leadership in the black community and the nation, but he has tried to impact mainstream politics and his message and his power have been diffused by the strength of mainstream resistance to change.

The United States does not have a labor movement which in so many Western countries is the progressive voice. Thomas Geoghegan (1991), writing about unions in the United States, states that without a labor movement, it doesn't seem possible for Democrats to ever again elect a president. He notes that the New Deal did not so much redistribute income as it did power. The unions arose, and they redistributed income. However, today with only 16 percent of the workforce unionized, the role of unions is diminished. Concrete proposals for resurrecting and strengthening unions are available, and in due time, trade unionism in the United States will be revitalized through rank-and-file organizing and changes in restrictive legislation.

The Republican party has heralded a new populism by ostensibly identifying with the needs of workers and the middle class against the alleged excesses in spending and special-interest politics of the Democrats. The Republican party believes that it can attract black voters with a combination of the right kinds of social programs and a conservative emphasis on traditional American values of hard work and "pulling yourself up by your bootstraps" (Lemann, 1991). It is ironic that both the Republican and Democratic parties are vying for the support of the black voter. This was particularly evident in the Senate confirmation hearings of Judge Clarence Thomas to the U. S. Supreme Court, in 1991 where both parties were vulnerable to the issues of race and neither felt it could afford to alienate potential black support.

In order to return to power, the Democratic party must capitalize on the common interests of diverse groups. Thus, it must form new coalitions by strengthening its traditional base and recapturing its traditional allies and by extending this base to women's groups, environmental groups, and diverse ethnic and racial populations. Instead of upholding traditional family values, for example, the Democrats need to straightforwardly embrace changing family patterns in work, procreation, marital status, and sexual preference. The changing demography of the nation also provides additional opportunities for unity and pluralism among diverse groups, without assimilation as a sole strategy.

The immigration patterns today are very different from the Europeans who came to the United States around the turn of the twentieth century. People from Asia, Africa, South and Central America, and Eastern Europe are seeking refuge and opportunities in the United States. The Democratic party, torn apart by racial conflicts since the 1960s, has an opportunity to provide leadership by forging new alliances among these diverse population groups. Arguments about multicultural curriculum in education and criticism of "political correctness" reflect the threat posed to the status quo by the emergence and empowerment of diverse ethnic and racial groups.

The need for interracial harmony is not merely rhetoric; it affects the quality of life for all Americans. The issue of racial integration or separatism continues to be a subject of heated debate. On an ideological and pragmatic level, hope for the future of the nation and the Democratic party lies in the ability to unify and meet the needs of working-class and middle-class citizens of different ethnic, racial, and cultural heritages. The increase in black political leadership is a positive beginning and a hopeful sign. However, this leadership has yet to be translated into empowerment for low-income black citizens or structural change. As noted earlier, the best hope for change emanates from the grass-roots level with elected officials supporting and encouraging citizen activism.

The unfinished business of the civil rights movement is evident, and there is need for renewal to achieve enduring change. Blauner (1989) believes that present-day black politics is pragmatic rather than ideological. But it is not too idealistic to expect that, utilizing new political strategies and a moral perspective, black political and grass-roots leadership can recapture the spirit, vision, and ideology of the 1960s civil rights movement in the current decade. As Marable (1991) states, the full extent of black progress cannot be measured solely in terms of civil rights legislation and voting rights. Rather, it is

. . . at the juncture of faith and political ambition, of spirit and struggle, that the black freedom movement must revive itself, casting aside the parochial chains of chauvinism and isolation. . . . In the process we will discover that the proverbial promised land of full equality and economic equity can be achieved, but only in concert with other groups of the oppressed—especially Hispanics, Native Americans, Arab-Americans, Asian/Pacific Americans, and the unemployed and economically and socially disadvantaged of all ethnic backgrounds (p. 23).

Today, there are hundreds of issues that can and do engage Americans. These include civil rights, abortion rights, environmental issues, antiwar protests, adequate and accessible low-cost housing, health care for all citizens, taxes, quality child care, job security and plant-closing legislation, full-employment policies and expanded earned-income tax credits, and universal welfare rights and entitlements, to name a few. Rather than disparate struggles, there is the need for unity and solidarity. In economic development, there is the need for trade unionism and corporate ownership by unions, worker-controlled, nonprofit businesses and resident owned, cooperatively managed low-income housing. This, then, brings back the need for many different strategies to effect social change. At a minimum, the need is for creative ideas, for grass-roots movements, for advocacy for organizational change, and for progressive coalitions that influence electoral politics. As a part of these requirements, there is the need for a more militant approach to change and the establishment of goals that expand the rights of the oppressed.

The list of progressive battles that continue to be fought does not get shorter—but it does change, somewhat. The rights of the mentally ill, and progress in the deinstitutionalization movement, capture public attention through media coverage of the homeless, primarily. Recent pressure to return the chronically mentally ill to custodial, institutional facilities is a conservative move backward in the social control and rights of this population. This is a political solution to "get rid of the mentally ill homeless" and an indictment of the so-called failure of the deinstitutionalization movement, when in fact the movement has not failed at all. Not only are progressive programs often designed for failure, they are often labeled failures, either when they succeed or to prevent them from succeeding. There is also recent awareness that certain private for-profit psychiatric hospitals may have "systematically misdiagnosed, mistreated and abused patients to increase . . . profits from insurance claims" (Kerr, 1991). The role of privatization pervades all aspects of social policy at the present time.

The need for universal health care is now on the national agenda and will be moving forward in many different directions simultaneously, not because the Bush administration is moving, but because there is movement from the grass roots. There is opportunity for progressive action here. All citizens need guaranteed health care, and all elderly need to resist the creation of social class divisions and dissension within their ranks.

Over 900 community action agencies continue to provide social services to the rural and urban poor, and these organizations need progressive support because they are always under siege and few other social agencies are totally committed to helping the poor. Head Start continues to be one of the most needed and fulfilling examples of affirmative action in the nation. The civil rights movement needs to regroup to move the rights of minorities forward. Minority-group children continue to drop out of school in record numbers, and the quality of public education has improved little. Efforts at overcoming school segregation are largely stalled throughout the nation, and there is disillusionment among blacks and progressive whites about school integration as a civil rights goal. There is compelling evidence that crime, drugs, and the inadequacies of the criminal justice system are racial issues, just as teen pregnancy, unemployment, inadequate welfare, and poor education are racial and sexist issues, as well. In 1990, the poverty rate rose sharply and declining incomes forced 2 million more people below the federal poverty level—$10,419 for a family of three (U.S. Census Bureau, 1990).

The spirit of conservatism is very much alive in the 1990s in the United States.[2] The white backlash to preserve the status quo that helped kill the social movements of the 1960s is very active today. Protection of traditional family structure and the work ethic still continues, and attacks on art, academia, and the so-called softness of the criminal justice system are prevalent. I have written how the social legislation of the era has also taken its share of attacks. The power structure does not really pay attention to social change efforts until they are effective. Attempts to suppress social change and undermine social programs since the 1960s attests to the effectiveness of the 1960s movements. That is why it is so important to counteract conservative and neoconservative rhetoric. The concept of "political correctness" is a current whipping boy, mocked by conservatives as a way to attack social change being brought about through the introduction of multicultural content in elementary, secondary and higher education.

For the last two decades, progressives have retreated as conservatives defined the social agenda. The "morality" of the 1980s has enhanced the concept of a just society, not by example, but by its opposite. Thus, there have been lessons about what not to do (e.g., deregulation of business, tax breaks for the rich, denigration of the poor, cutbacks in social programs, and so on) to achieve social justice and equality. The Republicans had redefined populism and readopted the posture of protecting and supporting the rights of the "silent majority" against the alleged effete snobs and intellectuals on the left.

Notwithstanding external constraints, such as downturns in the economy, and political attacks, progressives are not totally above reproach. Charges of elitism and top-down structure are well founded in some instances. Some writers, such as Dick Cluster (1979) and Stewart Burns (1990), also identify, for example, the splintering and splitting of leftist groups, intraorganizational contention and righteousness, and the need for balance between ideology and long-term plans and programs within progressive movements.

Michael Lerner (1988) cites self-doubt, anti-intellectualism, and anti-leadership components as additional progressive failings. Todd Gitlin and Michael Kazin (1988) argue that "the left lost initiative after the sixties partly because it failed to address the new anxieties and demands of a society which the movement had helped to change. The country is moving left, right, and center all at the same time. The right got as far as it did because—it swarmed into a political vacuum—a vacuum that remains to be filled" (p. 93).

SOCIAL POLICY AND SOCIAL CHANGE

While both need to work together, electoral politics and social movements serve different ends. We depend on government and elected officials to enact social policy that is progressive and that serves social justice goals. But we are aware that social change does not occur in this way. Rather, social movements create social change. No one knows for sure what causes social movements but it has been suggested that the frustrations and bitterness that are created because of discrepancies between ideals and reality are a likely starting point. Perhaps the 1960s social movements were a reaction against McCarthyism and the oppression and hyprocisy of the 1950s, as well as the many other factors that have been discussed throughout this book. But how much frustration is enough or too much, and what other social and/or economic conditions must be present for democracy and democratic processes to be sustained and enhanced?

In contrast with social reform brought about through social legislation, social change has several different characteristics: a restructuring of relationships and a redistribution of power and wealth is expected, particularly for women and minorities, and the working class; new definitions of normality and deviance should be included so that stigma and oppression of differences are eliminated; and above all, social change is hegemonic. That is, dominant cultural themes and beliefs and societal institutions must be restructured to accommodate the changes in relationships noted above.

This includes, foremost, structural change in such areas as education, religion, and communications. As we have seen in our discussions of the 1960s, social reform in the United States levels the outcomes of social movements and smooths out its radical elements in the enactment of social policy.

Morality and the principles of a just society are incorporated into progressive social legislation. Certainly, political economy and social control theories provide powerful explanations of social policy. But ideological direction provides the criteria against which social policy and the quality of life should be evaluated. If the post–Civil War period was the First Reconstruction, and the civil rights movement was the Second Reconstruction, the events and frustrations of the last two decades establish the basis for the Third Reconstruction. It is only a matter of time before the Third Reconstruction becomes a reality. This will involve new and creative partnerships between diverse racial and ethnic groups; between the very poor, the working class, and the middle class; between labor, church groups, and community-based organizations; between neighborhoods and regions; and between all women. We have seen in discussions of privatization that in the last two decades traditional partnerships between government and business, where business holds the balance of power, has not resulted in betterment of the economy and the standard of living for all citizens. Rather, new partnerships between government, labor, and community-based organizations are needed, as well as empowerment of citizens through local control of such arenas as education, economic development, and consumer-directed health care programs.

In the meantime, there is a crisis in our cities once again with social problems that disproportionately victimize people of color. Although crime, drugs, and alienation are not new phenomena, there are no ready solutions—not even proposals for solutions at the present time. Cities and states are financially bankrupt, and the federal government continues its campaigns of sloganism and disinformation and its policies of immoral neglect.

Having identified a plethora of problems it is not difficult to be prescriptive—what is needed seems obvious: new leadership emerging from the grass-roots level in the women's movement, for blacks and other minorities; a revitalized and democratized labor movement; new political parties or a Democratic party that recognizes government as an active, spending, redistributing agent of egalitarian social change (even George Will [1992] understands this); acknowledgement and celebration of changes in society, such as new ethnic and racial groups and changes in family structure; new coalitions of voters and special interest groups; recognition of drugs, crime, unemployment and chronic poverty for what they are in the context of sexist and racist public policies; and identification of a class struggle in the liberation of the poor and oppressed.

Although Marable (1991) speaks for blacks, his words have universal meaning:

Ethnic pride and group awareness constitute a beginning stage, not an end unto itself, for a richer understanding of the essential diversity and pluralism that constitutes America. That awareness of diversity must point toward the restructuring of the elaborate systems of ownership and power that perpetuate the unequal status of these ethnic groups and oppressed social classes. This leap of awareness depends on our willingness to define our political, educational, and social goals in a way that is truly majoritarian, that speaks for the commonwealth of the whole society, that realizes a new level of struggle for the black freedom movement (p. 23).

And Pollitt (1991) states in reference to women:

We need to create a militant movement outside of the realm of representative politics. This is what AIDS activists have done. If ACT UP can force the F.D.A. to change its drug protocols, women can force change through action. One-third of women sexually harassed at work? We can clog the court with cases, we can confront harassers at the workplace as a group, we can boycott and take to the streets. We can picket hospitals that refuse to perform abortions—as 90 percent of them now do (p. 541).

We can do what the civil rights movement did: Utilize courage; combine moral imperative with actions; develop leadership from the grass roots; and make a commitment for the long haul. As Harrington (1988) said, it takes the stamina and conviction of a long-distance runner to meet the challenges of progressive social change.

NOTES

1. The table below provides a summary of major differences between the 1960s and 1980s on selected variables:

Variables	1960s	1980s
Economy	vigorous economic growth	deinvestment; deindustrialization
Race	civil rights movement	attacks on gains in civil rights; increased racial conflict
Gender	women's movement	feminization of poverty
Social Class	War on Poverty	wider gap between rich and poor; rich get richer; "underclass"; declining standard of living
Moral Imperative	social justice and equality	Social Darwinism; the alleged immorality of the poor

2. Joe Conason (1992) describes the vitality, tactics, and strategies of the religious right-wing in electoral politics; and Bruce Shapiro (1992) notes how the New Alliance Party and Dr. Lenora Fulani fill a vacuum when an honest progressive agenda is absent in politics.

Bibliography

ABC News and Associated Press/Media General. August 1988; November 1988; January 1989. Data provided by the Roper Center at the University of Connecticut.

Abramovitz, M. *Regulating the Lives of Women*. Boston: South End Press, 1988a

Abramovitz, M. Why Welfare Reform Is a Sham, *The Nation*. Sept. 26, 1988b, 221, 238–241.

Alexander, R. The Right to Treatment in Mental and Correctional Institutions. *Social Work* (March 1989) *34*, 2, 109–12.

American Association of Homes For The Aged (AAHA). *Nursing Home Reform: Current Regulations, OBRA–1987*. Washington, D.C.: AAHA, 1988.

Anderson, S., Black Leadership Gap: Eyes on the Prizes, Not the People. *The Nation*, Oct. 16, 1989, 405, 422–425.

Anderson, E. *Streetwise: Race, Class, & Change in an Urban Community*. Chicago: The University of Chicago Press, 1990.

Angier, N. Study Finds Uninsured Receive Less Hospital Care. *New York Times*, September 12, 1990.

Applebome, P. Civil Rights Campaigns are Facing New Agendas. *New York Times*, April 2, 1990.

Applebome, P. Rights-Bill Backers Issue Call to More Transcendent Battle. *New York Times*, April 3, 1991.

Arnold, M. The Good War That Might Have Been Won. *New York Times Magazine*, September 29, 1974.

Bachrach, L., ed. *Deinstitutionalization*. San Francisco: Jossey-Bass, 1983.

Bachrach, L. Deinstitutionalization and Women: Assessing the Consequences of Public Policy. *American Psychologist* (October 1984) *39*, 10, 1171–77.

Belcher, J. Rights Versus Needs of Homeless Mentally Ill Persons. *Social Work* (September–October, 1988) *33*, 5, 398–402.

Bell, D. *And We Are Not Saved*. New York: Basic Books, 1987.

Benson, M. Disabled Have High Hopes for New Civil Rights Bill. *Times-Picayune*, March 17, 1991.

Berman, P. Still Sailing the Lemonade Sea. *New York Times Magazine*, October 27, 1991.

Bickman, L., and Dokecki, P. Public and Private Responsibility for Mental Health Services. *American Psychologist* (August 1989) *44*, 8, 1133–37.

Billingsley, A. The Struggle for Mental Health. In Evans, D., and Claiborn, W., eds., *Mental Health Issues and the Urban Poor*. New York: Pergamon, 1974.

Birnbaum, M. The Right to Treatment. *American Bar Association Journal* (1960) *46*, 499–505.

Blackburn, J. The War in Vietnam and the War on Poverty. In Everett, R., ed., *Anti-Poverty Programs*. Dobbs Ferry, N.Y.: Oceana Publications, 1966.

Blauner, B. *Black Lives, White Lives: Three Decades of Race Relations in America*. Berkeley: University of California Press, 1989.

Block, F.; Cloward, R.; Ehrenreich B.; and Piven, F. *The Mean Season*. New York: Pantheon, 1987.

Bloom, B. *Stability and Change in Human Characteristics*. NY: Wiley, 1964.

Bluestone, B., and Harrison, B. *The Deindustrialization of America: Plant Closings, Community Abandonment, and the Dismantling of Basic Industry*. New York: Basic Books, 1982.

Bok, M. Styles of Adaptation and Hospital Outcomes among Chronic Older Mental Patients. *Journal of Gerontology* (1971) *26*, 1.

Bok, M. *Community Action Agencies and Economic Development*. Washington, D.C.: National Association of Community Action Agencies, 1989.

Bok, M. *Meeting New Challenges: A Survey of Community Action Agencies in 1990*. Washington, D.C.: National Association of Community Action Agencies, 1990.

Bowles, S., Gordon, D., and Weisskopf, T. An Economic Strategy for Progressives. *The Nation* (February 10, 1992), 145, 163–65.

Boynton, R. Princeton's Public Intellectual. *New York Times Magazine*, September 15, 1991.

Boyte, H. *Common Wealth: A Return to Citizen Politics*. New York: Free Press, 1989.

Branch, T. *Parting the Waters: America in the King Years 1954–63*. New York: Simon and Schuster, 1988.

Brennan, T. "PC" and the Decline of the American Empire. *Social Policy* (Summer 1991) 16–29.

Bronfenbrenner, U. Head Start, A Retrospective View. In Zigler, E., and Valentine, J., eds., *Project Headstart*. New York: Free Press, 1979.

Brooks, A. Law and the Chronically Mentally Ill. In Bowker, J., ed., *Services for the Chronically Mentally Ill: New Approaches for Mental Health Professionals*. Vol. 1. Washington, D.C.: Council on Social Work Education, 1988.

Brooks, T. *Walls Come Tumbling Down: A History of the Civil Rights Movement—1940–1970*. Englewood Cliffs, N.J.: Prentice-Hall, 1974.

Brown, A. *Modern Political Philosophy: Theories of the Just Society*. London, England: Penguin Books, 1986.

Brown, K., and Fellin, P. Practice Models for Serving the Homeless Mentally Ill in Community Shelter Programs. In Bowker, J., ed., *Services for the*

Chronically Mentally Ill: New Approaches for Mental Health Professionals.
Vol. 1. Washington, D.C.: Council on Social Work Education, 1988.

Burnham, M. The Great Society Didn't Fail. *The Nation* (July 24/31, 1989) 122-24.

Burns, E. The Future of Health Care. *Public Welfare* (Spring 1976) 33-37.

Burns, S. *Social Movements of the 1960s: Search for Democracy.* Boston: Twayne Publishers, 1990.

Burtless, G. Public Spending for the Poor: Trends, Prospects, and Economic Limits. In Danziger S., and Weinberg, D., eds., *Fighting Poverty: What Works and What Doesn't.* Cambridge: Harvard University Press, 1986.

CAFCA. *The State Plan of Action for Connecticut's Fourteen Community Action Agencies and Their Network.* July 1982.

Campbell, D., and Frey, P. The Implications of Learning Theory for the Fade-Out of Gains from Compensatory Education. In Hellmuth, J., ed., *The Disadvantaged Child.* Vol. 3. New York: Brunner/Mazel, 1970.

Campbell, J. Economic News Grim from State. *Hartford Courant*, June 29, 1991.

Carling, P. Major Mental Illness, Housing, and Supports: The Promise of Community Integration. *American Psychologist* (August 1990) *45*, 8, 969-75.

Carter, S. *Reflections of an Affirmative Action Baby.* New York: Basic Books, 1991.

Chamberlain, J. *Farewell to Reform: The Rise, Life and Decay of the Progressive Mind in America.* Chicago: Quadrangle Books, 1965.

Civil Rights Act of 1964 with Explanation. Commerce Clearing House, 1964.

Clark, K., and Hopkins, J. *A Relevant War Against Poverty.* New York: Harper and Row, 1969.

Cloward, R., and Ohlin, L. *Delinquency and Opportunity: A Theory of Delinquent Gangs.* Glencoe, Ill.: Free Press, 1960.

Cloward, R., and Piven, R. Toward a Class-Based Realignment of American Politics: A Movement Strategy. *Social Policy* (Winter 1983) 3-14.

Cluster, D., ed. *They Should Have Served That Cup of Coffee.* Boston: South End Press, 1979.

Cohen, W. National Health Insurance Proposals. *Public Welfare* (Summer 1974) 7-20.

Cohen, M. Social Work Practice with Homeless Mentally Ill People: Engaging the Client. *Social Work* (November 1989) *34*, 6, 505-512.

Coleman, J. *Equality of Educational Opportunity.* Washington, D.C.: U. S. Department of Health, Education and Welfare, 1966.

Community Services Administration (CSA). *A Summary of Community Action Agency Resources in Connecticut: July 1, 1974–June 30, 1975.* CSA, Region I, 1976.

Conason, J. The Religious Rights Quiet Revival. *The Nation* (April 29, 1992) *541*, 553-59.

Congress and the Nation, 1965-1988, Vols. 11-V11. Congressional Quarterly Service, 1965-1988.

Connecticut Association for Community Action (CACA). *Community Action in Connecticut: A Review of Connecticut's Fourteen Community Action Agencies and Their Programs.* CACA, 1986.

Connery, R., and contributors. *The Politics of Mental Health.* New York: Columbia University Press, 1968.

Cooper, J. M., Jr. *Pivotal Decades: The United States 1900-1920.* New York: Norton, 1990.

Cox, A. *The Court and the Constitution*. Boston: Houghton Mifflin, 1987.

Danziger, S., and Weinberg, D. *Fighting Poverty: What Works and What Doesn't*. Cambridge: Harvard University Press, 1986.

Datta, L. Another Spring and Other Hopes. In Zigler, E., and Valentine, J., eds., *Project Head Start: A Legacy of the War on Poverty*. New York: Free Press, 1979.

Davis, C. Season of Change for Health Services. *HCFA Forum* (October 1981) 22–30.

Dawley, A. *Struggles For Justice: Social Responsibility & the Liberal State*. Cambridge, Mass: Harvard University Press, 1991.

DeParle, J. Democrat's Invisible Man Specializes in Making Inequity To Poor Easy To See. *NY Times*, August 19, 1991, p. A12.

Domhoff, W. *Who Rules America Now?* Englewood Cliffs, N.J.: Prentice-Hall, 1983.

Donovan, J. *The Politics of Poverty*. New York: Pegasus, 1973.

D'Souza, D. *Illiberal Education: The Politics of Race and Sex on Campus*. New York: Free Press, 1991.

Edsall, T., and Edsall, M. *Chain Reaction: The Impact of Race, Rights, and Taxes*. New York: Norton, 1991.

Egbert, R. Follow Through: Fulfilling the Promise of Head Start. In Hellmuth, J., ed., *The Disadvantaged Child*. Vol. 2. New York: Brunner/Mazel, 1968.

Ehrenreich, B. *Fear of Falling*. New York: Pantheon, 1989.

Eizenstadt, S. How to Make Medicaid Popular. *New York Times*, October 5, 1991.

Ellwood, D., and Summers, L. Poverty in America: Is Welfare the Answer or the Problem? In Danziger, S., and Weinberg D., *Fighting Poverty: What Works and What Doesn't*. Cambridge: Harvard University Press, 1986.

Enthoven, A. A "Cost-Unconscious" Medical System. *New York Times*, July 13, 1989.

Fager, C. *Selma 1965: The March That Changed the South*. New York: Scribner's, 1974.

Faludi, S. *The Undeclared War Against American Women*. New York: Crown, 1992.

First, R.; Roth, D.; and Arewa, B. Homelessness: Understanding the Dimensions of the Problem for Minorities. *Social Work* (March–April 1988) *33*, 2, 120–26.

Fisher, R. Privatization and Community Organization: The Case of Houston, Texas. Paper presented at the annual program meeting of the Council of Social Work Education, New Orleans, La., March, 1991.

Fletcher, A. For Civil Rights, It's Back to the Future. *New York Times*, August 19, 1990.

Flynn, R. Race, Neighborhood Still Affect Who Gets A Loan. *Hartford Courant*, Oct 30, 1991.

Foley, H. National Trends in the Financing of Mental Health Programs. In Evans, D., and Claiborn, W., eds., *Mental Health Issues and the Urban Poor*. New York: Pergamon, 1974.

Franklin, J. H. *From Slavery to Freedom: A History of Negro Americans*. New York: Vintage, 1967.

Franklin, J. H. *Racial Equality in America*. Chicago: University of Chicago Press, 1976.

French, L. Victimization of the Mentally Ill: An Unintended Consequence of Deinstitutionalization. *Social Work* (November–December 1987) *32*, 6, 502–6.

Freudenheim, M. Debating the Canadian Health "Model." *New York Times*, June 29, 1989.

Gallaway, R., and Vedder, R. *The Failure of the War on Poverty*. Washington, D.C.: National Forum Foundation, 1985.

Gaskins, R., and Wasow, M. Vicious Circles in Civil Commitment. *Social Work* (March 1979) *24*, 2, 127–31.

Geoghegan, T. *Which Side Are You On? Trying to Be for Labor When It Is Flat on Its Back*. New York: Farrar, Strauss and Giroux, 1991.

Gil, D. *Unravelling Social Policy*. Cambridge, Mass.: Schenkman Books, 1976.

Gitlin, T. and Kazin, M. Transcending the Sixties: Two Thoughts Forward, One Thought Back: The Rise and Rapid Decline of the New Ex-Left. *Tikkun* (January/February 1988) *3*, 1, 49–52, 92–93.

Glazer, N. *The Limits of Social Policy*. Cambridge: Harvard University Press, 1988.

Goldberg, G., and Kremen, E. The Feminization of Poverty: Only in America? *Social Policy* (Spring 1987) 3–14.

Golden, T. III, Possibly Violent, and No Place to Go. *New York Times*, April 2, 1990.

Goldman, H. The Demography of Deinstitutionalization. In Bachrach, L., ed., *Deinstitutionalization*. San Francisco: Jossey-Bass, 1983.

Goleman, D. New Way to Battle Bias: Fight Acts, Not Feelings, *N.Y. Times*. July 16, 1991, p C2, C8.

Gordon, C. Health Care the Corporate Way. *The Nation*, March 25, 1991, 376–80.

Gould, L., ed. *The Progressive Era*. Syracuse, N.Y.: Syracuse University Press, 1974.

Greenhouse, L. A Divided Supreme Court Ends the Term with a Bang. *New York Times*, July 1, 1990.

Greenhouse, L. Morality Play's Twist. *New York Times*, November 2, 1991.

Greenhouse, S. Long-Term Tax Rise is Urged. *NY Times*, January 27, 1992.

Griffith, J., ed. *Federalism: The Shifting Balance*. American Bar Association, 1989.

Grob, G. *Mental Institutions in America: Social Policy to 1875*. New York: Free Press, 1973.

Grob, G. Historical Origins of Deinstitutionalization. In Bachrach, L., ed., *Deinstitutionalization*. San Francisco: Jossey-Bass, 1983.

Gurin, A. Governmental Responsibility and Privatization: Examples from Four Social Services. In Kamerman, S., and Kahn, A., eds., *Privatization and the Welfare State*. Princeton, N.J.: Princeton University Press, 1989.

Hamilton, C., and Hamilton, D. Social Policies, Civil Rights, and Poverty. In Danziger, S., and Weinberg, D., eds., *Fighting Poverty: What Works and What Doesn't*. Cambridge: Harvard University Press, 1986.

Hampton, H., and Fayer, S. *Voices of Freedom*. New York: Bantam, 1990.

Harrington, M. *The Other America*. New York: Macmillan, 1962.

Harrington, M. *The New American Poverty*. New York: Penguin, 1984.

Harrington, M. *The Long-Distance Runner*. New York: Holt, 1988.

Hartman, A. Homelessness: Public Issue and Private Trouble. *Social Work* (November 1989) *34*, 6, 483–84.

Health Care Financing Administration (HCFA) Finds Medicaid Costs Could Exceed $250 Billion. *Gerontology News*. Washington, D.C.: GSA, November, 1991.

Heclo, H. The Political Foundations of Antipoverty Policy. In Danziger, S., and
    Weinberg, D., eds., *Fighting Poverty: What Works and What Doesn't*. Cam-
    bridge: Harvard University Press, 1986.
Hellmuth, J., ed. *The Disadvantaged Child*. Vols. 1, 2, 3. New York: Brunner/Mazel,
    1967, 1968, 1970.
Henwood, D. Recovery? Not by a Long Shot. *The Nation*, September 9, 1991.
Hilts, P. U. S. Returns to 1820's in Care of Mentally Ill, Study Asserts. *New York
    Times*, August 12, 1990.
Hollingshead, A., and Redlich, F. *Social Class and Mental Illness*. New York: Wiley,
    1958.
Holmes, S. With Glory of Past Only a Memory, Rights Panel Searches for New
    Role. *New York Times*, October 10, 1991.
Hunt, J. McV. *Intelligence and Experience*. New York: Ronald Press, 1961.
Ivins, M. Looking for Work: The United States of Statistics. *The Progressive*
    (February, 1992) *56*, 2, 46.
Johnson, A., and Kreuger, L. Toward a Better Understanding of Homeless
    Women. *Social Work* (November 1989) *34*, 6, 537–40.
Joint Commission on Mental Illness and Health. *Action for Mental Health*. New
    York: Basic Books, 1961.
Kahn, A. *Social Policy and Social Services*. New York: Random House, 1973.
Kamerman, S. The New Mixed Economy of Welfare: Public and Private. *Social
    Work* (January–February 1983) *28*, 1, 5–11.
Kamerman, S., and Kahn, A. Child Care and Privatization under Reagan. In
    Kamerman, S., and Kahn, A., eds., *Privatization and the Welfare State*.
    Princeton, N.J.: Princeton University Press, 1989.
Katz, M. *The Undeserving Poor*. New York: Pantheon Books, 1989.
Kerr, P. Chain of Mental Hospitals Faces Inquiry in Four States. *New York Times*,
    October 22, 1991.
King, M. L., Jr. *Stride Toward Freedom*. New York: Harper and Row, 1958.
King, M. L., Jr. *Why We Can't Wait*, New York: Harper and Row, 1964.
Kirp, D. Rationing Life and Death. *The Nation*, March 5, 1990.
Kleiman, C. Women Must Make Saving For Retirement a Priority. *Hartford
    Courant*, March 18, 1991.
Kohl, H. The Politically Correct Bypass Multiculturism and the Public Schools.
    Social Policy (Summer 1991) 33–40.
Kolata, G. Racial Bias Seen on Pregnant Addicts. *New York Times*, July 19, 1990.
Koroloff, N., and Anderson, S. Alcohol-Free Living Centers: Hope for Homeless
    Alcoholics. *Social Work* (November 1989) *34*, 6, 497–504.
Kozol, J. *Death at an Early Age*. Boston: Houghton Mifflin, 1967.
Kozol, J. *Rachel and Her Children*. New York: Crown Publishing, 1988.
Kozol, J. *Savage Inequalities*. New York: Crown Publishing, 1991.
Kramon, G. Medical Insurers Vary Fees to Aid Healthier People. *New York Times*,
    March 24, 1991.
Kultgen, P., and Habenstein, R. Processes and Goals in Aftercare Programs for
    Deinstitutionalized Elderly Mental Patients. *Gerontologist* (April 1984) *24*,
    2, 167–73.
Kuttner, R. *The End of Laissez-Faire: National Purpose and the Global Economy*.
    New York: Knopf, 1991.

Lappé, F. *Rediscovering America's Values*. New York: Ballantine Books, 1989.

Lemann, N. The Unfinished War. *Atlantic Monthly* (1988) *262*, 6, 37–56, part I; and (1989) *263*, 1, 52–71, part II.

Lemann, N. *The Promised Land: The Great Black Migration and How It Changed America*. New York: Knopf, 1991.

Lerner, M. The Legacy of the Sixties for the Politics of the Nineties. *Tikkun* (January/February 1988) *3*, 1, 44–48, 87–91.

Leutz, W.; Abrahams, R.; Greenlick, M.; Kane, R.; and Prottas, J. Targeting Expanded Care for the Aged: Early SHMO Experience. *Gerontologist* (February 1988) *28*, 1, 4–17.

Levin, H., ed. *Community Control of Schools*. Washington, D.C.: Brookings Institution, 1970.

Levin, L. What Proposals for National Health Insurance Ignore. *Social Policy* (Summer 1991) *22*, 1, 42–45.

Levine, I., and Rog, D. Mental Health Services for Homeless Mentally Ill Persons: Federal Initiatives and Current Service Trends. *American Psychologist* (August 1990) *45*, 8, 963–68.

Levitan, S. *The Design of Federal Antipoverty Strategy*. Ann Arbor: University of Michigan, Institute of Labor and Industrial Relations, 1967.

Levitan, S. *The Great Society's Poor Law: A New Approach to Poverty*. Baltimore: Johns Hopkins Press, 1969.

Lewis, A. Politics and Decency. *New York Times*, April 15, 1991.

Liptzin, B. Canadian and U. S. Systems of Care for the Mentally Ill Elderly. *Gerontologist* (April 1984) *24*, 2, 174–78.

Lukas, J. A. *Common Ground*. New York: Vintage, 1986.

MacKay, M. *The Progressive Movement of 1924*. New York: Octagon, 1966.

Mandell, B. The National Welfare Rights Movement: The Social Protest of Poor Women, by Guida West. Book review in *Journal of Progressive Human Services* (1990) *l*, 1, 106–16.

Mann, A., ed. *The Progressive Era: Liberal Renaissance or Liberal Failure*. New York: Holt, Rhinehart and Winston, 1964.

Marable, M. Black America in Search of Itself. *The Progressive* (November 1991) 218–23.

Marris, P., and Rein, M. *Dilemmas of Social Reform*. New York: Atherton, 1969.

McDermott, C. Empowering the Elderly Nursing Home Residents: The Resident Rights Campaign. *Social Work* (March 1989) *34*, 2, 155–57.

McGuire, T. Outpatient Benefits for Mental Health Services in Medicare. *American Psychologist* (May 1989) *44*, 5, 818–24.

Mechanic, D. *Mental Health and Social Policy*, 3rd ed. Englewood Cliffs, N.J.: Prentice-Hall, 1989.

Megan, K. Nursing Home Restraints at Issue. *Hartford Courant*, November 23, 1991.

Meissner, H., ed. *Poverty in the Affluent Society*. New York: Harper and Row, 1973.

Mendelsohn, R. Is Head Start a Success or Failure? In Hellmuth, J., ed., *The Disadvantaged Child*. Vol. 3. New York: Brunner/Mazel, 1970.

Miller, D. *Women and Social Welfare: A Feminist Analysis*. New York: Praeger, 1990.

Miller, S. M. Reawakening the 60s: Strategies for the 80s. *Social Policy* (Fall 1986) 40–44.

Miller, S. M., and Mishler, E. Social Class, Mental Illness, and American Psychiatry. In Riessman, F.; Cohen, J.; and Pearl, A., eds., *Mental Health of the Poor*. New York: Free Press, 1964.

Miller, S. M., and Riessman, F. *Social Class and Social Policy*, New York: Basic Books, 1968.

Mills, C. W. *The Power Elite*. N.Y.: Oxford University Press. 1956.

Morris, A. *The Origins of the Civil Rights Movement*. New York: Free Press, 1984.

Moyers, B. The LBJ, Civil Rights Champion, Segregation Boded Disintegration. *The Hartford Courant*, November 13, 1988.

Moynihan, P. D. *Maximum Feasible Misunderstanding*. New York: Free Press, 1969.

Mulvihill, J. A Plan to Improve the Nation's Health by the Year 2000. *Hartford Courant*, September 9, 1990.

Murray, C. *Losing Ground: American Social Policy, 1950–1960*. New York: Basic Books, 1984.

Myers, S. L., Jr. Black Leaders Have Justification to Fear Plot to Discredit Them. *Hartford Courant*, April 1, 1990.

NAACP Legal Defense and Educational Fund. *The Unfinished Agenda on Race in America*. New York: LDF Survey Department, 1989.

National Advisory Council on Economic Opportunity. Critical Choices for the Eighties. *Clearing House Review* (November 1980).

National Association for Community Development (NACD). *An Interpretive History of the 1969 Economic Opportunity Act Amendments*. Washington, D.C.: NACD, 1970.

National Association of Social Workers (NASW). National Health Care Proposal by NASW Would Save U. S. Billions, Analysts Find. *National Association of Social Workers News*. (February 1991) *36*, 2, 1 and 14.

National Commission on Social Security (NCSS). *Medicare and Medicaid in America's Future*. Washington, D.C.: NCSS, 1981.

Newman, F.; Griffin, B; Black, R.; and Page, S. Linking Level of Care to Level of Need: Assessing the Need for Mental Health Care for Nursing Home Residents. *American Psychologist* (October 1989) *44*, 10, 1315–24.

Newman, H. Medicaid and National Health Insurance. *Public Welfare* (Summer 1974) 21–27.

Newman, J.; Bok, M.; and Morales, J. The Family Support Act of 1988 and Myths about the Poor. Paper presented at the Council on Social Work Education Annual Program Meeting, New Orleans, March 17, 1991.

O'Brien, D. *Neighborhood Organization and Interest Group Processes*. Princeton, N.J.: Princeton University Press, 1975.

O'Brien, G. R. Partnership Is the Solution to Health-Care Crisis. *Hartford Courant*, January 17, 1991.

Omnibus Budget Reconciliation Act of 1987 (P. L. 100–203). *HCFA Legislative Summary*, April 1988.

Orfield, G. *The Closing Door: Conservative Policy and Black Opportunity*. Chicago: University of Chicago Press, 1991.

Ozawa, M., ed. *Women's Life Cycle and Economic Insecurity*. New York: Praeger, 1989.

Palmer, J.; Smeeding, T.; and Torrey, B. *The Vulnerable*. Washington, D.C.: Urban Institute, 1988.

Pear, R. Rich Got Richer in 80's; Others Held Even. *New York Times*, January 11, 1991a.

Pear, R. Low Medicaid Fees Seen as Depriving the Poor of Care. *New York Times*, April 2, 1991b.

Pear, R. Higher Fees to Doctors May Not Help Medicaid. *New York Times*, April 3, 1991c.

Pear, R. Panel Says Medicaid Should Increase Doctor Payments to Medicare Levels. *New York Times*, July 2, 1991d.

People for The American Way. *Justice Denied: The Human Impact of the Supreme Court's Civil Rights Retreat*. Washington, D.C.: People For the American Way, 1990.

Perkey, B. Public and Private Responsibility for Mental Health Services: A Report on the Tennessee Task Force. *American Psychologist* (August 1989) *44*, 8, 1148–50.

Perry, B. ed. *Malcolm X. The Last Speeches*. New York: Pathfinder, 1989.

Phillips, K. *The Politics of Rich and Poor*. New York: Random House, 1990.

Piven, F. The Politics and Professionalism of Citizen Participation. In Cahn, E., and Passett, B., eds., *Citizen Participation*. N.Y.: Praeger, 1971.

Piven, F., and Cloward, R. *Regulating the Poor: The Functions of Public Welfare*. New York: Vintage, 1971.

Piven, F., and Cloward, R. *Poor Peoples' Movements: How They Succeed. Why They Fail*. New York: Pantheon, 1977.

Piven, F., and Cloward, R. The American Road to Democratic Socialism. *Democracy* (Summer 1983) *3*, 3, 58–68.

Piven, F., and Cloward, R. The Contemporary Relief Debate. In Block, F.; Cloward, R.; Ehrenreich, B.; and Piven, F., *The Mean Season*, New York: Pantheon, 1987.

Plotke, D. Talk Democracy: How To Reframe the Public Debates. *Social Policy* (Fall 1990) *21*, 2, 26–36.

Plotnick, R., and Skidmore, F. *Progress against Poverty: A Review of the 1964–1974 Decade*. New York: Academic Press, 1975.

Pollinger, K., and Pollinger, A. *Community Action and the Poor: Influence vs. Social Control in a New York City Community*. New York: Praeger, 1972.

Pollitt, K. "Fetal Rights"—A New Assault on Women. *The Nation*, March 26, 1990, 409–18.

Pollitt, K. Women Scorned. *The Nation*, November 4, 1991, 540–41.

Powledge, F. *Free At Last?* Boston: Little, Brown, 1991.

Quint, M. Racial Gap Found in Mortgages, *NY Times*, October 22, 1991.

Rachlin, S. The Influence of Law on Deinstitutionalization. In Bachrach, L., ed., *Deinstitutionalization*. San Francisco: Jossey-Bass, 1983.

Rawls, J. *A Theory of Justice*. Cambridge, Mass.: Belknap Press, 1971.

Reed, A. The Underclass Myth. *The Progressive* (August, 1991) *55*, 8, 18–20.

Reich, R. *The Resurgent Liberal*. New York: Random House, 1989.

Reich, R. *The Work of Nations: Preparing Ourselves for 21st-Century Capitalism*. New York: Knopf, 1991.

Reiff, R. The Social Responsibility of Community Mental Health Centers. In Evans, D., and Claiborn, W., eds., *Mental Health Issues and the Urban Poor*. New York: Pergamon, 1974.

Report on the National Advisory Commission on Civil Disorders. New York: Dutton, 1968.

Richmond, J.; Stipek, D.; and Zigler, E. A Decade of Head Start. In Zigler, E., and Valentine, J., eds., *Project Head Start: A Legacy of the War on Poverty*. New York: Free Press, 1979.

Riessman, F. *The Culturally Deprived Child*. New York: Harper and Row, 1962.

Rockwell, P. Fighting the Fires of Racism. *The Nation*, December 11, 1989, 714–18.

Rossi, P. The Old Homeless and the New Homelessness in Historical Perspective. *American Psychologist* (August 1990) *45*, 8, 954–59.

Rustin, B. From Protest to Politics: The Future of the Civil Rights Movement. *Commentary* (February, 1965) *39*, 2, 25–31.

Salem, D.; Seidman, E.; and Rappaport, J. Community Treatment of the Mentally Ill: The Promise of Mutual-Help Organizations. *Social Work* (September–October 1988) *33*, 5, 403–8.

Shadish, W. Policy Research: Lessons from the Implementation of Deinstitutionalization. *American Psychologist* (July 1984) *39*, 7, 725–38.

Shadish, W. Private Sector Care for Chronically Mentally Ill Individuals: The More Things Change, the More They Stay the Same. *American Psychologist* (August 1989) *44*, 8, 1142–47.

Shapiro, B. Doctor Fulani's Traveling Snake-Oil Show. *The Nation* (May 4, 1992), 585–94.

Shapiro, W. Unfinished Business. *Time*, August 7, 1989, 12–15.

Sikora, F. *Until Justice Rolls Down: The Birmingham Church Bombing Case*. Tuscaloosa: University of Alabama, 1991.

Simons, L. Privatization and the Mental Health System: A Private Sector View. *American Psychologist* (August 1989) *44*, 8, 1138–41.

Sleeper, J. *The Closest of Strangers: Liberalism and the Politics of Race in New York*. New York: Norton, 1990.

Smith, V., and Eggleston, R. Long-Term Care: The Medical Versus the Social Model. *Public Welfare* (Summer 1989) *47*, 3, 26–30.

Smyer, M. Nursing Homes as a Setting for Psychological Services. *American Psychologist* (October 1989) *44*, 10, 1307–14.

Sommers, I.; Baskin, D.; Specht, D.; and Shively, M. Deinstitutionalization of the Elderly Mentally Ill: Factors Affecting Discharge to Alternative Living Arrangements. *Gerontologist* (October 1988) *28*, 5, 653–58.

Sommers, I. and Baskin, D. Community Care and Social Exclusion of the Chronically Mentally Ill. *J. Progressive Human Services* (1991) *2*, 2, 35–48.

Sosin, M. Legal Rights and Welfare Change, 1960–1980. In Danziger, S., and Weinberg, D., eds., *Fighting Poverty: What Works and What Doesn't*. Cambridge: Harvard University Press, 1986. pp. 283–286.

Spar, K. *The Community Services Administration: Programs, History and Issues, 1964–1980*. Washington, D.C.: Congressional Research Services, Library of Congress, 1980.

Spivack, M. State Courts: Taking a Stand for Civil Liberties. *Hartford Courant*, September 9, 1990.

Starr, P. The Meaning of Privatization. In Kamerman, S., and Kahn, A., eds., *Privatization and the Welfare State*. Princeton, N.J.: Princeton University Press, 1989.

Starr, P. *The Social Transformation of American Medicine*. New York: Basic Books, 1982.

Steele, S. A Negative Vote in Affirmative Action. *New York Times Magazine*, May 13, 1990.

Surber, R.; Dwyer, E.; Ryan, K.; Goldfinger, S.; and Kelly, J. Medical and Psychiatric Needs of the Homeless—A Preliminary Response. *Social Work* (March–April 1988) *33*, 2, 116–19.

Terry, D. As Medicaid Fees Push Doctors Out, Chicago Patients Find Fewer Choices. *New York Times*, April 12, 1991.

Thomas, J. C. *Between Citizen and City*. Lawrence: University Press of Kansas, 1986.

U. S. Code Congressional and Administrative News. 88th Congress (1963); 88th Congress (1964); 89th Congress (1965); 96th Congress (1972); 99th Congress (1975); Omnibus Budget Reconciliation Act (1981, 1987).

U. S. Bureau of Census, Department of Commerce, 1987, 1989, 1990.

U. S. Department of Health and Human Services (USDHHS). *National Head Start Bulletin*. Washington, D.C.: USDHHS, 1989, 1990.

U. S. Department of Health and Human Services (USDHHS). *Project Head Start: Statistical Fact Sheet*. Washington, D.C.: Administration for Children, Youth and Families, Office of Human Development Services, USDHHS, 1991.

Urofsky, M. *The Supreme Court and Affirmative Action*. New York: Scribner, 1991.

Valentine, J., and Stark, E. The Social Context of Parent Involvement in Head Start. In Zigler, E., and Valentine, J., eds., *Project Head Start*: A Legacy of the War on Poverty. New York: Free Press, 1979.

Viorst, M. *Fire in the Streets*. New York: Simon and Schuster, 1979.

Volgenau, G. 25 Years After Riot, Watts Is Worse, Some Say, *Hartford Courant*, August 10, 1990.

Westinghouse Learning Corporation. *The Impact of Head Start: An Evaluation of the Effects of Head Start on Children's Cognitive and Affective Development*. Washington, D.C.: Office of Economic Opportunity, 1969.

White, S. The National Impact Study of Head Start. In Hellmuth, J., ed., *The Disadvantaged Child*. Vol. 3. New York: Brunner/Mazel, 1970.

Who's Entitled? *New York Times* editorial, February 6, 1991.

Wilk, R. Involuntary Outpatient Commitment of the Mentally Ill. *Social Work* (March–April 1988) *33*, 2, 133–37.

Wilkerson, D. Compensatory Education: Defining the Issues. In Hellmuth, J., ed., *The Disadvantaged Child*. Vol. 3. New York: Brunner/Mazel, 1970.

Wilkerson, I. A Remedy for Old Racism Has New Kinds of Shackles. *New York Times*, September 15, 1991.

Will, G. Bush's Speech Was a Lot of Noise, Not the Humdinger He Promised. *Hartford Courant*, January 30, 1992.

Williams, J. *Eyes on the Prize: America's Civil Rights Years, 1954-1965*. New York: Viking, 1987.

Williams, L. Cutting the Budget: A Lot of Talk, Little Action. *Hartford Courant*, January 26, 1992.

Williams, L., and Bixby, L. Poll Shows Affirmative Action Supported in Theory Only. *Hartford Courant*, February 26, 1989.

Wilson, W. J. Cycles of Deprivation and the Underclass Debate. *Social Service Review* (1985) *59*, 541-59.

Wilson, W. J. *The Truly Disadvantaged*. Chicago: University of Chicago Press, 1987.

Winschel, J. In the Dark . . . Reflections on Compensatory Education 1960-1970. In Hellmuth, J., ed., *The Disadvantaged Child*. Vol. 3. New York: Brunner/Mazel, 1970.

Women in Peril: The Feminization of Poverty. *National NOW Times*, February-March 1989.

Zigler, E., and Anderson, K. An Idea Whose Time Had Come: The Intellectual and Political Climate for Head Start. In Zigler, E. and Valentine, J., eds., *Project Head Start: A Legacy of the War on Poverty*. New York: Free Press, 1979.

Zigler, E., and Valentine, J., eds. *Project Head Start: A Legacy of the War on Poverty*. New York: Free Press, 1979.

Index